Advance praise for the book

'Dinkar Srivastava's book is timely and a must-read for those who wish to understand Pakistan. Muslim League's Two-Nation Theory had enormously negative consequences for the Indian subcontinent, especially the Indian Muslims. The author has also brought out the struggle of Muslims for united India. Maulana Madani's message of composite nationalism is as relevant today as it was before Partition.'

Maulana Mahmood A. Madani, President, Jamiat Ulama-e-Hind

'*Pakistan: Ideologies, Strategies and Interests*, by Ambassador Dinkar Srivastava, goes beyond the humdrum examination of event-based developments pertaining to that country and constitutes a fascinating study of the underlying motivating factors that govern its actions, derived, as the title suggests, from ideologies, interests, etc. The credibility of the arguments adduced and the conclusions drawn in the book are compelling as they rest both on the author's considerable firsthand professional expertise on Pakistan and on the writings of several Pakistani scholars which are liberally cited. Accordingly, this book must be at the top of the reading list of those interested in knowing what makes Pakistan tick and comprehending where it is headed.'

Satish Chandra, former Indian High Commissioner to Pakistan and Deputy National Security Adviser

'Dinkar Srivastava covers Pakistan's trajectory from pre-Partition days to the contemporary period. A fascinating account of the mindset of the Pakistan Army and its Afghanistan and Kashmir policies.'

General N.C. Vij, former Chief of Army Staff

'The book is a timely reminder of the relevance of Maulana Madani's call for composite nationalism as we Indians grapple with the selective killing of Hindus in Pahalgam following Pakistan Army chief General Munir's attempt to revive the extinct Two-Nation Theory. The interpretation of Islam based on Prophet Mohammad's constitution of Riyasat-e-Madina by the head of Deoband, India's largest seminary, was a resounding rejection of the Two-Nation Theory.'

Sultan Shahin, Founder Editor, NewAgeIslam.com

'Who were the people who conceived of the idea of Pakistan; after birth, what have its ruling ideologies been; what are the influences and forces that transformed the Pak polity and society to be inextricably grounded in radical religious beliefs which continue to spawn extremism; what is the modus operandi of the Army, which is the state in Pakistan, for disabling democracy and making successive elected governments redundant; how have the Army, the sole custodian of Pakistan's nuclear weapons stock, and the ISI, flourished by perpetuating their singular objective of taking over Kashmir through a proxy war carried out through unceasing cross-border terrorism... Answers to these and many other questions and concerns are contained in this deeply researched and well-written book by a veteran diplomat known for his admirable understanding of India–Pakistan relations. A must-read narrative for policymakers and students of international relations. Highly recommended.'

N.N. Vohra, former Governor of Jammu and Kashmir (2008–2018)

Pakistan

PAKISTAN

Ideologies, Strategies and Interests

DINKAR P. SRIVASTAVA

BLOOMSBURY
NEW DELHI • LONDON • OXFORD • NEW YORK • SYDNEY

BLOOMSBURY INDIA
Bloomsbury Publishing India Pvt. Ltd
Second Floor, LSC Building No. 4, DDA Complex, Pocket C—6 & 7,
Vasant Kunj, New Delhi, 110070

BLOOMSBURY, BLOOMSBURY INDIA and the Diana logo
are trademarks of Bloomsbury Publishing Plc

First published in India 2025

ISBN: HB: 978-93-61316-74-6; eBook: 978-93-61317-78-28
2 4 6 8 10 9 7 5 3 1

Typeset in Adobe Garamond by Manipal Technologies Limited
Printed and bound in India by Thomson Press India Ltd

MIX
Paper | Supporting responsible forestry
FSC® C010615

To find out more about our authors and books visit www.bloomsbury.com and sign up for our newsletters

To
Dr Khan Saheb and Badshah Khan

Contents

1

Introduction

MOST OF THE EXISTING literature on Pakistan is about war and diplomacy and its civil–military rulers. However, this does not explain the multiple crises facing the country today. In May 2023 Imran Khan's supporters attacked the Army General Headquarters (GHQ) in Rawalpindi and the Corps Commander's residence in Lahore. The Pakistan Army regards itself as a defender of not only its territory but also its ideological frontiers; its legitimacy is now being challenged. The country underwent elections, but the outcome was contested. There is growing inequality, food shortages and a threat to internal stability by a host of jehadi groups. Is there a common thread behind the repeated eclipse of democracy, neglect of socio-economic development and rise of the praetorian state?

This book seeks to explore deeper impulses behind the creation of Pakistan and its subsequent evolution. The ideology of Pakistan is cited in the judgements of its Supreme Court. It is not defined but has produced major political consequences. The book looks at the interplay of ideology, interests and strategies followed by successive civil and military regimes in Pakistan. Though the book traces the history of Partition, its focus is on contemporary Pakistan, covering a wide canvas from Muhammad Ali Jinnah to the present.

This book does not go into the question of theology, nor does it make any comment on any religion. It brings out the cynical exploitation of religion for political ends by the Muslim League before Partition, and Pakistan's rulers since then. The first victims of this ideology were Pakistan's minorities. Now, it haunts the majority community, which has to conform to a conservative interpretation of Islam.

Pakistan has no history – it is based on an idea. It celebrates Muslim rule in the subcontinent, but this was based in Delhi. It denies the historical legacy of the region that is today's Pakistan. Sindh is called Bab-ul-Islam (Gateway of Islam), celebrating the victory of the Arab invader Muhammad bin Qasim over the Hindu ruler Raja Dahir in the early eighth century CE. Karachi has a port named after him. Mahmoud Ghazni and Muhammad Ghori, who came from Afghanistan, are heroes in Pakistan's historiography; the country's missiles are named after them. Pakistan is reliving the past in which it identifies itself as the aggressor in the subcontinent. It regards itself as inheriting the mantle of Muslim rule in India. But it does not accept Akbar, the greatest Mughal. Iqbal's conception of a state for Muslims in north-west India excluded most of the Muslims of undivided India. The ideology of Pakistan denies both history and geography.

British policy played a major role in Partition. However, the idea of a separate Muslim identity was also strong in the minds of the Muslim elite of north India, the *Ashrafs*. Three eminent personalities who contributed to building this identity were Sir Syed Ahmad Khan, Iqbal and Jinnah.

Sir Syed Ahmad Khan was a product of the period which saw the destruction of the Muslim power in India by the British. He advocated English education to elevate the status of Muslims in the new order. He also spoke about an inevitable conflict between Hindus and Muslims in case of the departure of the British, in a speech in Meerut in 1888. While the first goal was unexceptionable, was the second necessary? Hindu and Muslim soldiers had fought together in the war of 1857.

Iqbal and Jinnah came later. Iqbal was critical of the idea of nationalism but demanded a separate state for Muslims in the north-western part of India. He stressed the role of religion in a state according to Islam. Jinnah propounded his Two-Nation Theory in 1940. These different strands of thinking gave rise to the idea of a separate state for Muslims of the subcontinent. The state was to be based on religion.

Freedom movements the world over were marked by resistance to colonial powers. The Muslim League leaders advocated collaboration with the British. Iqbal criticized the idea of nationalism when it was sweeping through Asia and the Arab world. He feared it would undermine the unity of Islam. Pan-Islamic thinking was also strong in Maududi's thinking, the founder of Jamaat-e-Islami. Zia-ul-Haq encouraged transnational Islam, which provided the ideological underpinning for Pakistan's policies in Afghanistan and Jammu and Kashmir.

Jinnah's speech of 11 August 1947 provided an enlightened view of Pakistan's future, which was a departure from the Two-Nation Theory. But he never returned to this vision of an inclusive state. Liaquat Ali Khan got the Objectives Resolution adopted in 1949, laying the foundation of an Islamic Pakistan.

While Pakistan's domestic policy is heavily influenced by ideology, its foreign policy reflects a pragmatic strain. Consider how Pakistan seamlessly shifted alliances from the capitalist United States to communist China. However, its policies closer to home, in Afghanistan and Kashmir, are driven by ideology.

While the role of ideology has strengthened, the space for rational choices has become more limited. Pakistan threatened to use nuclear weapons during the Kargil war. Prime Minister Imran Khan revived the spectre in a debate in the National Assembly in the aftermath of the Pulwama terror attack and India's response in Balakot. Such behaviour is not part of any definition of deterrence. No country would accept total destruction for a limited stake.

The Ideology of Pakistan

The ideology of Pakistan has different meanings for different stakeholders. *Ashrafs* – the Muslim elite of north India saw themselves as descendants of past rulers who came from Arabia and Central Asia. They were willing to accept Partition, rather than be a minority in a united India. Why did Maududi oppose Pakistan's creation? Why did he change his mind later?

There is debate whether Pakistan was conceived of as a 'Muslim' state or an 'Islamic' state. The former view emphasizes a territorial dimension – a homeland for the Muslims of the subcontinent – while the latter emphasizes the Islamic identity of the state. Are these two concepts mutually exclusive? However, this debate between the two conceptions of Pakistan is a later construct. In the minds of the makers of Pakistan, there was no contradiction between these two strands.

The Two-Nation Theory was based on 'irreconcilable differences' between Hindus and Muslims. The ideology of Pakistan projected this into inter-state relations after Partition. Its external manifestation was hostility to India; its internal fallout was the rise of a praetorian state where all other functions of government became subservient to maintaining a strong army. This has led to the periodic eclipse of democracy, the appropriation of a large chunk of the budget for the defence of the country, and neglect of socio-economic development.

The breaking away of East Pakistan as Bangladesh in 1971 showed that religion was not a sufficient glue to hold the country together. Paradoxically, Pakistan moved closer to an Islamic identity after the 1971 war. Zulfikar Ali Bhutto brought Liaquat's Objectives Resolution, which laid down the vision of an Islamic Pakistan into the body of the country's third Constitution. Religious parties called for the ouster of Bhutto's government by raising the slogan of 'Nizam-e-Mustafa' (Order of Prophet). Under Zia, this became part of the state philosophy. In recent history, Imran Khan called for Riyasat-e-Madina. Both these concepts call for a society based on the tenets of Islam. Thus, over the decades, the role of religion in the state and society has deepened.

The Road to Partition

This section examines the Two-Nation Theory and the Lahore Resolution adopted at the 1940 session of the All-India Muslim League. By describing Muslims as a separate nation, the resolution elevated them from a minority in united India. This marked the first step towards Partition.

The Lahore Resolution did not mention 'Pakistan'. However, it raised the demand for a separate territory for the Muslims in the north-western and eastern 'zones' of the country. The description of the new political entity as 'independent states' in which 'the constituent units shall be autonomous and sovereign' clearly implied more than one state. Jinnah later tried to change this to the singular noun 'state' at the Muslim League convention of 1946. The chapter on the Lahore Resolution covers this little-known episode based on the writings of one of the senior-most Muslim League leaders, Chaudhry Khaliquzzaman. The issue remains at the heart of the demand for more political space by Baloch, Pashtun, Sindhis and Muhajir. However, the denial of the separate identity of these different national or ethnic groups has become part of the ideology of Pakistan.

This section also covers the constitutional schemes introduced by the British. The Cripps Mission included the 'opt-out' provision for provinces, which was close to the Muslim League's demand for separate state(s) for Muslims. The nexus between the British policy and the Muslim League's stance became clearer in the Cabinet Mission Plan. A later chapter will revisit the controversy about Jawaharlal Nehru's statement of 10 July 1946. This is supposed to have triggered the Muslim League's rejection of the plan and killed the last chance to keep India united. Was the Cabinet Mission Plan a blueprint for India's unity or a plan for its Balkanization?

Jinnah and the Muslim League were not the sole representatives of the Muslims; there were Muslims who fought for a united India, such as Maulana Abul Kalam Azad and Rafi Ahmed Kidwai, whose contribution is well known and will be looked at in another chapter. In 1938, Maulana Hussain Ahmad Madani wrote a treatise called *Muttahida Qaumiyat* (composite nationalism) as a rejoinder to Iqbal and the Muslim League. Allah Bakhsh Soomro in Sindh and the Khan Brothers in the North-West Frontier Province (NWFP) made tremendous sacrifices for a united India.

Jinnah's speech of 11 August 1947 is covered in a separate chapter, given its importance. The chapter examines his speech from the point of view of a dissenter, a supporter and the establishment. Khan Abdul Wali Khan, the son of Khan Abdul Ghaffar Khan (Badshah Khan) was a dissenter. Justice Muhammad Munir, who would go on to be the chief justice of Pakistan and would author the Munir Commission report on anti-Ahmadi riots in Punjab in the early 1950s, was a Jinnah supporter. The views of the establishment figures of the period are reflected in the speech of Maulana Shabbir Ahmad Usmani in the debate over the Objectives Resolution in the Pakistan Constituent Assembly. Jinnah's speech, the only time he spoke of the Pakistani state making no distinction between citizens on the grounds of faith, was a radical departure from the Muslim League's policy of promoting the communal divide. Khaliquzzaman has explained Jinnah's reasons for doing so. What were they?

Faith, Politics and Interests

The Objectives Resolution introduced by Liaquat and adopted by Pakistan's Constituent Assembly in 1949 proclaimed divine sovereignty over the entire universe. This gave religion an overarching role in the state and society, and affirmed the vision of Pakistan as an Islamic state. The Chapter 'Divine Sovereignty' in this book brings out the views of the majority as well as minority members on the resolution in the debate in the Pakistan Constituent Assembly.

The Muslim League opposed the idea of majority rule in an undivided India. After Partition and the emergence of Pakistan, the opposition to majority rule took a new form – denying East Pakistan its due share in the government. This time, it was the fear of the 'Muslim' majority, and East Pakistan soon emerged as the 'other nation'. That chapter brings out Pakistan's internal dynamics for more than two decades until the independence of Bangladesh.

Pakistan's government appointed the Munir Commission to look into the causes and consequences of the anti-Ahmadiya riots in the early 1950s. The book covers the deliberation of the Munir Commission in the Chapter titled 'Who Is a Muslim'. Justice Munir's courageous stand saved Ahmadiyas in the 1950s. They were declared non-Muslims under Bhutto.

The chapter on minority rights also covers Maududi's testimony before the Munir Commission. He had initially opposed Pakistan's creation. Justice Munir questioned why he changed his position, and Maududi's answer was revealing – the minority population in West Pakistan (the entire modern-day Pakistan) dropped from a substantial 26 per cent in 1947 to 2.88 per cent by the time of the 1951 census. The largest minorities in Pakistan were Hindus and Sikhs. Pakistan had achieved ideological purity, which satisfied the founder of the Jamaat-e-Islami.

Nationality, Language and Ideology

Urdu was part of the ideology of Pakistan; its imposition played a major part in creating a sense of alienation in the Bengali-speaking eastern wing of the country. However, the nationality issue did not go away with the separation of East Pakistan. The book covers it in four different chapters on Balochistan, Sindh, Khyber Pakhtunkhwa and the Muhajir population.

The repeated military operations in Balochistan testify that nationality remains a potent issue even after Bangladesh broke away. Despite its rich mineral and gas resources, Balochistan remains the most backward province economically in Pakistan.

Sindh is a divided province. The influx of Muhajirs (the migrants from India who came to Pakistan) and forced migration of Hindus changed the demographic composition of Sindh soon after Partition. Today, it is home to the Pakistan People's Party (PPP) and the Muttahida Qaumi Movement (MQM, formerly the Muhajir Qaumi Movement). Though the PPP has retained its hold in Sindh, its national footprint is shrinking.

Muhajirs lost their political ascendancy with the deaths of Jinnah and Liaquat soon after Pakistan's creation. The introduction of language quotas in 1972 undermined their position in the bureaucracy. The launch of Operation Clean-up against the MQM in 1992 was a watershed – the Pakistan Army had turned against Muhajirs who had created Pakistan.

The NWFP under the Khan Brothers – Khan Abdul Jabbar Khan and Khan Abdul Ghaffar Khan – had opted to be part of India in 1947, before the British moved the goalpost and called for a public referendum. Today, their secular legacy has faded. Though the Awami National Party may have been wiped out in Khyber Pakhtunkhwa, the rise of the Pashtun Tahafuz Movement (PTM) shows that the idea of Pashtun nationalism remains alive.

Ideologies, Interests and Strategies

The Pakistan Army plays the role of both priest and soldier. It has promoted the role of religion in the state and society. Its views have an imprint on Pakistan's domestic as well as external policies. Its Afghanistan and Kashmir policies, as well as the nuclear doctrine, have largely remained the army's domain even during the spells of civilian government. But the choice of jehadi groups to promote Pakistan's interests abroad has led to the rise of an extremist philosophy and sectarianism at home. The chapter also examines radicalization within the army, which has made its chiefs fear for their lives.

The army is the sole custodian of nuclear weapons in Pakistan. The country stresses that its nuclear doctrine is India-specific. This view is rooted in a vision of perpetual conflict with India and a desire to seek parity with its neighbour, which is seven times bigger. This is ideology; not an expression of nuclear deterrence based on a cold calculation of risk management.

Pakistan's rhetoric that Kashmir is the unfinished agenda of Partition is an extension of the Two-Nation Theory. Though Pakistan has appropriated the Kashmir cause, it seldom talks about the part of Kashmir it has occupied illegally. The chapter on Jammu and Kashmir brings out the sweeping changes Islamabad made inside Pakistan-occupied Kashmir and Gilgit-Baltistan in 2018, a year before the abrogation of Article 370 by India.

The chapter on Jammu and Kashmir also covers the Kargil war, based on contemporary Pakistani accounts. Was the civilian Prime Minister Nawaz Sharif kept informed by General Pervez Musharraf when he launched Operation Koh-e-Paima to 'liberate' Jammu and Kashmir in 1999? What was Sharif's reaction when he learned that the army had crossed the Line of Control? The chapter also covers a ruling by the Pakistan Supreme Court which came out just when the military adventure in Kargil had become public – the court remarked that the people of Gilgit-Baltistan were denied fundamental rights and representative institutions.

While Pakistan claims that the Kashmir issue is rooted in the history of Partition, there was no such justification for conflict with Afghanistan. In the 1990s, Pakistan's generals propounded the theory of 'strategic depth' in Afghanistan, which implied treating a sovereign state as its hinterland. After the recent falling out between Kabul and Islamabad, Pakistan has built a fence along its Afghanistan border.

Pakistan is in the throes of its worst economic crisis. Generous assistance from the World Bank and the International Monetary Fund (IMF) temporarily spared it from the consequences of elite profligacy. The chapter examines the structural problems behind Pakistan's recurring troubles.

If Islam defined the polity, Pakistani rulers chose a different basis for the economy. The beauty of Islam is the idea of equality, but their laissez-faire economic policies accentuated inequalities. There is no single ideology that explains the country; there are, indeed, plural ideologies of Pakistan.

Imran Khan has arguably emerged as the most popular leader in Pakistan today, with a religious appeal combined with resistance to the West. He is a creation of the army, who now challenges his creator. What explains his hold on the Pakistani imagination? This phenomenon is covered in a separate chapter.

The concluding chapter looks to the future. Pakistan is indeed a victim of global warming, caused by the emissions of developed countries. However, its economic crisis is self-inflicted. Do Pakistan's ideologies equip it to cope with the challenges of the twenty-first century?

Sources

This book examines the speeches of Iqbal, Jinnah and Muslim League leaders in detail to understand the ideology behind their conception of a state for 'Muslim India'. It considers both international and Indian sources, essential to any discussion of Partition. Pakistan's independence journey is covered primarily through Pakistani sources, including debates in the Constituent Assembly in 1949 on the Objectives Resolution and discussions in the Pakistan National Assembly on the Simla Agreement.

I have drawn upon Urdu writings, including Sir Syed Ahmad Khan's *Asbab-e-Baghawat-e-Hind*, Hussain Madani's *Muttahida Qaumiyat Aur Islam*, Maududi's *Masla Qaumiyat* and Qudratullah Shahab's *Shahabnama*. Shahab, an Indian Civil Service officer, headed the Pakistani Governor-General/President's secretariat for eleven years. All translations are the author's own.

Apart from military and political leaders, the book considers the writings of two eminent Pakistani jurists. One is Justice Munir, who represented Pakistan on the Boundary Commission deliberations during Partition. The other is Justice Dorab Patel, one of the few dissenting judges in Bhutto's trial, later appointed chairman emeritus of the Human Rights Commission of Pakistan, where he made significant contributions to the promotion of human rights. I had the privilege of knowing him personally while I was posted at the Indian Consulate in Karachi.

The events leading up to the separation of East Pakistan are analysed based on the writings of Sherbaz Mazari, the leader of the opposition till 1977, who later refused the offer of prime ministership made to him by General Zia in 1980. He was a Baloch sardar (leader) and his writings provide insight into the conditions of Balochistan. Bhutto addressed him as his 'Toomandar' (feudal lord) in the debate in the Pakistan National Assembly. It was my privilege to know Mazari during my stint in Karachi. I also had the honour of meeting Sardar Akbar Khan Bugti, who had invited me home for dinner in Quetta.

While Pakistan has moved towards a stronger Islamic identity, an alternative view – rooted in a secular, plural conception of the state – was offered by the Khan Brothers but is often overlooked. In the aftermath of 9/11, this forgotten strand is more relevant than ever.

2

The Ideologies of Pakistan

> 'Is religion a private affair?' 'Is it possible to retain Islam as an ethical ideal and to reject it as a polity in favour of national polities in which [the] religious attitude is not permitted to play any part?'
>
> –Iqbal, in his presidential address to the Muslim League's annual session of 1930[1]

PERHAPS THE MOST IMPORTANT element that shapes, and constrains, the evolution of Pakistan's polity is the ideology of Pakistan. In a country that does not have a history, ideology is important in defining national identity. The idea of a separate identity of the Muslim community preceded the demand for a separate state. In the world view of the *Ashrafs* of north India, this was rooted in Arabia and Central Asia. They were also conscious of the privileged position of Muslims as past rulers of the country. One of the most eloquent proponents of this view was Sir Syed Ahmad Khan, who saw an inevitable conflict for the throne of India between Hindus and Muslims, in case of the departure of the British. Iqbal, in his presidential address at the Muslim League conference in 1930, demanded a separate state for Muslims in the north-western part of India. He stressed that in Islam, 'Church and State are organic to each other.' Jinnah described Hindus and Muslims as 'two irreconcilable nationalities' in his speech at the Lahore session in 1940. The thinking of these three eminent persons gave birth to the idea of a separate state for Muslims of the subcontinent, to be based on religion.

The term 'ideology' is usually associated with a political philosophy. Democracies with multi-party systems do not have a 'state' ideology, though different parties may have their own beliefs or value systems.

Many countries have a state religion. The Two-Nation Theory blurred the distinction between faith and politics. This has affected every aspect of Pakistan's polity. It also carried the legacy of pre-Partition politics into the foreign policy of the new state. Perennial conflict with its neighbour, India, has become a part of the ideology of Pakistan.

The liberals in Pakistan point to a different ideology, reflected in Jinnah's famous speech of 11 August 1947, which laid out an enlightened vision of that country's future. The idea died down quickly. In February 1948, Jinnah affirmed that the Constitution of Pakistan would be based on Islamic sharia. Six months after Jinnah's death, Prime Minister Liaquat Ali Khan got the Objectives Resolution adopted in the Constituent Assembly in 1949. This laid down the objectives of the founding of the state. It proclaimed the sovereignty of the divine over the lay and ecclesiastical domains. This restricted the role of the elected Parliament and placed minority rights on a tenuous footing. It also assigned the state the role of 'enabling Muslims' to 'order their lives in the individual and collective sphere' in accordance with the tenets of Islam. Religion became the business of the state, contrary to Jinnah's famous speech.

Zulfikar Ali Bhutto brought the Objectives Resolution into the operative part of the country's third Constitution. General Zia-ul-Haq introduced Nizam-e-Mustafa, based on sharia law. Imran Khan upholds 'Riyasat-e-Madina' as the model for Pakistan. The central idea of a state based on religion has endured and become stronger. This has been reinforced by state intervention.

The ideology of Pakistan is cited in judgements of the Supreme Court of Pakistan but is not defined.[2] The absence of a definition makes its influence more pervasive. The court, in its judgement of 1972, justified the banning of Khan Abdul Wali Khan's National Awami Party (NAP) by the Bhutto government on the grounds that it had worked against the 'ideology of Pakistan'[3]. The ideology sealed the fate of the country's largest opposition party, which ruled two provinces, NWFP and Balochistan, before it was outlawed. The Supreme Court used the term in its judgement even before the third Constitution was formally adopted.

Fifteen years later, Bhutto's Pakistan People's Party was at the receiving end. His daughter Benazir Bhutto filed a writ petition in the Supreme Court in 1987. She was apprehensive that the reference to 'the Islamic ideology' in the Political Parties Act could be used to deny her party a chance to participate in elections. While the Supreme Court agreed that political parties were necessary for the functioning of democracy, the chief justice stated: 'The concept of *Islamic ideology* is interwoven with the *Ideology of Pakistan* and is inseparable as it is the foundation of the *two-nation theory*.' [Emphasis added][4]

These two judgements by Pakistan's Supreme Court, delivered fifteen years apart, show the hold of ideology on that country. According to Justice Dorab Patel, the ideology of Pakistan mentioned in the Supreme Court's judgement referred to the Two-Nation Theory. He was a judge of the Pakistan Supreme Court who had given a very courageous dissenting judgement in the Bhutto case at the height of Gen. Zia's martial law. There have been breaks in the history of democracy in Pakistan, but the ideology continued to shape government policy and decisions of the highest judiciary even when the Constitution was yet to be framed or remained suspended.

There are conflicting views on the role of ideology. Ayub Khan mentioned in his memoirs that man's 'greatest yearning is for an ideology for which he should be able to lay down his life'. He added, 'Such an ideology with us is obviously that of Islam. It was on that basis we fought for and got Pakistan, but having got it, we have *failed to* define that ideology in a simple and understandable form.'[5] [Emphasis added] Justice Muhammad Munir said he heard the term for the first time in 1953 when he was holding an inquiry on the Punjab disturbances on the Ahmadiya issue.[6] He was the author of the Munir Commission report which gave an enlightened interpretation of Islam.

The term 'Ideology of Pakistan' may not have been used by the founders of Pakistan, but the ideas now recognized as part of this existed before the term was coined. These include the Two-Nation Theory, Iqbal's thoughts, the Lahore Resolution, and increasingly, Maududi's thoughts. Maududi was the founder of Jamaat-e-Islami. Though he does not figure in Pakistan's official narrative, his thinking has deeply influenced the evolution of Pakistan's polity.

Urdu was as much part of the ideology of Pakistan as Islam. This was expressed by Jinnah in his speech in Dhaka in 1948. He described Urdu as the best in Muslim tradition and close to the Arab language and culture. Urdu was equated with religion. The language spoken by 7.2 per cent of the people of the country was given precedence over Bengali, which was the language of the majority (54.6 per cent) of the population, according to the 1951 Census of Pakistan.[7] The ideology based on religion denied ethnic or linguistic identities, which were dismissed as 'parochial tendencies'. This remains at the root of continuing discontent in Balochistan and Khyber Pakhtunkhwa, even after the secession of East Pakistan.

The ideology of Pakistan has weakened democracy. In a democracy, sovereignty rests with the people. The Objectives Resolution, which is now the cornerstone of Pakistan's Constitution, proclaimed that sovereignty belongs to the divine. This has undermined the authority of the elected institutions and governments. In Pakistan's turbulent history, street protests by religious groups have brought down governments enjoying majority. The dismissal of Nawaz Sharif's government in 2017 by the Supreme Court was a technicality; the government's functioning was made impossible by the agitation launched by Barelvi cleric Khadim Rizvi with the tacit support of the army. Democracy is part of the Constitution of the Islamic Republic of Pakistan, but the ultimate arbiter of the fate of governments is the ideology of Pakistan.

Why Pakistan? Was it created for the protection of the Muslim minority in India? The *Ashrafs* – the Muslim elite – believed that they were heirs to the Muslim rulers of the past. They saw power as a privilege that had to be restored to the community. This was not a 'minority' question as it is commonly understood. Muslims were actually the majority in the north-western and eastern parts of the subcontinent – the regions which became Pakistan eventually. These provinces were run by governments headed by Muslim chief ministers. The status of the minority was an issue for the Muslims of northern and central India from where the Muslim League leaders came. At the Lahore session in 1940, the League formally buried the demand for minority protection. Jinnah said that Muslims were not a minority; they were a 'nation'.

Pakistan ka Matlab Kya? (What Is the Meaning of Pakistan?)

Qudratullah Shahab was an Indian Civil Service officer who headed Pakistan's governor-general and president's secretariat for eleven years under three heads of state – Governor-General Ghulam Mohammad,

President Iskandar Mirza and President Ayub Khan. In his memoir *Shahabnama*, he devoted a chapter debating the idea of Pakistan, titled 'Pakistan ka Matlab Kya? (What Is the meaning of Pakistan?)' He summed up ideas, events and actors who played a role in creating Pakistan. He described Pakistan as a 'positive step towards completion of the 1857 War of Independence'. He added that it was the 'gradual and logical conclusion of Sir Syed Ahmad Khan's Aligarh Movement'. He said it was 'an expression of Allama Iqbal's dream, which he presented in his speech at Allahabad'. Shahab gave credit to Jinnah's speech at the most critical juncture in Lahore in 1940. He projected it as a struggle against the Hindu majority, rather than the British rule. This is a faithful reflection of the Muslim League's policies.

In conclusion, Shahab summed up the meaning of Pakistan as he began the chapter – by describing the reaction of his Kashmiri cook Rezwan, as they listened to the broadcast of the Partition plan by Lord Mountbatten along with Nehru, Baldev Singh and Jinnah on All India Radio on 3 June 1947. When asked by Shahab about his understanding of Pakistan, Rezwan replied, 'Pakistan ka matlab kya? La ilaha illallah.'[8] The line was written by Asghar Soudai of Sialkot. Shahab said Soudai adopted 'the shortcut of crores of Muslims like Rezwan'. The issue is not the verse of the Holy Quran. It is the attempt to derive legitimacy for a political movement in terms of religion. This was the Muslim League's message conveyed in simple terms, which could be understood by the cook, the driver and the Indian Civil Service (ICS) sahib alike.

Two-Nation Theory

The origin of the Two-Nation Theory precedes the creation of the Muslim League. In Lucknow in 1887, Sir Syed said, 'From our hands, the country was taken by the government into its own.' He added, 'Our nation is of the blood of those who made not only Arabia but Asia and Europe, to tremble. It is our nation which conquered with its sword the whole of India, although its peoples were all of one religion.'[9] The description of Muslims as a 'nation' was the essence of the Two-Nation Theory. In Sir Syed's conception, they were foreigners who conquered the land and were distinct from its 'peoples who were all of one religion'. In a speech in Meerut in 1888, Sir Syed Ahmad

Khan cast Hindus and Muslims as two separate nations. He said that in the event of the departure of the British, 'one of them should conquer the other and thrust it down'. This preceded Jinnah's statement in the Lahore session of the Muslim League, that Hindus and Muslims are two irreconcilable nationalities, by half a century.

'Restoring Muslims' special status in India's political hierarchy through access to modern education and winning concessions from the British was the basic thrust of Sir Syed's politics.'[10] Muslims' special status as past rulers was also strong in Maududi's thoughts. He opposed the creation of Pakistan, because 'this would result in handing over the dominion of the Mughals to the Hindus'. Maududi hoped to halt the rise of Hindu power in India by converting the whole of India to Islam, rather than the alternative of creating a relatively small separate Muslim state.[11]

The Two-Nation Theory was initially confined to seeking safeguards for Muslim minorities. This was later transformed into a demand for recognizing Muslims as a separate 'nation'. Iqbal gave a call for a consolidated north-west Indian Muslim state in 1930. The Lahore Resolution of 1940 adopted this as the Muslim League's official position and also added an eastern zone to Iqbal's demand, which was limited to the north-west. This was not based on any historical experience; no such state existed in the past. Muslims had coexisted with Hindus in the subcontinent for centuries. There was a conscious attempt to escape history.

It may not have been a coincidence that the Two-Nation Theory emerged towards the end of British rule. Since Iqbal's 1930 speech, Muslim League leaders had made it clear that they were unwilling to accept the democratic principle of majority rule. They stressed the special position of Muslims. If they could not rule, Partition was the solution. The Two-Nation Theory validated this.

Poet, Philosopher and Ideologue

In Pakistan's official narrative, Iqbal is considered the best exponent of the ideology that led to the creation of Pakistan. He explored the relationship between religion and the state in his presidential address at the Muslim League conference in 1930. He cited the example of the

Reformation in Europe and stated that Luther's revolt 'would eventually mean the complete displacement of [the] universal ethics of Jesus by the growth of a plurality of national and hence narrower systems of ethics'.[12] Iqbal saw Luther's revolt weakening the Vatican's hold and leading to the rise of the nation state. He did not want the same fate to befall Islam. He was keen to preserve the unity of the Islamic *Ummah* (community of Muslims) at the expense of nationalism.

Iqbal added, 'At the present moment, the national idea is racializing the outlook of Muslims, and thus materially counteracting the humanizing work of Islam.'[13] He ignored both the secular and ideological differences which had already taken shape within the fold of Islam. The speech was made more than a decade after the Arab revolt against the Ottoman Empire during the First World War. The revolt arose in Arabia, the heart of Islam, and was led by the sons of the Sharif of Mecca. By the time Iqbal made his 1930 speech, Turkey, under Kemal Atatürk, had abolished the Caliphate. The idea of nationalism was gaining ground in Muslim countries, as it was in various colonies. Iqbal sought to stem this tide in the subcontinent. His repeated criticism of nationalism must have been convenient for the British, who were trying to suppress national awakenings from the Middle East to the Indian subcontinent. The sectarian schism within Islam had taken place more than a millennium ago with the rise of the Shia faith. If it was difficult for him to accept plurality within Islam, it was even more difficult to accept it between different religions.

Iqbal added, 'In the world of Islam, we have a universal polity whose fundamentals are believed to have been revealed.' Interestingly, he described religion not as an individual's faith, but as a 'polity'. In stressing the universal nature of the polity, he indicated a strong preference for pan-Islamic thinking. By describing that the 'fundamentals' of this polity have been 'revealed', he was also constricting the role of an elected legislature in reforming the society.

Iqbal in his speech further stated, 'In Islam, God and the universe, spirit and matter, church and State, are organic to each other.' Couched in metaphysical terms, Iqbal was reinforcing the role of religion in politics. This went against the fundamental principle of Reformation, which was the separation of state and religion.

Iqbal posed the question, 'Is religion a private affair?' He opposed treating it as a private matter. This would have implications for both majority and minority communities. The subsequent history of religious movements in Pakistan, and the role assumed by the government in regulating religious practice, shows the danger of what Iqbal was propagating. Declaring Ahmadiyas as non-Muslims was an early manifestation of this trend. Pakistani liberals may have a sense of discomfort with the state of affairs in the country today, where the state has assumed the role of regulating the life of an individual citizen in accordance with religious injunctions. Iqbal's thoughts provided a philosophical validation much earlier.

Iqbal further added, 'The religious ideal of Islam, therefore, is organically related to the social order which it has created.' By linking religion with the social order, Iqbal made social reforms difficult, as they often involve challenging religious beliefs. He did so at a time when contemporary Turkey and Persia – one a Sunni state and the other Shia – were trying to break free from the orthodoxies of the past. Iqbal was more conservative than Sir Syed, who wanted political power for Muslims but advocated social reform.

Iqbal's hold on the Pakistani psyche cannot be explained by his speeches or philosophical musings alone. He wrote beautiful poetry in Urdu, which carried an enduring message easily understood by the masses. Pervez Hoodbhoy, a leading Pakistani commentator, pointed out that Iqbal wrote stirring poems that 'arouse Muslim supremacy, calling upon ascetic warriors to lead the world'.[14]

An example of such writing is the couplet, 'Who has smashed the idols of worship? Who has cut the Armies of the unbeliever?' Hoodbhoy added, 'The Islamic narcissism filling his Urdu verses goes subterranean, and the dagger and sword return to their sheaths when he writes in English.'[15]

Iqbal and Maududi

Iqbal's portraits adorn Pakistan's government offices and military establishments. However, the establishment maintains some distance from Maududi, who founded Jamaat-e-Islami. At different points in history, both Ayub Khan and Nawaz Sharif made sarcastic remarks about him for opposing the creation of Pakistan.

Despite this, Iqbal's and Maududi's ideas share striking similarities. Both believed that religion and politics are inseparable – religion encompasses all spheres of an individual's life. However, a key difference remained: Iqbal closely followed the British lead in politics, while Maududi pursued an independent course.

Both Iqbal and Maududi opposed the territorial concept of nationalism. They saw Muslims as part of the Islamic *Ummah*, transcending national boundaries. Iqbal wrote poetry rejecting Maulana Madani's call for Muttahida Qaumiyat (composite nationalism), which saw Hindus and Muslims as part of the same nation. Madani, in his brilliant treatise, rejected Iqbal's idea of basing nationalism on religion. Citing Arabic usage and verses (*āyāt*) from the Quran, he demonstrated that while millat referred to a religious community, the word 'qaum' denoted a group of people and was neutral in terms of faith. This is explored in greater detail in the chapter on Muslims for United India. Though Iqbal opposed Muslim nationalism rooted in a *watan* (country), he nevertheless called for a separate state for Muslims of north-west India.

Maududi wrote the treatise *Masla Qaumiyat* (*The Problem of Nationalism*) in support of Iqbal's position. He described Maulana Madani's position, equating *qaum* with *watan*, as 'absolutely wrong and baseless'.[16] He mocked the idea that 'nationalism' could help India achieve freedom from foreign rule. He wrote that the Quran described a group of Muslims as a *jamaat* or *hizb*, which means a 'party' of people who belong to a religion.[17] He described the Muslim *ummah* (community) as an 'international party'.[18] Maududi provided an exclusivist definition in which Muslims could not share an identity with people of other religions. Instead, they were part of the *ummah*, which transcends national borders. This challenges both plural societies and allegiance to a state within defined borders.

Maududi was more logically consistent than Iqbal. He opposed Partition, believing it would mean abandoning the Mughal legacy and reducing Muslim rule to a corner of the subcontinent. However, after Partition, he endorsed the concept of Pakistan. His testimony to the Munir Commission explained the reason for this change. He was a strong advocate of ideological purity and opposed a Muslim state with a mixed population. The sharp decline in Pakistan's minority population soon after Partition changed his mind. This is explored in detail in the chapter on minorities in Pakistan.

Farzana Shaikh, an eminent expert on Pakistan, wrote that for both Iqbal and Maududi, the idea of a Muslim state had little or nothing to do with the idea of a Muslim nation. According to her, 'What made an independent Muslim State imperative was to restore to Muslims the privilege of power both believed was a divinely sanctioned prerogative.'[19] The urge for separate statehood did not arise from any need to protect the minorities. In Muslim-majority provinces, the community already held power after the elections of 1937. Separate statehood would only worsen their problems in Muslim-minority provinces.

Rejection of democracy was a strong strand in the ideology Iqbal propounded. This was also shared by Maududi. Both strongly advocated that Ahmadiyas were non-Muslims. The electoral success of the Jamaat-e-Islami may be limited but its influence on Pakistan's polity has been profound. Maududi looms larger after his death.

Jinnah

Jinnah, in his Lahore speech in 1940, stated that the Hindus and Muslims 'belong to two different civilizations which are based mainly on conflicting ideas and conceptions'. He was emphasizing their differences to justify a separate territorial settlement for Muslims. He had elevated Muslims from a minority to a separate nation, that needed its own territory. He expressed his opposition to entering any Constituent Assembly, as this would have implied accepting a common Constitution in a unified country.

Jinnah did not clarify the nature of the state; the Lahore Resolution did not mention Pakistan. However, by the time of the 1946 elections, there was no ambivalence, at least not in his actions on the ground. In an agreement reached on 24 November 1945, he assured the Pir Sahib of Manki Sharif: 'Every law in Pakistan will be in consistency with Islamic sharia and not repugnant to the Quran and the Sunnah.'[20]

Jinnah's speech of 11 August 1947 is cited by his admirers as an enlightened vision of Pakistan. As mentioned earlier in the chapter, the promise held out by this speech did not last. Pakistan's establishment maintains an embarrassed silence about it.

Divine Sovereignty

The Objectives Resolution of 12 March 1949 is a major milestone in the evolution of the ideology of Pakistan. This was a formal statement of the state policy adopted by the Constituent Assembly of Pakistan. It was introduced by Prime Minister Liaquat Ali Khan and represented the government's intervention to shape the ideological frontiers of the new state. The preamble to the resolution stated: 'Whereas sovereignty over the entire universe belongs to Allah Almighty alone and the authority which He has delegated to the state of Pakistan, through its people for being exercised within the limits prescribed by Him is a sacred trust.'

The preamble made it clear that Pakistan would be an Islamic state. The resolution was not introduced in response to street agitation; Liaquat faced no challenge from the clergy or the army. The description of Muslim League leadership as 'modernist' following a 'secular' agenda is inherently flawed.

The resolution also curtailed the role of the elected legislature. As 'sovereignty' belongs to Allah, it is not derived from a popular mandate expressed through the legislature. The evolution of Pakistan's polity has shown the legislature's role curtailed by both religious forces and the establishment. The foundation was laid by the Objectives Resolution.

Liaquat said Pakistan will not be a theocracy. In a theocracy, the clergy controls the state. Muslim League leaders wanted to retain state power for themselves. They distanced themselves from the clergy but adopted the same principles the clergy demanded. The government of the new state was to be based on religion.

The language of the Objectives Resolution made it clear that the state would have a role in 'enabling' Muslims to 'order their lives' in accordance with the teachings and requirements of Islam. Religion was not a matter of an individual's choice, nor was the state's role limited to the public sphere. It covered both individual and collective spheres.

The Objectives Resolution, which laid the foundations of an Islamic Pakistan, has continued to exert a powerful appeal. It has been part of every Constitution adopted since – 1956, 1962 and the current Constitution adopted in 1973 under Bhutto, who projected himself as a modern leader fighting the Mullahs. The Eighth Amendment to the third Constitution, adopted under Zia-ul-Haq, gave the resolution mandatory force, overriding fundamental rights. Though most of the political architecture of Zia's period has been demolished, this aspect has remained untouched.

Erosion of Democracy, Rise of the Centralized State and Role of the Army

The eclipse of democracy took place under the civilian leadership long before Gen. Ayub Khan staged his military coup. Neither the Muslim League's internal structure and working nor its constitutional demands reflected the principle of democracy. After Partition, the League acted as both the political party and the electoral college for individuals seeking high government offices. Ayub's military coup did not displace an elected government – neither the Pakistan Constituent Assembly nor the governor-general, whom he displaced, was elected.

Is democracy part of Pakistan's ideology? The idea of democracy in united India was anathema to the Muslim League leaders, as they feared this would give an advantage to the Hindu majority. After Partition, Liaquat Ali Khan decided to go slow on federal elections, and instead held elections in the provinces first. The Muslim League's fear of facing the electorate deepened after its crushing defeat in the 1953 provincial elections in East Pakistan. The erosion of democracy took place with the acquiescence of the judiciary. Justice Munir, who provided an enlightened interpretation of Islam in the Munir Commission report, also validated the suspension of the Constituent Assembly by Governor-General Malik Ghulam Mohammad under the 'doctrine of necessity'. This was later used to justify military rule.

The Muslim League's demand in pre-Partition India for 'parity' between the minority and majority communities was opposed to the principle of democracy. Muslims constituted 25 per cent of the population, while Hindus made up 75 per cent. After Partition, the idea of 'parity' between the two wings was used to negate the numerical majority of East Pakistan by creating a 'One Unit' system in West Pakistan. This was a clear denial of democracy.

Ayub Khan took up the task of defining the ideology of Pakistan. In his book *Friends Not Masters*, he posed the question whether 'religion has to have a say in matters both temporal and secular'. His second question was how to 'define the duties of the state and those of the individual'. The third question was 'What is the definition of a "Momin" [true believer]?'[21] The military ruler was asserting that the state and the Constitution should determine who qualifies as a true believer and sought to keep that prerogative in the hands of the state.

Ayub Khan ruled Pakistan for eleven years. He devised a system of basic democracy based on an extremely limited franchise. The first elections under universal franchise were held in Pakistan in 1970. The military ran the country as a unitary state, centralizing all power in the national capital. Ayub Khan handed over power to Gen. Yahya Khan on 25 March 1969. Yahya dissolved the 'One Unit' system and ordered elections based on universal suffrage. The change was forced by events – agitation in East Pakistan had intensified. Though the political structure had changed, Pakistan's ideology remained at the core of Yahya's governance. Under Article 20(2) of the Legal Framework Order issued by Yahya, 'the Constitution to be made by the National Assembly had to preserve "Islamic ideology which is the basis of creation of Pakistan"'.[22]

The 1973 Constitution: Old Order Changeth Not

After the separation of Bangladesh, Pakistan adopted its third and current Constitution in 1973. The breaking away of the largest province with the highest Muslim population had exposed the hollowness of the Two-Nation Theory. Yet the makers of the new Constitution clung to the 'ideology of Pakistan' more tenaciously than before. Bhutto made the Objectives Resolution an integral part of the Constitution.

The 1973 Constitution declared Islam to be the state religion. It included provisions to remove inconsistencies between existing laws and the Holy Quran and Sunnah, and to prohibit future laws repugnant to the Holy Quran and Sunnah.[23] The 'repugnancy clause' established the primacy of religion over the lay domain – all laws have to conform to religious injunctions. Bhutto introduced these changes when he was at the zenith of his power. There was no street agitation at that stage. The description of Pakistani rulers as a 'Westernized, secular elite' is misleading.

There was continuity in another key area – the attempt to create Pakistan as a centralized state. The distribution of powers between the Centre and the provinces was heavily weighted in favour of the former. Provinces were given residuary powers. But as Justice Munir stated, with 'the federal and the concurrent list having exhausted practically all important subjects of legislation', it was difficult to see what these residuary subjects were.[24] A centralized state has become part of the ideology of Pakistan.

The limited powers of the provinces became even more constrained in emergencies under the new Constitution. Justice Munir wrote, 'Under Art. 232 the President could proclaim a state of Emergency, and such proclamation gave the center the power to legislate on residuary subjects as well. Thus the center acquired power over the provinces, and the center meant Mr. Bhutto.'[25]

Pakistan hosted the second conference of the Organisation of Islamic Cooperation (OIC) in Lahore in 1974. Bhutto had discovered a new source of funding and legitimacy for Pakistan. It was to gravitate increasingly towards the Middle East. Its quarrels lay in South Asia. Its ideological inspiration came from Arabia's past. This identity would deepen under Zia.

Nizam-e-Mustafa (Order of the Prophet)

The 1977 elections were seen as rigged and brought street protests from an alliance of opposition parties. The Pakistan National Alliance (PNA), led by religious parties, raised the demand for Nizam-e-Mustafa, which broadly denotes the system of governance in early Islam. Its proponents called it Islamic democracy.

Justice Munir has debated the concept of Nizam-e-Mustafa in his book *From Jinnah to Zia*. He wrote, 'If we want a form of government that was in force during the Islamic republic, the first question that arises is whether the democratic government was in force in that period.'[26] His own answer was in the negative. He said, 'Democracy as a form of government is essentially a Western idea.' He added, 'In Nizam-e-Mustafa there were no parties, nor there can be now unless democracy is separated from religion belying the claim that in Islam religion cannot be separated from politics. And if you have parties in

Islam the result will be that Islam will be divided into sects which is not a very desirable result.'[27]

Justice Munir courageously advocated a secular state but was not optimistic about the prospect of democracy in Pakistan. Munir wrote, 'the obvious course for Pakistan is to have a secular State, and in doing so it will be realizing the ideal that Quaid-i-Azam had placed before us'. On the other hand, Shahab endorsed the idea that the meaning of Pakistan was *La ilaha illa Allah*. He equated the state with religion. It seems that Shahab's view has won so far.

Shahab, having served three autocratic rulers, as head of the governor-general and president's secretariat, seemed to have discovered his democratic leanings only after quitting the government. Looking back over Pakistan's journey since its creation, Shahab concluded that 'Martial law should sound its last bugle for the setting sun and smilingly return to the barracks forever. Political process without any restrictions should start afresh in the country.'[28] However, there was no change in his thinking that Islam should be central to public life in Pakistan. He advocated a pan-Islamic view of Pakistan's mission. He wrote, 'Encouragement of Islam in Pakistan is not only in our interests but will also prove handy in Afghanistan and Central Asia.'[29] Shahab was the ultimate insider; his writings show that the impulse for the Islamization of Pakistan came from within the establishment.

While Ayub was critical of the role of religious parties, Zia co-opted them. Jamaat-e-Islami gave a push for the Deobandi school, with its stress on a puritanical version of Islam. Both the Pakistan Army and the clergy supported the transnational definition of Islam based on the concept of Islamic *ummah*. It was useful to the army in raising cadres and financing for Jehad in Afghanistan and Jammu and Kashmir. This was also closer to the conception of an Islamic emirate favoured by the religious parties.

Zia's period saw two major events on Pakistan's western border – the Soviet intervention in Afghanistan and the Iranian Revolution. Zia used the opportunity to join the Afghan Jehad to get military and economic assistance. At home, he gave a free hand to various Sunni groups. The introduction of sharia law by Zia led to the question – whose version of sharia? This intensified the sectarian divide and gave birth to the Shia organization Tehreek Nifaz-e-Fiqh-e-Jafaria. The competition among the religious groups gave rise to extremism. It was not trouble in Afghanistan which brought terrorist groups to Pakistan. The Taliban went from madrassas in Pakistan to Afghanistan. Mullah Umar was a product of the Binori mosque in Karachi.

After Zia's death in a plane crash, elections brought Benazir Bhutto to power. Benazir Bhutto's PPP was allied with JUI (Jamiat Ulama-e-Islam), while the Pakistan Muslim League (PML) of Nawaz Sharif was allied with JI (Jamaat-e-Islami). Thus, both mainstream parties had entered into alliance with religious parties. Democracy returned to Pakistan, but the role of religion in politics had grown again.

The defining event of the new millennium was the 9/11 attack on the Twin Towers in New York. Pakistan played an ambivalent role despite its alliance with America. It was no coincidence that Osama bin Laden was found living in Abbottabad, close to the Pakistan Military Academy, and 70 kilometres from Islamabad. Mullah Umar also received sanctuary in Pakistan. The fact that he lived in that country for more than a decade after his escape from Afghanistan came to light in the course of an intra-Taliban leadership tussle. Pakistan may see these events differently. After the US launched Operation Enduring Freedom in Afghanistan in October 2001, there were demonstrations in support of the Taliban in Pakistan, and Osama bin Laden was proclaimed a hero. Public discourse in the country veered towards extremism.

Musharraf accommodated religious parties in power while taking action against the mainstream opposition parties, Nawaz Sharif's PML(N) and Benazir Bhutto's PPP. The PML(Q) government, which came to power in Islamabad in 2002, was supported by an alliance of religious parties, called the Muttahida Majlis-e-Amal (MMA). The MMA was rewarded for siding with the PML(Q) – 'King's Party' at the federal level – by being allowed to form governments in the two border provinces, NWFP and Balochistan. This provided the Taliban and Al-Qaeda with a friendly ecosystem in Pakistan.

After the fall of the Musharraf government, the PPP and PML(N) came together to pass the Eighteenth Amendment to the Constitution in 2010. This clawed back some space for democracy by repealing Article 58(2)(b), which allowed the president to dismiss the prime minister. But they left untouched Article 2A, which had made the Objectives Resolution an integral part of the Constitution and deepened the role of

Islam in the state and society in Pakistan. They had chosen democracy but not Justice Munir's enlightened vision of Pakistan.

The Eighteenth Amendment to Pakistan's Constitution in 2010 devolved more powers to provinces. Their share in the revenue was increased by the Seventh National Finance Commission award. However, the Pakistan Army's role in governance has been institutionalized. The army's role in national politics provides a centralizing impulse.

While civilian politicians and the military were the earliest supporters of a state founded on religion, the judiciary has also joined in. It is ironic that Musharraf – a former army chief and president – was sentenced to death for high treason, while the cleric of Islamabad's Lal Masjid (the Red Mosque), who challenged the writ of the state in the national capital, was set free. It was during this period that Tehriq-e-Taliban Pakistan (TTP) rose to power.

Riyasat-e-Madina

Imran Khan came to power in 2018 with the military and religious groups' support. In an address in November 2019, he gave a call for Riyasat-e-Madina as the model for Pakistan. The phrase refers to the first state established by the Holy Prophet, which is considered a model of Islamic governance.

Imran Khan is now in jail, but commands a large following, as the results of the 2024 elections have shown. The rhetoric of piety and concern for welfare of the poor touches a deep chord in the minds of the electorate. However, various poverty alleviation and employment generation schemes received 3 per cent of the total projected tax revenues, while the 'national security' sector was allocated 40 per cent.[30]

Democracy, Nationality and Ideology?

Altaf Gauhar, in his biography of Ayub Khan, explained the quick acceptance of the military coup: 'Muslim jurists regard power as a "gift of Allah", hence its own justification. To question the possession of power was to invite disorder.'[31] There was very little resistance to the three coups by Ayub, Zia and Musharraf. The ideology has legitimized power. While democracy had weak roots in Pakistan, political parties have contributed to weakening it further. The opposition tries to take the battle to the streets by organizing 'Long Marches' to demand the resignation of the party in power. The agitation outside the Parliament is used to invite military intervention.

The ideology of Pakistan does not accept national or ethnic parties but is sympathetic to religious groups. Khaled Ahmed, a noted Pakistani commentator, pointed to the contrast between Pakistan's treatment of the TTP on one hand and nationalist groups like the Baloch Liberation Front (BLF) on the other. Though both have challenged the authority of the state, the former is treated more leniently. Ahmed argues, 'The TTP was ideologically driven and the BLF secular. The Taliban had the same ideology as Pakistan's, and its claims were corrective of a misguided state; while the BLF did not resonate with the Muslim mind in Pakistan.'[32] Ahmed questions: 'And why should the Taliban version of sharia be more persuasive than the sharia proclaimed by the Constitution of the Islamic Republic of Pakistan? Because the Taliban sharia was more "authentic".'[33] The state faces competition from non-state actors who are now defining the ideology of Pakistan as much as the establishment.

The Communist Party of India had supported the creation of Pakistan. While the left movement took root in India, it did not survive in Pakistan. The combination of religion and military alliance with the US was too powerful for the Communist Party to resist, which was seen as atheist. Much before Pakistan joined the US-led military bloc in 1954, the army was purged of officers suspected of leaning to the Left. This included Colonel (later Maj. General) Akbar Khan who led the tribal invasion in Jammu and Kashmir in 1947–48.

Economy

Jinnah mentioned the problem of poverty among Muslims, but did not outline how the state would tackle this problem. The Two-Nation Theory also did not provide any blueprint for the new state's economic future. The absence of any socio-economic programme was to mark the philosophy of the Muslim League.

Post-Independence, Pakistan adopted a laissez-faire model of the economy which gave rise to inequalities. This was against the Islamic principle of equality. Pakistan has different ideologies pervading political and economic domains. While the polity was to be based on Islam, the economy followed the capitalist model.

Afghanistan and Jammu and Kashmir

Pakistan did not allow its changing foreign policy alignments to affect its domestic politics. It made a seamless switch from an alliance with the US in the 1950s to an 'all-weather friendship' with China since the 1960s. However, this pragmatic approach gives way to a more ideological position while dealing with its neighbours. Pakistan lays its claim over Jammu and Kashmir on religious parameters. This is an ideological position, though the element of interest cannot be denied. In Afghanistan's case, Pakistan risked its relations with the US to bring the Taliban back to power in 2021. Support to the Taliban continued despite its ideological kin, the TTP, emerging as a threat to Pakistan's internal security as far back as 2007. This goes beyond the mere pursuit of interest. Pakistan's choice of an ideologically driven cadre to undermine the fledgeling democracy established in Afghanistan after 9/11 is an expression of ideology. This policy has now been reversed by Islamabad. The TTP wants to establish an Islamic emirate in Pakistan, which Islamabad promoted in Afghanistan but resisted at home. The TTP has been more consistent; Pakistan has used ideology as a tool for foreign policy.

Alternate Constructs

In his book *Muslim Zion: Pakistan as a Political Idea*, Faisal Devji has debated if Pakistan is a Muslim Zion.[34] These are the only two countries founded based on religion. But the similarities end here. Unlike the Jewish diaspora, the Muslims of the Indian subcontinent were not forced into exile. The Muslim League chose to sacrifice the interests of Muslims of Muslim-minority regions to get a state in the Muslim-majority areas. Israel has accepted the Right to Return for the Jewish community. Pakistan closed the door to further immigration of Muslims soon after the partition.

Aitzaz Ahsan, in his book *The Indus Saga and the Making of Pakistan*, has tried to anchor Pakistan's identity in a territorial concept based on the Indus. He has also challenged the assumption that Muslims came from outside. This late realization is a refreshing change from the writings of Sir Syed Ahmad Khan who claimed subcontinental Muslims were descendants of the Arab invaders. He describes 'Indus person' as 'a family man, an enlightened non-fundamentalist Muslim'.[35] He argues that Iqbal's conception was Pakistan as a Muslim state instead of an Islamic state. This appears to be a romantic construct. The demand for Pakistan did not arise from the 'Indus man'; it was raised by Muslims from provinces where they were in the minority, outside what Aitzaz Ahsan calls the Indus region. Iqbal resisted territorial nationalism as he feared this would weaken the unity of the Islamic world. This was the antithesis of Aitzaz Ahsan's conception of the Indus man rooted in the indigenous tradition.

Most of the Hindus were forced to flee Pakistan despite being the 'Indus man'. The population of Hindus in Karachi, which is the heart of the Indus region, declined from 51 per cent in 1947 to 2 per cent in 1951. Aitzaz Ahsan's writing is an attempt to give Pakistan the historical depth it lacks without acknowledging the history of communal politics followed by the Muslim League in undivided India, and the trajectory that the country has taken since Partition.

Pakistan: A Homeland for Muslims or an Islamic State?

The debate over Pakistan as a territorial concept or an Islamic state is a recent one. The proponents of the idea of Pakistan did not necessarily see a conflict between these two strands of Pakistan's ideology. Iqbal's address of 1930 included both strands. He demanded a separate state for Muslims in the north-west but stressed the organic link between religion and state.

Jinnah, in his speech at the Karachi Bar Association in February 1948, declared that Pakistan's future Constitution would be based on the sharia. Any doubt about the nature of the state was settled after the adoption of the Objectives Resolution in 1949. This has since emerged as the cornerstone of Pakistan's Constitution. It now affects the lives of the majority and the minority communities. Religion was not to be a private affair, as Iqbal had said. The Objectives Resolution granted a role in an individual's personal life to the state.

The issue of national or linguistic identities remains unresolved. The space for democracy has been narrowed by demands of religious groups for the polity and the economy to conform to religious injunctions. The limited electoral influence of religious parties is no index of a liberal order; mainstream parties have outflanked them by assuming their agenda. The intervention of the higher judiciary has repeatedly reinforced ideology's role in the state. Both the military and civilians undermine democracy. The National Assembly was dissolved based on Imran Khan's advice in 2022 to avoid the No Confidence vote. In the 2024 elections, 'independent' candidates supported by Khan's Pakistan Tehreek-e-Insaf (PTI) won the largest number of seats but were forced to sit in opposition.

While the army claims to be the custodian of Pakistan's ideology, its legitimacy is being challenged as shown by the events of 9 May 2023 after an attack on the Army GHQ in Rawalpindi. The median of Pakistan's politics has veered towards an increasingly intolerant society based on a narrow interpretation of religion. There has been a steady progression from the Objectives Resolution to Nizam-e-Mustafa to Riyasat-e-Madina. Ideology has trumped interest; it cannot be challenged as it is equated with faith.

PART 1

The Road to Partition

3

Two-Nation Theory

'Now suppose the English ...were to leave India', 'Is it possible that under these circumstances, two nations – the Mahomedans and the Hindus – could sit on the same throne and remain equal in power? Most certainly not. It is necessary that one of them should conquer the other and thrust it down.'

–Sir Syed Ahmad Khan, Meerut, 1888

THE PASSAGE IS FROM Sir Syed Ahmad Khan's speech in Meerut in 1888. He was criticizing the Congress's demand for a representative government and control over the budget. He said, 'These proposals of the Congress are extremely inexpedient for the country, which is *inhabited by two different nations.*' [Emphasis added] He cast Hindus and Muslims as two 'different nations' who could not cohabit as equals – 'one of them should conquer and thrust down the other'. This preceded Jinnah's 1940 speech at the All-India Muslim League session by over half a century. Jinnah said, 'It is a dream that the Hindus and Muslims can ever evolve a common nationality.' He stressed that they indeed 'belong to two different civilizations which are based mainly on conflicting ideas and conceptions'.[1]

The *Ashrafs*, Muslim elite of north India, saw themselves as heirs to the Muslim rulers, and foreign to this land. Eighteenth-century theologian Shah Waliullah said, 'We are an Arab people whose fathers have fallen in exile in the country of Hindustan, and our Arabic genealogy and Arabic language are our pride.'[2] A century later, this sentiment was echoed by Syed Ahmad Barelvi who said, 'We must repudiate all those Indian, Persian and Roman customs which are contrary to the Prophet's teaching.'[3]

The creation of separate electorates reinforced the idea of a distinct identity and political aspirations of Muslims of the subcontinent. The demand was made by Muslim notables in October 1906. But the inspiration for the demand came from the British. This was the reaction to protests against the partition of Bengal in the previous year. The British wanted to sap the strength of any future agitation by creating a communal divide. While the partition of Bengal was later annulled, separate electorates continued. It also had a much wider impact on the entire country. The delegation's meeting with Viceroy Lord Minto was followed by the founding of the Muslim League in Dhaka in December 1906.

Two decades later, the Khilafat movement, launched to protest the abolition of the Turkish Caliphate brought the two communities together for a short period. Mahatma Gandhi's support made it a broad-based movement, which the Khilafat Committee asked him to lead. However, its lasting impact was to stress the role of religion in politics and pan-Islamic ideas. As Khaliquzzaman has remarked, most of the Muslim League leadership came from the ranks of those who participated in the Khilafat movement. He was one of these leaders, who became president of the Pakistan Muslim League after Jinnah's death.

The idea of Muslims being a separate 'nation' was supported by Iqbal in his 1930 presidential address at the Allahabad session of the All-India Muslim League. Jinnah made a formal statement at the Lahore conference of the Muslim League in 1940. His speech elevated the Muslim demand from safeguarding minority rights in united India to a separate nationality requiring an independent state. The transformation in the League's position followed the changing contours of British policy. It fostered a separate Muslim identity to block India's political evolution, and they used it to divide the country when the British were leaving India.

Sir Syed Ahmad Khan

Sir Syed had witnessed the events of 1857 described as 'mutiny' or 'gadar' by the British, and the 'first war of independence' by Indian historians, and wrote *Asbab-e-Baghawat-e-Hind* (*The Reasons for India's Rebellion*) in 1859, almost immediately after the uprising.

In this book, he examined the causes behind the traumatic event which led to the overthrow of the old order. Dismissing all popular theories surrounding the event, he argued that the distribution of chapatis (flatbread) in the cantonments could not have been a cause as it was not accompanied by any secret message.[4] He also ruled out the confiscation of Awadh by the East India Company as a cause.[5] He was sceptical of the theory that the establishment of foreign rule over an ancient country was the reason for the revolt.[6]

Sir Syed rejected the role of religion and the call for jehad as the reason for the uprising.[7] He wrote that 'those who raised the flag of "Jehad" were "kharab" [bad] people, with "bad soul" and "bad conduct", who spent time "drinking wine", "dancing" and "merrymaking".' He added, 'In this "hungama" (uproar), nothing happened which was in accordance with religion.'[8]

Sir Syed mentioned that two 'fatwas' (religious edicts in accordance with Islamic tradition) were printed in Delhi: the first one was issued when the 'Namakharam Army' from Meerut reached Delhi. The second fatwa called for jehad, but it was 'without doubt, not authentic'.[9]

Sir Syed's description of the rebel soldiers as 'namakharam' makes it clear that his sympathies lay with the East India Company, and not the last Mughal emperor for whom the rebel soldiers – Muslims and Hindus alike – fought. He described Bahadur Shah Zafar as 'Dilli ka Badshah' (King of Delhi). At points in the book, he was even more disparaging and called him the 'deposed King of Delhi'.[10] He described the East India Company as 'our government' which was odd. While the events of 1857 eventually resulted in the exile of the last Mughal emperor, Sir Syed was writing about the causes that led to the uprising before he was deposed.

Sir Syed treated the last Mughal emperor and the rebel soldiers more severely than British historians. The Company ruled in the name of the Mughal emperor. The book *Ideologies of the Raj*, a part of the new Cambridge History of India series, describes Bahadur Shah Zafar as the 'legitimate authority'. Its author, Metcalf says: 'For half a century, the British had themselves endeavoured to use the power of that name to secure their own position, while in 1857 the rebel soldiery, in turn, forced their way into his fort in order to command that legitimate authority.' He adds:

> Although the British could not legally try the king for treason, in as much as he was the king and they his vassals, nevertheless the trial, and Bahadur Shah's subsequent banishment to Burma, enabled the British

> at last to represent themselves as the unquestioned rulers of India. A new order had begun.[11]

The British account accepts Bahadur Shah Zafar was the legitimate authority and does not use the pejorative term 'namakharam' for the rebel soldiers who fought for him.

Sir Syed initially stressed Hindu – Muslim unity. For example, in a speech on 27 January 1884 at Gurdaspur, he said, 'We [i.e. Hindus and Muslims] should try to become one heart and soul, and act in union.'[12] However, he was to disregard this opinion soon. He called upon the Muslim landed class to keep away from the Congress, which was demanding a voice in shaping the country's budget, selection to government jobs through competition and election to local bodies. He said Muslims may not be able to compete with 'Bengalis'. He added that they may not win the elections as Hindus were in the majority in most towns. This last statement was an indication that his universe was limited to provinces in north and central India. In west and east India, where Muslims were in the majority, they would have an advantage in the elections.

In his Lucknow speech in 1887, Sir Syed stressed the special position of Muslims as past rulers:

> We are those who ruled India for six or seven hundred years. (Cheers.) From our hands, the country was taken by Government into its own. Is Government so foolish as to suppose that in seventy years we have forgotten all our grandeur and our empire?[13]

Sir Syed in his Meerut speech in 1888 mentioned an inevitable conflict between Hindus and Muslims as discussed at the beginning of the chapter. Referring to Hindus and Muslims as separate nations, he added: 'Until one nation had conquered the other and made it obedient, peace could not reign in the land. This conclusion is based on proofs so absolute that no one can deny it.'[14]

In the Meerut speech, Sir Syed told the Muslim aristocracy that their interests lay in cultivating the British, citing religious grounds. 'No Mahomedan can say that the English are not "people of the book". Now, God has made them rulers over us. Therefore, we should cultivate friendship with them, and should adopt that method by which their rule may remain permanent and firm in India, and may not pass into the hands of the Bengalis.' Sir Syed added: 'If we join the political movement of the Bengalis our nation will reap loss, for we do not want to become subjects of the Hindus instead of the subjects of the "people of the book". And as far as we can we should remain faithful to the English Government.'[15]

The Muslim League was born nearly two decades after Sir Syed delivered his 1888 speech. His twin axioms – a collaboration with the foreign ruler and casting the interests of Muslims and Hindus as inherently contradictory – would capture the League's politics. His concern about the upliftment of the Muslim community by providing them with modern education is commendable. But he embraced English education, and not the Western values of separation of religion and state. He opposed the national movement and nascent steps towards democracy as he feared Muslims would become 'subjects of the Hindus'.

Separate Electorate

The demand for a separate electorate was voiced after the partition of Bengal by Lord Curzon in 1905. Both developments were linked to British attempts to divide the Indian polity. The nature of the electorate did not signify much when the elected government had little power. This was three decades before provincial assemblies were given limited powers under the Government of India Act, 1935.

The idea of a separate electorate for Muslims was not a spontaneous demand. Chaudhry Khaliquzzaman mentioned in his memoir *Pathway to Pakistan* that William Archbold, principal of the Muhammedan Anglo-Oriental (MAO) College in Aligarh, wrote to Nawab Mohsinul Mulk stating that, 'in his opinion, it would be wise for the Muslims to claim nomination or representation on the basis of religion'.[16]

Mohsinul Mulk, who was associated with MAO College, organized a Muslim delegation following his meeting with Mr Dunlop Smith, secretary to Lord Minto, who was Curzon's successor as viceroy of India. The Secretary of State in London sanctioned approval before the delegation, headed by Agha Khan, met with Minto in October 1906 to demand a 'separate electorate' for the Muslims.

Khaliquzzaman claimed, 'This system of safeguard of minority interest was unique and unknown to a democratic system of representation in any other country at that time.'[17] His statement shows that separate electorates were a departure from democracy as practised in other countries. For the next four decades the Muslim League sought to not secure Muslims' democratic rights but fought for reservations in jobs in excess of their share in the population. Iqbal in his address to the Muslim League conference in 1930, and Jinnah in his speech at the Lahore session of the Muslim League in 1940, cautioned against democracy even after the demand for separate electorates had been conceded. They feared that democracy would go in favour of the Hindu majority.

Khilafat Movement

For Turkey, the abolition of the Ottoman Caliphate was an internal decision to move the country towards a modern state system. For the British, it was a foreign policy issue. Turkey had sided with Germany in the First World War. The title 'Caliphate' was used to claim the allegiance of Indian Muslims to the Turkish cause and incite them to rebel against the British authority. For Indian Muslims, it became an emotive issue, and Mahatma Gandhi supported it as an expression of solidarity with them.

The position taken by Khilafat movement supporters in India must have looked anachronistic to the Arabs. Turkish rule evokes bitter memories in the Arab world. The Arabs have an older history and association with Islam than the Turkic tribes, which came to Anatolia around the eleventh century CE. The seat of the Caliphate had remained in Arab lands – Syria, Iraq and Egypt – under the Omayyads, Abbasids and Fatimids until the Turkish sultan assumed the title. Just when the Arabs were preparing to enjoy their freedom from Turkish rule, the Indians seemed to suggest that their bondage should be perpetuated.

The supporters of the Khilafat movement sent out delegations to Afghanistan and Arabia to gather support for their stand but did not have much success in convincing the Muslims of other countries to rise in defence of the Caliphate. The mission sent to Kabul failed to win over the king of Afghanistan. Its leader, Maulana Ubaidullah, had to leave that country. A mission sent to Saudi Arabia, the heart of Islam, had even less success as the Sharif of Mecca handed over Maulana Mahmud Hasan and his followers to the British, who sent them to Malta as internees.[18]

The Khilafat issue was taken up at the Delhi session of the Muslim League in 1918. A resolution was moved for the protection of the Khilafat. Khaliquzzaman writes:

> Mr Jinnah then raised a Point of Order and gave his opinion that under the Muslim League Constitution, it had no right to dabble in the foreign politics of the Government. Everyone was taken aback. Both Rahman and I joined issues with him on the question and finding the members opposed to his views he left, followed by the Raja of Mahmudabad.[19]

Jinnah stood aside from the Khilafat movement not because of any commitment to secular values but because he did not want the League to interfere in a foreign policy matter, which was the government's prerogative to decide. Taking up the cause of preserving the Caliphate amounted to going against British policy. Neither Jinnah nor the landed aristocracy like the Raja of Mahmudabad could countenance this. After all, the Muslim League had come so far only because of British patronage. How could Jinnah go against its imperial interests? This caution guided Jinnah's actions and the Muslim League's decisions until the end of British rule in India. This was the higher principle that overruled even the pull of communal politics, which remained the basis of the Muslim League's policy.

The Poet

Iqbal wrote the famous poem *Saare Jehan Se Achha Hindostan Hamara* in 1904. It included the stanza, 'Mazhab nahin sikhata aapas men bair rakhna. Hindi hain ham, watan hai Hindostan hamara.' These lines emphasized religious harmony (religion does not teach enmity). Iqbal said, 'We are Indians, and India is our country.' The sense of belonging to a nation was rooted in 'Hindostan', which was described as watan or country. This was a territorial definition of nationhood; not one based on religious identity. Over the next twenty-five years, however, Iqbal was to assume a completely different position.

In his presidential address to the 1930 session of the All-India Muslim League, he described Muslims as 'the only Indian people who can fitly be described as a "nation" in the modern sense of the word'. He differentiated them from the Hindu majority and repudiated the territorial definition of nationhood. He said,

> …Nor should the Muslim leaders and politicians allow themselves to be carried away by the subtle but fallacious argument that Turkey and Persia and other Muslim countries were progressing on national, i.e. territorial, lines. The Muslims of India were differently situated. The countries of Islam outside India are practically wholly Muslim population. The minorities there belong, in the language of the Quran, to the 'people of the Book'.

Iqbal denied the contemporary trend in Muslim countries, which were progressing along 'national, i.e. territorial lines'. His sweep of history also ignored centuries of strife among the 'people of the Book'. This included the dispersion of the Jews, the Crusades and the increasing friction between Palestinians and Jewish settlers, which had begun in the aftermath of the Balfour Declaration and the end of the First World War. His allusion to the phrase was rooted in a religious context.

Iqbal was born in 1877. For most families in northern India, memories of 'Ghadar' (the 1857 'mutiny') were still fresh, when Hindu and Muslim soldiers had fought together to restore the authority of the last Mughal emperor. The ageing king was perhaps only a symbol, but the choice of symbol was important. The Hindu soldiers did not turn to ancient India but accepted the Mughal emperor as their rightful ruler. This shared legacy did not find any reflection in Iqbal's thoughts; he stressed their differences.

Sir Iqbal witnessed the Khilafat movement, which was supported by the Congress under Mahatma Gandhi. Jinnah and the Muslim League had stood aside. Iqbal, deeply concerned with maintaining pan-Islamic unity, nevertheless distanced himself from the movement. In both his opposition to nationalism and his aloofness from the Khilafat movement, he was close to the British position.

Iqbal's 1930 address presented two contradictory thoughts. He began by differentiating between the principles of Reformation, as they evolved in Europe, and the context of Islamic societies. He said that Reformation resulted in a 'polity evolved on national lines, i.e. on lines which recognize territory as the only principle of political solidarity'. He added, 'In Islam, God and the universe, spirit and matter, Church and State, are organic to each other.' By defining nationhood based on religion, he not only broke from Western thought but also contemporary Islamic societies like Turkey and Persia. He had also distanced himself from the idea expressed in his poetry – 'Hindi hain ham, watan hai Hindostan hamara'. Being Indian was identified with 'watan' or country, which was a territory. It did not have a religious connotation.

Iqbal began his speech opposing nationalism based on territorial lines but ended with a call for establishing an Indian Muslim state based on territorial consolidation:

> I would like to see the Punjab, North-West Frontier Province, Sind, and Balochistan amalgamated into a single State. Self-government within the British Empire, or without the British Empire, the formation of a consolidated North-west Indian Muslim State appears to me to be the final destiny of the Muslims, at least of North-West India.

While calling for a single state for Muslim India, Iqbal made two significant omissions. There was no reference to Bengal. Nor did he give much thought to the situation of Muslims in provinces where they may be in a minority. Worse, he was making the demand on behalf of Muslim-majority provinces, where their majority already provided the Muslims a safeguard against any future dispensation based on elections.

Iqbal was from Punjab. The Muslim League would only gain power in that province in 1946. Iqbal was prepared to accept the partition of Punjab, with the exclusion of the Ambala Division in order to achieve a religiously homogenous population. Later, the Muslim League would oppose the partition of provinces even while demanding the partition of the country.

Was Iqbal arguing for autonomy for Muslim-majority provinces within India or for partition of the country? His words, 'Self-government within the British Empire, or without the British Empire', could encompass both ideas. He referred to the British Empire; the four provinces he mentioned were part of British India. Even if we accept the interpretation as advocating autonomy, not independence and partition, this was to be within the British Empire – not necessarily British India. His thrust was towards partition and independence. This is reinforced by his use of the word 'state', not 'province', for the consolidated entity in north-west India.

Iqbal's 1930 speech was made against the backdrop of the Simon Commission's visit in 1928. The commission's report suggested replacing the Central Legislative Assembly with an assembly of the representatives of federal states. The British would have retained their hold on the Executive, unfettered by the work of the Central Assembly. Presented in the garb of federation, this was a scheme for a confederation of different states and provinces that would weaken India's unity. The Congress opposed it, while Iqbal said, 'I give my wholehearted support to this view of the matter…'

Iqbal was opposed to constitutional scheme with a strong Centre. He said, 'What is called "residuary powers" must be left entirely to self-governing states, the Central Federal State exercising only those powers which are expressly vested in it by the free consent of federal states.' His formula was devised to ensure maximum autonomy for Muslim-majority provinces – a position the League consistently pursued until 1947.

Iqbal tried to allay the Hindu fear that the creation of autonomous Muslim states would mean the introduction of a kind of religious rule in such states. He said, 'I have already indicated to you the meaning of the word religion, as applied to Islam. The truth is that Islam is not a Church. It is a State conceived as a contractual organism long before Rousseau ever thought of such a thing…'

Iqbal had extended the hold of religion over the lay sphere by claiming that Islam was a state. This placed minority rights on a precarious perch. Such rights as they would enjoy were not part of a covenant the minorities had accepted voluntarily but were subject to norms alien to their faith.

Iqbal was even critical of the Lucknow Pact, which had legitimized a separate electorate in an agreement with Congress. Under the pact, Muslims got twice the weightage of their percentage of the population in Muslim-minority provinces like Uttar Pradesh, Bihar and the Central Provinces. The pact was predicated on a slight reduction in the weightage of the Muslim population in the Muslim-majority provinces.

It was designed to ensure the protection of Muslims, Hindus and Sikhs in areas where they were in a minority.

Iqbal was critical of a slight reduction in the weightage of the Muslim majority in Punjab and Bengal, though this did not change the political balance. In both provinces, the premiers were Muslims. Iqbal equated the interests of the Muslims of India with the interests of the Muslims of Punjab. There was no reference to the interests of Muslims in states where they were in a minority. His speech mentioned the British prime minister's admission in a debate in the House of Commons that it was difficult to reconcile the system of the separate electorate with Britain's democratic traditions.

Iqbal's thoughts had a deep influence on the politics of the Muslim League. His philosophy was rooted in the past and rejected the values of democracy and enlightenment. He said, '[The] principle of European democracy cannot be applied to India without recognizing the fact of communal groups.' His speech was indeed a celebration of communal politics.

In Iqbal's view, the welfare of the Muslim minority demanded not only a separate electorate for them but also their recognition as a separate 'nation'. While rejecting the territorial basis of nationalism, he made a contradictory demand for a separate territory consolidating the Muslim-majority states of Punjab, Sindh, North-West Province and Balochistan. Scarcely any thought was given to the impact of such a step on the Muslims in areas where they were in minority. Nor did he recognize that religion could not subsume or suppress ethnic and linguistic differences. The values underlying the political construct he suggested continue to cast a shadow on the politics of Pakistan.

Jinnah gave voice to the Two-Nation Theory at the Lahore session of the All-India Muslim League in 1940. With the British departure drawing closer, the question raised by Sir Syed Ahmad fifty-two years earlier at Meerut about the nature of political order if the English left India was revived. As Islamabad-based political economist Niaz Murtaza commented in *Dawn*, the Muslim mindset was based on 'an absurd sense of superiority claiming a divine birthright to rule others...'[20] If they could not rule, they preferred Partition. The minority problem could have been settled in a democratic framework, but League leaders had consistently ruled this out. Partition made the minority problem worse and led to the uprooting of millions.

The British were not ready to give up their Indian empire in 1940. They were using the Muslim League to stall the Congress's demand for assurance of absolute freedom at the end of the Second World War. It was only when the British realized they could no longer hold their Indian empire that they decided to partition it. There was a convergence between British aims and the League's demand. The Muslim League was a willing accomplice, with the Two-Nation Theory providing an ideological cover. This is discussed in the following chapters on the Lahore Resolution and the Cabinet Mission Plan.

4

Lahore Resolution

'It is perfectly true that the word "State" was substituted for the word "States". Whether it was done validly and legally has only an academic interest....'

–Nawab Ismail Khan, in a letter to Chaudhry Khaliquzzaman on the Lahore Resolution[1]

THE RESOLUTION ADOPTED BY the All-India Muslim League at Lahore in March 1940 is considered to have laid the foundations of the new state, though it did not mention Pakistan specifically. The resolution called for a separate homeland for 'Mussalmans of the Indian subcontinent' but went beyond the idea of a Muslim 'nation' to call for 'states' in the north-western and eastern zones of India. In both respects – in setting apart Muslims as a separate 'nation' and giving it a territorial definition – this reflected what Iqbal had stated in his presidential address in the Muslim League session a decade earlier, in 1930. But now, it was no longer a matter of an individual's vision but the collective demand of the party. Iqbal's speech had mentioned Punjab, North West Frontier Province, Sindh and Baluchistan. The Lahore Resolution added an 'eastern zone'.

The original Lahore Resolution envisaged a plurality of 'independent states'. Jinnah later replaced 'states' with 'state', creating an abiding controversy that persists even after the creation of Bangladesh.

There is overwhelming evidence that the inspiration for the Lahore Resolution came from the Viceroy's office. This was reminiscent of the British orchestrating the demand for separate electorates from Muslim notables nearly four decades earlier in 1906. The timing of the resolution – within days of the Congress's demand for complete independence at the Ramgarh session on 19 March 1940 – could not have been better from the British point of view. Though Jinnah or the Muslim League had hardly any credentials to represent 'Muslim India' after the League's defeat in the 1937 elections, the resolution served to show that Indian opinion was divided, and pitted the minority against the majority.

The events in the subcontinent were taking place against the background of the war which had broken out in Europe in September 1939. While the Congress Working Committee adopted a resolution on 11 August 1939 not to assist in the war effort, the Muslim League passed a resolution on 27 August, adopting a wait-and-watch attitude and confining itself to the demands for 'Muslim India' to be met without delay.[2] On 3 September, following the German attack on Poland, Britain declared war. On the same day, the Viceroy, Lord Linlithgow, committed India to the war and appealed to the Indian people for their sympathy and support. He invited Gandhi Ji, Jinnah and the Chancellor of the Chamber of Princes, the Maharaja of Nawanagar, Sir K.S. Digvijaysinhji for separate meetings. There followed a series of meetings over the next six months, leading up to the adoption of the Lahore Resolution.

The Congress wanted an unambiguous declaration for 'absolute freedom for India at the end of the war', and the liberty to frame 'her own constitution by means of a Constituent Assembly'. The Viceroy was only ready to give an undertaking that at the end of the war, the British government 'would be willing to enter into consultations with the representatives of the several communities, parties and interests in India, and with the Indian princes', with a view to 'framing of such modifications in the plan embodied in the Government of India Act as might seem desirable'.[3] This fell short of the Congress's demand. The offer of setting up a consultative committee or temporary expansion of the Viceroy's Executive Council to accommodate Indians was not acceptable to the Congress. At most, the British were willing to co-opt them into the government symbolically, without any commitment for the future. The Congress resigned from the provincial governments in October 1939 and, at the Ramgarh session on 19 March 1940, adopted a resolution insisting on 'nothing short of complete independence' and the demand for a Constituent Assembly. This decision closed the door for negotiations with the British and left the field open to the Muslim League.

The British priority was to secure cooperation for the unimpeded war effort while postponing the decision on India's future constitutional status until after the war. The Muslim League's stance perfectly complemented British aims. It was willing to cooperate on the recruitment of troops and to raise the communal question, which helped the British delay a future settlement. On 24 February 1940, Jinnah conveyed to the Viceroy the Muslim League Working Committee's demand that 'no commitment would be made with regard to the future constitution of India, or any interim settlement be reached with any other party, without the approval and consent of the Muslim League'.[4] The League sought not only participation in decision-making but also a veto over India's future.

The Lahore Resolution originated from a paper written by Sir Zafarullah Khan, a member of the Viceroy's Executive Council. According to Ayesha Jalal, 'Zafarullah's note was seen by Jinnah.'[5] Linlithgow wrote to the Secretary of State, Lord Zetland, on 12 March that, 'It had been written specifically for adoption by the Muslim League with a view to it being given full publicity.'[6]

Khaliquzzaman traced the origin of the resolution to his meeting a year earlier with Lord Zetland in London in March 1939. H.V. Hodson goes back further to a pamphlet published by Sir Sikandar Hayat in July 1938 under the title *Outlines of a Scheme of Indian Federation*. What is unmistakable is that the British had prior knowledge of the draft before it was introduced and adopted in the Muslim League's 1940 session.

The resolution did not mention 'partition' or 'Pakistan'. But this was inherent in the demand for 'independent States in the north-western and eastern zones of India'. It could not be more specific in the midst of the war effort, which the Muslim League had promised to support. The party could not afford to be inconvenient to the British, on whose patronage it depended.

It was extraordinary that the Muslim League claimed to represent Muslims and demanded a separate homeland on their behalf after a poor showing in the previous elections.[7] In his speech at the Lahore session, Jinnah rejected Gandhiji's offer to join the Constituent Assembly to decide India's future. As he put it sarcastically, this would have meant 'Brother Gandhi has three votes and I have only one vote', as Muslims constituted 25 per cent of India's population. The implied demand for 'parity' with the majority, which constituted 75 per cent of the population, not only went beyond the universally understood norms of minority protection, but also negated the principle of democracy. Post-Partition, West Pakistan would use the principle of 'parity' to deny the numerical majority of East Pakistan, leading to the eventual break-up of the country.

The British needed Jinnah to stymie the Congress's demand for independence by raising the communal issue. Jinnah played the role of spoiler to perfection. In turn, the British rewarded the Muslim League leadership by pandering to their extravagant demands without a representative credential.

V.P. Menon served as the reforms commissioner and later became constitutional adviser to the viceroy, giving him an insider's view of the negotiations. After Independence, he became Secretary of the Ministry of States under Patel. He has given an interesting account of the meeting between the viceroy and Jinnah on 13 March, when the latter conveyed that 'both from the Muslim point of view and that of His Majesty's Government, there was every reason for cooperation between the two'. Jinnah said, 'if the British Government could not improve on its present solution for the problem of India's constitutional development', he 'would have to fall back on some form of partition of the country'. He added that the 'Muslims were not a minority but rather a nation; and secondly, that democracy for all India was impossible'.[8]

The Viceroy sketched out three possibilities arising out of the constitution embodied in the Government of India Act of 1935 – removal of Hindu – Muslim differences, conflict between them, and third, 'there might be some tripartite arrangement by which the presence of His Majesty's Government, in a manner as little out of tune with Indian aspirations as possible, would be needed in India, longer even than some imagined'. Jinnah said, 'the third of these possibilities was an excellent one so far as he was concerned', and 'he was in favour of a Muslim area run by Muslims in collaboration with Great Britain'.[9] Jinnah was ready to accept indefinite prolongation of the British rule in the subcontinent and partition of the country, with the Muslim area run under British tutelage.

Menon's account of the meeting between the Viceroy and Jinnah finds an uncanny reflection in Jinnah's speech and in the Lahore Resolution itself, adopted barely ten days later. The League played down the issue of immediate independence from British rule. Instead, Jinnah held out the assurance that the recruitment of soldiers from Muslim-majority provinces for the British Army would continue unimpeded. These were the overriding priorities of the British government at the moment. British support was crucial to the rise of the Muslim League; they had to be responsive to the core interests of their patron.

Jinnah, in his speech at Lahore, stressed that he was invited by the viceroy, apart from Gandhiji, for a meeting to explain the war aims. Jinnah said he was surprised at his 'promotion'; earlier, the British were only 'running after Gandhi'. Jinnah's aim in highlighting the invitation was not only to emphasize the Muslim League's position as an equal partner with the Congress in any dialogue but also to consolidate his position within the party. The prime ministers of Muslim-majority provinces nominally supported the Muslim League's position at the Centre, but fiercely preserved their independence at the provincial level. The provincial level was the only level that mattered to them, because the British did not allow any power-sharing with Indians at the Centre. To these provincial leaders, Jinnah was a 'spokesman' for Muslim demands at the Centre, not necessarily the arbiter of their fate. The invitation from the viceroy to Jinnah for dialogue was useful to elevate his status within 'Muslim India'.

The British did not see Jinnah as the 'sole spokesman' of Muslims. In February, the viceroy also consulted Sir Sikandar Hayat Khan and A.K. Fazlul Haq. Punjab, which contributed 55 per cent of British India's army recruits, was particularly crucial. Jinnah had little control over the province, run by Sir Sikandar Hayat and his Unionist Party.

In his memoirs, Chaudhry Khaliquzzaman recalled suggesting to Lord Zetland in March 1939 that Muslim areas be partitioned from India: 'You may partition the Muslim areas from the rest of India and proceed with your scheme of federation of the Indian provinces without including the Muslim areas, which should be independent from the rest.'

Zetland did not respond, but the conversation was conveyed to the viceroy. Khaliquzzaman later obtained a transcript of the discussion from the British and reproduced it in his memoirs: '...that Lord Zetland gathered that the idea in your minds was of a federation of Muslim

Provinces and States in North-West India; a further federation of Bengal and Assam, and possibly more than one federation of the other Provinces and States in the remaining part of India.'

His suggestion for two Muslim federations in the east and west, separate from the rest of India, was reflected in the 1940 Lahore Resolution. His reference to 'more than one federation of the other Provinces and States in the remaining part of India' hinted at India's Balkanization. Since the transcript of his discussion with Zetland was passed on to the Viceroy, 'Lord Linlithgow knew before the Pakistan Resolution was passed what next step the Muslim League was likely to take'.[10]

Khaliquzzaman later reported the conversation to Jinnah, who asked, 'Have you weighed the consequences?' Jinnah assured him that 'he was not opposed to it but it had to be examined in all its bearings'. The British and the League were working in tandem for Partition. Later attempts by Khaliquzzaman and some historians to shift the blame for Partition onto the Congress do not hold up to scrutiny.

Hodson's account of Sir Sikandar Hayat's 1938 pamphlet, *Outlines of a Scheme of Indian Federation*, adds further context. The pamphlet proposed a three-tier system of provinces, regions and a central authority. Of the seven regions suggested, two closely resembled what later became Pakistan.[11]

All three proposals – Sikandar Hayat's 1938 scheme, Khaliquzzaman's 1939 suggestion and Sir Zafarullah Khan's 1940 draft – were shared with the British beforehand. Though differing in details, they aligned broadly with what the British later proposed as the Cabinet Mission Plan in 1946. Initially hesitant to endorse the League's demands, the British had no qualms about dividing India when their imperial withdrawal became inevitable.

Sir Sikandar Hayat's proposal differed from the final Lahore Resolution. He told British administrator Edward Penderel Moon that he published his plan to pre-empt 'something worse'. Hodson, quoting Moon, noted: 'The "something worse" to which he referred was the idea of Pakistan.'[12]

Hodson added,

> Some months later, Mr Moon suggested to the Punjab Premier that the Pakistan concept might after all be the best solution. Sir Sikandar turned

> upon him, his eyes blazing with indignation, and exclaimed: 'How can you talk like this? You have been long enough in Western Punjab to know the Muslims there. Surely, you can see that Pakistan would be an invitation to them to cut the throat of every Hindu *bania*....'[13]

'Nine years later, Pakistan did mean a massacre. But Sir Sikandar was dead.'[14]

Hodson stated that Sir Sikandar supported the Lahore Resolution 'for tactical reasons' to 'keep his followers together while the mad dream, as he saw it, of total partition faded'. However, as Hodson observed, 'the dream, the chimera, the students' scheme that was to become reality'.[15]

Jinnah's Speech

Jinnah said in his speech that 'it is a dream that the Hindus and Muslims can ever evolve a common nationality'. 'To yoke together two such nations under a single state, one as a numerical minority and the other as a majority, must lead to growing discontent and final destruction of any fabric that may be so built up for the government of such a state.' Though he did not mention 'Pakistan' or 'partition', he was ruling out the coexistence of Hindus and Muslims in a single state.

Jinnah added, 'Muslim India cannot accept any constitution which must necessarily result in a Hindu majority government. Hindus and Muslims brought together under a democratic system forced upon the minorities can only mean Hindu Raj. Democracy of the kind with which the Congress High Command is enamoured would mean the complete destruction of what is most precious in Islam.' Rejection of a common constitution meant separate statehood. Ironically, Jinnah was making the statement in Lahore, which was being ruled by a coalition of Muslims, Hindus and Sikhs under Sikandar Hayat's Unionist government. The best defence of minority rights in a democracy is forming cross-party and cross-denominational linkages.

Jinnah also said, 'Mussalmans are not a minority as it is commonly known and understood.' 'Even today, according to the British map of India, out of eleven provinces, four provinces where the Muslims dominate more or less...'. He left out the provinces where Muslims were a minority. The callous neglect of the fate of Muslims in minority provinces and of their Hindu and Sikh counterparts in Muslim-majority provinces would have disastrous consequences during Partition. The Muslim League had developed a mutual hostage theory for minority protection, which was spelt out by Khaliquzzaman in his speech at the Lahore session. None of this survived the communal frenzy unleashed by the League's demand for partition based on religion.

Of the four Muslim-majority provinces mentioned by Jinnah to buttress his argument that Muslims were not a minority but a nation, three were ruled by chief ministers who opposed the League's philosophy. The NWFP had elected a Congress government headed by Dr Khan Saheb. Sindh was ruled by Allah Bakhsh Soomro who organized a conference in Delhi to oppose the Lahore Resolution. Punjab was ruled by Sikandar Hayat who headed a coalition government of Hindus, Muslims and Sikhs. Only in Bengal did the League have a presence as a junior partner in the government headed by Fazlul Haq who led the Krishak Praja Party.

Jinnah's speech also left out nationalist Muslims in other parts of India who had chosen to throw in their lot with the 'Hindu Congress', as he described it. The Congress not only had a Muslim president but also many other leaders who contributed to independent India's development.

While repudiating the idea that Muslims were a minority, Jinnah said, 'Mussalmans are a nation according to any definition of a nation, and they must have their homelands, their territory and their state.' The reference to 'state' meant that Jinnah's aim was not simply an autonomous zone within the Union. It is also worth noting that Jinnah talked not of a single homeland but of homelands for Mussalmans. This is also in consonance with the resolution adopted at the Lahore conference, which mentioned 'Independent states'.

Lahore Resolution

Pakistan's official narrative describes the Lahore Resolution as the moment the idea of a separate state was born, though the text does not mention 'Pakistan' or 'partition'. Ayesha Jalal has argued that Jinnah used it as a bargaining counter.

The resolution was adopted in March 1940, after the outbreak of the Second World War and the viceroy's 18 October 1939 declaration that a new constitutional scheme would be explored post-war. The Muslim League always operated by positioning itself between British interests and the Congress's stance, leaning towards the former. Calling for independence would have placed it alongside the Congress, risking the loss of British support. Instead, it demanded statehood, but without explicitly calling for 'Pakistan' or 'partition' to avoid antagonizing the British, who had not yet decided to leave India.

Four aspects of the Lahore Resolution stand out. First, it assumed 'Muslim India' was a homogeneous 'nationality', despite ethnic and linguistic diversity among Muslim-majority provinces. Second, it spoke of multiple 'independent states', later changed by Jinnah to the singular. Third, it proposed 'territorial adjustments', raising concerns about future divisions within provinces. The League applied self-determination to partition India but denied the same principle within the new Muslim zones. Fourth, it promised minority protection in both Muslim- and Hindu-majority areas – an impractical idea, as Sikandar Hayat had warned Penderel Moon. After Partition, Khaliquzzaman's 'mutual hostage theory' collapsed when anti-Hindu and anti-Sikh violence erupted in Rawalpindi in March 1947.

The resolution welcomed the Viceroy's declaration that the Government of India Act, 1935 would be reconsidered. It stated, 'Muslim India will not be satisfied unless the whole constitutional plan is reconsidered de novo and that no revised plan would be acceptable to the Muslims unless it is framed with their approval and consent.' The League thus claimed sole authority to speak for 'Muslim India' while rejecting the 1935 Act without proposing an alternative.

The most famous section read:

> Resolved that it is the considered view of this Session of the All-India Muslim League that no constitutional plan would be workable in this country or acceptable to the Muslims unless it is designed on the following basic principle, viz, that geographically contiguous units are demarcated into regions which should be so constituted with such territorial adjustments as may be necessary that the areas in which the Muslims are numerically in a majority, as in the North-Western and Eastern Zones of India, should be grouped to constitute independent States in which the constituent units shall be autonomous and sovereign.

Having claimed Muslims were a separate nation, the League now demanded land and statehood. The resolution referred to 'geographically contiguous units' in the 'North-Western and Eastern Zones', grouped to form 'independent States'. Thus, it envisaged a plurality of such 'States'. Independent states could come into being only after the partition of the Union. There was no ambiguity on this score.

The ambiguity lay in whether the 'constituent units' would be 'autonomous and sovereign'. The terms have different meanings. The confusion was likely deliberate, to maintain the support of Muslim-majority provinces over which Jinnah had little control. These constituent units in the west included Punjab, Sindh, NWFP and Balochistan.

Sovereign Independent State or States?

Khaliquzzaman wrote in his memoirs that Jinnah tried to change the 'independent States' mentioned in the Lahore Resolution to a singular noun 'State' in the Muslim League convention in April 1946, claiming that the reference to the plural in the original version was a printing mistake. He said, 'The fundamental departure from the original resolution in using the word "State" in the singular calls for some explanation.'[16] He added that after Independence and Partition, controversy had arisen in the context of growing differences between East and West Pakistan in 1953. The secretary of the Bengal Muslim League, Abdul Hashim, had raised the question of the change from 'States' to 'State' in the Delhi convention of the Muslim League in 1946. Khaliquzzaman, who had by 1953 become Governor of East Pakistan, wrote to Nawab Ismail Khan to aid his memory. The latter had remained behind in Meerut, India.

Both Khaliquzzaman and Nawab Ismail Khan were associated with internal deliberations of the Muslim League at the highest level. Ismail Khan was a member of the Subjects Committee of the Muslim League, which drafted the resolution of the 1946 convention; the committee was chaired by Khaliquzzaman. The 1946 convention gave final touches to the Muslim League's demand for Pakistan on the eve of independence. Nawab Ismail Khan confirmed to Khaliquzzaman in October 1953, 'You are perfectly right that for the word "States" in the original resolution, the word "State" was substituted without any comments from anybody.'

Khaliquzzaman stated in his memoir, 'The Lahore Resolution having become the basic creed of the League could not possibly be amended by a subsidiary body, working under its Constitution...' 'Later when the council of the All-India Muslim League met to consider the proposals of the British government which contemplated a single State, no objection was raised that it was contrary to the basic creed of the League.'[17]

Nawab Ismail Khan wrote a second letter to Chaudhry Khaliquzzaman in November 1953, in which he stated, 'What has really astounded me in your letter is that Mr Jinnah ruled that the word "States" was a misprint...' 'If the word had been a misprint, as it is contended, how was it that it was not rectified when this resolution was converted into a creed of the League?'[18] He reproduced excerpts from the Muslim League constitution 'published under the direct supervision of Nawabzada Liaquat Ali Khan, which mentioned that "the North-Western and North-Eastern zones shall be grouped together to constitute independent *states* as a free national homeland".' [Emphasis added][19]

During my time at the Indian Consulate in Karachi in the early '90s, Muhajir friends told me the original resolution mentioned 'Qaumein' (nations), acknowledging the distinct identities of Baloch, Sindhis, Pashtuns, Punjabis and UP-Bihar Muslims – something the official narrative later suppressed. The ideology of Pakistan does not recognize ethnic diversity.

'Territorial Adjustments as May Be Necessary'

The resolution called for contiguous units with 'territorial adjustments as may be necessary'. Khaliquzzaman criticized this, arguing it weakened Pakistan's claim to undivided Punjab and Bengal. He added that had the provinces remained whole, India's access to Kashmir could have been blocked. However, the resolution made no mention of Kashmir or princely states.

A decade earlier, Iqbal had suggested excluding Ambala division from Punjab to ensure greater religious homogeneity in Muslim areas. Khaliquzzaman's logic was different – he believed minorities in Pakistan would safeguard Muslims in India. This 'mutual hostage' theory proved disastrous.

Mutual Hostage Theory

The resolution included a paragraph on reciprocal minority protection. Supporting it, Khaliquzzaman said: 'The Muslims in the minority Provinces should not be afraid as to what would happen to them after the partition of India into Hindu India and Muslim India. The same thing could happen to them as to the minorities in the Punjab and Bengal.'[20]

Penderel Moon raised this with Sir Sikandar Hayat Khan, who stated:

> He brushed it aside. The Baluchis and Awans of West Punjab, he said, wouldn't care at all about the lives of Muslims in Hindustan. The hostage idea was a mere fancy. Both sides would kill their own hostages. 'I do hope', he went on, 'I won't hear you talk like this again. *Pakistan would mean a massacre.*' [Emphasis added] [21]

Jinnah knew the predicament of Muslims in minority provinces. He was willing to abandon them. At the Cawnpore Muslim Students Federation Conference on 30 March 1941, 'He referred to the Round Table Conference, where he said that Mahatma Gandhi did not agree to allow 51 percent representation to Muslims in Punjab. When no adjustment could be made between the two communities, the Pakistan plan was devised. Speaking about the fate of Muslims in the non-Pakistan zone, he added that "*In order to liberate seven crores of Muslims where they were in a majority he was willing to perform the last ceremony of martyrdom if necessary and let two crores of Muslims be smashed.*"' [Emphasis added][22]

Jinnah was prepared to sacrifice Muslims in minority provinces for Pakistan. The fate of Hindus and Sikhs in Pakistan was not even mentioned. Jinnah's remarks also show that Pakistan had been in the making since the second Round Table Conference in 1931. He justified his position by recalling that Gandhi had refused to grant Muslims 51 per cent representation in Punjab. He omitted the fact that Muslims had already received double the representation warranted by their population in minority provinces.

A Bargaining Counter?

Ayesha Jalal has argued that the Lahore Resolution was simply 'a bargaining counter'.[23] She stated that Jinnah's politics revolved around the Centre, and the Lahore Resolution did not address the issue of the power compact at the Centre. This is a curious thesis. Jinnah's speech must be the definitive interpretation of the resolution. In his speech, he stressed that 'Mussalmans are a nation', and 'they must have their homelands, their territory and their state'. If he were bargaining, he never suggested as much. Jalal's thesis presumes something Jinnah never said while ignoring what he explicitly demanded. Once the League demanded 'Independent States', there was no need to define central power-sharing. Her argument is an attempt to absolve Jinnah of Partition.

Khaliquzzaman has written, 'I do not know how many people realize when it was that for the first time the Muslim League Working Committee decided to claim the division of India.' He elaborated that this decision was made in a meeting of the League Working Committee on 4 February 1940, when Mr Jinnah rejected Sir Sikandar's confederal scheme with the concurrence of the members. It was communicated to the Viceroy on 6 February 1940. 'Mr. Jinnah informed the Viceroy that the Muslim League in its open session at Lahore on 23 March was going to ask for the partition of the country as decided in our meeting two days earlier.'[24] Clearly, the demand for Pakistan was not a bargaining counter but the ultimate objective.

What was the meaning of the resolution calling for 'Independent States' without mentioning Pakistan or partition? Hodson said the 'intended meaning' was clarified in a later paragraph: 'This session further authorizes the Working Committee to frame a scheme of constitution in accordance with these basic principles, providing for the assumption finally by the respective regions of all powers such as *defence, external affairs, communications, customs and such other matters as may be necessary*.' [Emphasis added][25]

Defence, external affairs, communications and customs are subjects dealt with by governments of independent states, not provinces. The only ambiguity was the time frame – these powers were to be assumed 'finally'. The League avoided British displeasure by not explicitly calling for independence during the war. Its omission of 'Pakistan' or 'partition' was not moderation but strategy. The Congress was left to demand British withdrawal, while the League made clear what it sought to gain. Hodson described the Lahore Resolution as the 'Pakistan resolution'.[26]

Prof. Ishtiaq Ahmed, in his monumental work on Jinnah writes: 'It is important to underline that on 22 March 1940, Jinnah was solid as a rock in his demand for Partition to create separate Muslim states, which came to be known by the generic name of Pakistan, covering constellations consisting of several, two and one Muslim states.'[27]

Within a year of the resolution's adoption, Jinnah addressed the Aligarh Muslim University (AMU) students' union in March 1941, stating: 'Pakistan is not only a practical goal but the only goal if you want to save Islam from complete annihilation in this country.'

The resolution was made part of the League constitution in the August session of the Muslim League in April 1941.[28] This was the clearest indication that it was not a bargaining counter, but a formally defined Muslim League's goal. Distinguishing between tactical moves and non-negotiable demands is key to understanding subsequent developments. Those who argue that Jinnah's acceptance of the Constituent Assembly in 1946 implied commitment to Indian unity overlook the weight of his actions and statements since the Lahore Resolution, or even earlier, the Round Table Conference. No party enshrines a mere bargaining position in its Constitution.

The shift from 'states' to 'state' in the Lahore Resolution held profound implications for East Pakistan. This remains a live issue in Pakistan even after its eastern wing's separation.

5

Cripps Mission, Cabinet Mission Plan and Nehru's Statement of July 1946

'According to those close to Mr Jinnah, he evinced[a] deep sense of relief upon this return to his old tactical position, and upon his no longer bearing responsibility for a strategic compromise – the Cabinet Mission Plan… '

–H.V. Hodson, former Reforms Commissioner, in his book *The Great Divide*[1]

SIR STAFFORD CRIPPS WAS sent to India in March 1942, as the Japanese attack on India appeared imminent. Singapore had fallen on 15 February 1942; Rangoon on 8 March. Cripps arrived in India on 22 March. He brought a proposal for associating Indians with an interim government and a final settlement after the end of the war. The proposal showed that the British policy had veered towards endorsing the League's demand for a separate political entity for Muslims. This was rejected by both the Congress and the Muslim League. Their reasons were different. The Congress was opposed to the provision that gave the choice to provinces not to accede to the Union. As the Congress Working Committee's resolution described it, its acceptance beforehand would have been 'a severe blow to the conception of the Indian unity'.[2] The Muslim League Working Committee resolution declared that 'the only solution of India's constitutional problem is the partition of India into independent zones'. It was therefore opposed to entering 'a constitution making body, whose main object is the creation of a new Indian Union'.[3]

In the short term, Indians could join the Executive Council, but Britain would not transfer responsibility for the war effort during the interim period. The Cripps proposal suggested 'an elected body charged with the task of framing a new constitution for India' after the war. Indian states were invited to participate, but their involvement was voluntary. The British acceptance of the Constitution so framed was subject to 'the right of any province of British India that is not prepared to accept the new constitution to retain its present constitutional position'. This was the poisoned chalice offered to the Congress, where both provinces and princely states could stay out of the Union. Cripps also clarified that the short-term and long-term proposals were part of a package.

Penderel Moon said it was 'the first occasion on which the British publicly admitted the possibility of Partition'.[4] He recorded,

> This was a triumph for Jinnah. It put him in a very strong position, for if the Muslims of Muslim-majority provinces stood behind him, he could now, with the right to stay out conceded, bargain for the terms on which those provinces could come in and the dream of Congress Raj over the whole of India would never come true. Even the Muslims who did not want Pakistan were impressed by the importance of supporting Jinnah.[5]

The British priority was the war effort, which required continued recruitment from Punjab which was the main catchment area for the Indian army. Moon's supposition that 'Muslims of Muslim-majority provinces stood behind Jinnah' was wishful thinking. Punjab was ruled by Sikandar Hayat's Unionist government, which included Hindus and Sikhs. Sikandar Hayat dismissed Pakistan as 'Jinnistan', a pun on Jinnah's name, meaning 'abode of Jinns or ghosts'. The Muslim League had won just one seat in Punjab in 1937. Why pander to the League when its demand was anathema to both Congress and the Unionists? Jinnah was useful as a counterbalance to Congress, which sought independence after the war.

The Cripps proposal paralleled the Muslim League's Lahore demand by admitting the possibility of Partition but referred to provinces rather than 'Zones'. This contradicted the League's vision of Pakistan, which required the north-west and north-east to be herded into 'Zones'. In 1942, NWFP opposed Pakistan, and Punjab remained outside the League's control. A scheme of voluntary association where the choice rested with provinces was unlikely to produce Pakistan as demanded by the League. It also provided for a Constituent Assembly to frame a constitution for a new India, which was not there in the League's 1940 resolution. This was, of course, a symbolic gesture to the idea of India's unity; Cripps had clarified that the States and the provinces could stay out. But the Constituent Assembly, where the Congress would have had a majority was an anathema to the Muslim League.

Linlithgow left India in October 1943. He was succeeded as Viceroy by Wavell. By this time, the tide of war had turned in favour of the Allied forces. Nevertheless, it was also clearer that the British would not be able to deny or delay a substantial transfer of power to Indian hands.[6]

At the Karachi session of the Muslim League in December 1943, Jinnah invented a new slogan, 'Divide and Quit'. 'The League resolved to establish a "Committee of Action" to organize Muslims all over India to resist the imposition of a unitary constitution and to prepare for the coming struggle for the achievement of Pakistan.'[7]

The Cabinet Mission Plan and Nehru's Statement of 10 July 1946

The British government sent the Cabinet Mission to India in February 1946. The Muslim League accepted its plan on 6 June, and the Congress followed on 6 July.

The Cabinet Mission Plan proposed a united India with a weak Centre. Some argue that Jinnah's agreement to join the Constituent Assembly would have preserved India's unity. This school of thought blames Nehru's 10 July 1946 statement for provoking Jinnah to retract. In response to a press question, Nehru said the Constituent Assembly would be sovereign and take its own decisions. Jinnah seized this as a departure from the plan, leading the League to revoke its acceptance on 29 July.

Nehru is accused of losing the last chance to avert Partition when the League had accepted the plan. Maulana Abul Kalam Azad called Nehru's statement 'one of those unfortunate events which changed the course of history'. He said, 'Jawaharlal's statement was wrong,' adding, 'We had in fact agreed that the Central Government would be federal.'

'These matters could not be changed unilaterally by Congress without the consent of other parties to the agreement.'

The underlying assumption in Azad's criticism of Nehru's statement was that the Cabinet Mission Plan represented an attempt to shape an India united in a 'federal' structure. This view is also supported by British officers like Hodson and Penderel Moon, who fondly proclaim British attachment to India's unity. In Pakistan's official narrative, any suggestion that Jinnah was willing to accept something less than Pakistan is anathema. However, this view appeals to those uneasy with Partition's legacy.

To assess this issue, we must consider key questions. Did the Cabinet Mission Plan propose Indian unity? Was it truly a 'federal' plan? Was the Muslim League prepared to join the Constituent Assembly of a united India? If not, its acceptance was merely a tactic to control the Interim Government until Partition. The plan reflected a striking convergence between British policy and the League's demands.

The Cripps proposal included the possibility of 'provinces' opting out, posing a problem for Jinnah, who lacked control over Muslim-majority provinces. The Cabinet Mission Plan resolved this by allowing 'Zones' to opt out, mirroring the League's 1940 Lahore Resolution.

According to Penderel Moon, the provinces were to be divided into three Groups:

(a) The six provinces with non-Muslim majorities, excluding Assam, i.e. Madras, Bombay, Orissa, the Central Provinces, Bihar and the United Provinces;
(b) The Muslim-majority areas in the north-west: the Punjab, the North West Frontier Province, Sindh and Balochistan;
(c) Bengal and Assam

The grouping along communal lines closely followed the scheme envisaged in the Lahore Resolution adopted by the Muslim League in 1940. The fundamental principles were as follows:

(i) 'A Union Government was to deal with foreign affairs, defence and communications.
(ii) The Groups of Provinces, one of the predominantly Hindu provinces and the other of the predominantly Muslim provinces, to deal with such of the remaining subjects as the

provinces in the respective groups desired to be dealt with in common;

(iii) The Provincial Governments to deal with all other subjects and to have all the residuary sovereign rights;

(iv) The Indian States to take their appropriate place in this structure on terms to be negotiated with them.'[8]

There were two curious aspects of the Cabinet Mission Plan. The 'grouping of provinces' allowed them to adopt their own constitutions – an essential attribute of sovereignty – effectively conceding a de facto partition before discussions on a federal constitution even began. Provinces, however, lacked this privilege and had no choice but to join the grouping scheme. They were compulsorily placed into 'Zones' and could not opt out until after the zones were established and new elections were held. By then, the zones, with their own constitutions, would have consolidated power, making provincial secession more difficult. This resolved Jinnah's internal dilemma, as he still lacked control over the provinces. 'Zones' with separate constitutions did not constitute a 'united' India.

The 'Union' was not a federation but a weak confederation of independent states. The 'Union government' lacked financial powers even for its limited functions. Indian (princely) states were to 'take appropriate place in this structure on terms to be negotiated with them'. This left open many possibilities.

The grouping scheme on communal lines revived the Muslim League's demand in the Lahore Resolution, which called for Muslim-majority areas in the north-western and eastern parts of India to be grouped in zones constituting 'independent states'. The Cabinet Mission Plan fleshed this out while maintaining the principle of partition.

Hodson, who had served as reforms commissioner of the Government of India (1939–41), provided insight into the final years of British rule. The Cabinet Mission first met Jinnah on 16 April 1946, before consulting Gandhi and Congress leaders. It presented Jinnah with two options, described by Hodson as 'the choice between a small Pakistan with sovereignty and a big Pakistan in an all-India Union'.[9] Interestingly, both options included Pakistan. The second option indeed offered him a much bigger slice of territory, as it did not envisage any partition of Punjab or Bengal. Jinnah told them, 'If the Congress wants to make a suggestion to me, let them do so and I will consider it.'[10] The Mission then met Congress leaders.

Hodson records that the Mission reverted to the second alternative as the basis of negotiations – 'two federations linked in a minimal super-federal center'.[11] The Muslim League Council adopted a resolution conveying its acceptance of the Cabinet Mission Plan on 6 June, 'Reiterating that a sovereign Pakistan remained the unalterable objective of the Muslims'. The League statement mentioned that it had accepted the Cabinet Mission Plan, since 'the basis of Pakistan was inherent in the grouping of the Muslim areas in Sections B and C'. As recorded by Hodson, the League 'kept in view, however, the implicit opportunity of secession of provinces or groups from the Union, and reserved the right to revise its policy at any time if the course of events so required'.[12]

The Muslim League had already resolved on partition. The Cabinet Mission Plan merely reiterated the principle that independence would come with the subcontinent's division. The League's acceptance did not indicate a commitment to India's unity but an understanding that the plan contained the seeds of partition, masked by superficial unity.

Hodson's account is supported by Penderel Moon's memoir *Divide and Quit*:

> Hopes of a settlement were enormously raised when on June 6th Jinnah, abandoning his usual negative attitude, got the Muslim League to pass a resolution accepting the scheme and agreeing to join the constitution-making body. The acceptance, it is true, was stated to be '*in the hope that it would ultimately result in the establishment of complete sovereign Pakistan*', *which still remained the unalterable objective of the Muslims in India.* [Emphasis added][13]

While Moon argued this was a rejection of 'sovereign Pakistan', his own account suggests that the Muslim League's calculations were different. Jinnah's acceptance of the plan was not an endorsement of a united India but a tactical step. The League's ultimate goal was still 'the establishment of complete sovereign Pakistan'. The Cabinet Mission Plan allowed the

League to enter the Interim Government while positioning itself to counter the Constituent Assembly's attempt to establish a united India.

Penderel Moon described that the Cabinet Mission proposed 'that the Constituent Assembly should follow a certain procedure designed to meet Jinnah's objection to a single constitution-making body'.

> It was proposed that after an initial full meeting of a formal character, the Assembly should divide up into three sections – Section A consisting of the representatives of the five Hindu-majority provinces; Section B of the representatives of the Punjab, N.W.F.P. and Sind, and Section C of the representatives of Bengal and Assam. *These Sections would draw up constitutions for the Provinces included in each of them*... After the Sections would have drawn up the constitution of the Provinces, *Finally the Constituent Assembly would meet again as a whole to settle the Union Constitution*. [Emphasis added][14]

The adoption of the Groups' constitutions was to precede the adoption of the Union constitution. The only thing certain in this sequence was that the Groups would come into being *before* the process to 'settle the Union' constitution would have even begun. Given the tangled history of three-way negotiations between the British, the Muslim League and the Congress, there was no guarantee that the Union would be agreed to. But the Groups would have been established, nevertheless.

What was worse was that while an opt-out of the zones from the Union was an a priori assumption, there was no opt-out for the provinces. The NWFP, with its Congress ministry, and Assam, with Hindu-majority areas, did not have the choice to opt out of the zones. 'Thus the right of self-determination was being conferred on artificially created zones but denied to the existing provinces. Theoretically, a province would have the right to opt out of a group by a vote of its legislature after the new constitutional arrangements had come into operation.'[15] But this was, at best, a symbolic gesture. Thus, provinces were to be delivered to the Muslim League with their hands and feet tied. Princely states could join either zone or stay independent. This was a thinly disguised scheme for India's partition, rather than a blueprint for India's unity.

The Cabinet Mission Plan also imposed parity between Congress and the Muslim League at the federal level – an unprecedented equation of a 25 per cent minority with a 75 per cent majority. The League's claim to represent all Muslims was contested by Congress and leaders in Muslim-majority provinces like the NWFP and Punjab. A year earlier at the Simla conference, Khizr Tiwana's credentials to represent Punjab were recognized. Jinnah had derailed the conference by insisting on being the 'sole spokesman' for Muslims. The 1946 elections had improved the League's standing, but the population ratio remained unchanged. The British accepted the League's communal demands, making the Cabinet Mission Plan a denial of democracy.

The plan handed the Muslim League a larger Pakistan within a weak federal framework. It was the second of two options the Cabinet Mission had discussed with Jinnah before consulting Congress. Jinnah had first choice from the menu presented. This explains the League's acceptance on 6 June – uncharacteristically ahead of Congress's acceptance on 6 July. Normally, Jinnah waited for Congress's position before responding.

Congress faced a wrenching decision. Independence would come with de facto partition. Not only did the Muslim-majority zones have the option to secede, but princely states could also opt out, with a weak Centre unable to persuade them to join. Compounding this, the NWFP, governed by Congress, and Assam were forcibly grouped. The Cabinet Mission Plan was not a blueprint for unity but a thinly veiled scheme for Partition.

Aftermath

Wavell, who favoured the Muslim League, did not see Nehru's statement as a departure from the Constituent Assembly's procedure. In a telegram to Lord Pethick-Lawrence on 16 July 1946, he noted:

> From the full API report which has been telegraphed today, it does not repeat not appear that the Congress have definitely decided to disregard the procedure laid down for the Constituent Assembly or to try for instance to carry a decision on a major communal issue (such as initial groups in Sections A, B and C) by a bare majority, although individual passages read out of their context give the opposite impression.[16]

After Nehru's statement, Congress tried to mollify the League. Maulana Azad cited the Congress Working Committee's resolution of 8 August 1946, which reaffirmed its acceptance of the Cabinet Mission Plan in its entirety: 'The Committee wishes to make it clear that while they did not approve of all the proposals contained in this statement [Cabinet Mission Plan], they accepted the scheme in its entirety.' Azad remarked:

> We had hoped that this resolution of the Working Committee would save the situation. *Now, there was no longer any doubt that the Congress had accepted the Cabinet Mission Plan in its entirety.* If the Moslem League accepted our resolution, it could return to the early position without any loss of prestige. Mr Jinnah did not, however, accept the position... [Emphasis added][17]

The Congress had bent over backwards to accommodate Jinnah. Hodson described the resolution of the Congress Working Committee of 8 August as 'designed to appease the League'.[18] The Muslim League had rejected the Cabinet Mission Plan on 29 July, and did not reconsider it.

After the Congress's acceptance of the plan, the viceroy invited Nehru to form the Interim Government. Jinnah did not want the League excluded, despite rejecting the plan. He responded with the call for 'Direct Action' on 16 August, leading to massive violence. The constitutional lawyer had now turned to communal violence to press his demands. He must have realized that he no longer had a veto over negotiations. The British had granted him this privilege as long as he served their interests by deadlocking talks. Once they decided to leave, this was no longer necessary.

Viceroy Wavell sought to placate the League by inviting it to join the Interim Government, despite its rejection of the Cabinet Mission Plan. Jinnah agreed to join without committing to the Constituent Assembly. The League wanted a share in power without accepting the 'Union'. Wavell replied, 'Since the basis for participation in the cabinet is, of course, acceptance of the Statement of 16 May, I assume that the League Council will meet at a very early date to reconsider its Bombay resolution.'[19]

The League never revised its position on the Constituent Assembly but joined the Interim Government. If it could reverse its decision on the Executive, why not on the Constituent Assembly? It sought influence during the transition but refused to commit to a united India.

Jinnah seized upon Nehru's statement and used it as an excuse to blame the Cabinet Mission as well as the Congress. He said, 'the League had now no alternative but to revert to the national goal of Pakistan'. As Hodson has written, Jinnah was relieved that the compromise had not worked out:

> According to those close to Mr Jinnah, he evinced deep sense of relief upon this return to his old tactical position, and upon his no longer bearing responsibility for a strategic compromise – the Cabinet Mission Plan – which he had accepted only because he feared that if he rejected it, the Congress would be left not only in British favour as the time for independence approached, but also in actual power as the Interim Government of India.[20]

The British aided the League by shifting the goalposts. The Cabinet Mission Plan, announced on 16 May, was a package deal covering short-term and long-term plans. Wavell, however, allowed the League to join the Interim Government without committing to the Constituent Assembly, effectively modifying the plan.

The plan envisaged a divided India under a weak confederation. Even if the Union had materialized with a constitution, it would have been paralysed by the League's disproportionate influence, as seen in the Interim Government. A weak Centre would have also complicated the integration of princely states. Jinnah asserted in his 11 August 1947 speech: 'Any idea of a united India could never have worked, and in my judgement, it would have led us to terrific disaster.'[21] For him, sovereign Pakistan was the goal.

The League's initial acceptance and later rejection of the Cabinet Mission Plan did not mark a shift in its thinking. It had already decided on Pakistan. As mentioned earlier, Khaliquzzaman stated that the League Working Committee had resolved to demand partition even before adopting the Lahore Resolution. Liaquat Ali Khan, in a September 1945 speech at AMU, clearly outlined Pakistan's boundaries. In *Creating a New Medina*, Venkat Dhulipala cites Liaquat:

> the boundaries of Pakistan will be the present provincial boundaries of the Punjab, NWFP, Baluchistan and Sind in the northwest, and Bengal and Assam in the northeast ... *Those who think we are pitching our demand too high in order to bargain are gravely mistaken. This is not the maximum demand but the minimum demand of Muslim India.* [Emphasis added][22]

The 1945–46 elections were fought on the demand for Pakistan. The League could not abandon its goal. Pakistan was not an unintended consequence of negotiations – it was the objective.

Though Azad criticized Nehru for his 10 July 1946 statement, he held the Muslim League responsible for Partition. He recalled meeting League followers left behind in India as Jinnah departed for Pakistan on 14 August. Jinnah's farewell message urged them to be loyal Indian citizens. Azad wrote: 'Jinnah's parting message came as the last straw on the camel's back. It was now clear to them that the only result of Partition was that their position as a minority was much weaker than before. In addition, they had through their foolish action created anger and resentment in the minds of Hindus.'[23]

6

Muslims for a United India

'Inhabitants of India, regardless of their faith, should become united as Indians and form one nation to fight with the foreign nation which has damaged their common interests.'

–Maulana Hussain Ahmad Madani in
Composite Nationalism and Islam[1]

THE TWO-NATION THEORY WAS challenged by many eminent Muslim leaders and organizations, including Maulana Abdul Kalam Azad and Rafi Ahmed Kidwai. They fought for India's independence and stood for a united India. Azad 'saw himself as a Muslim, but more than that he declared himself a proud Indian and part of the indivisible unity called Indian nationality.[2] He was a devout Muslim and a great scholar of Islamic theology. But he anchored his 'notion of composite nationalism' in the 'early history of Islam'.[3] There were others too, who are now forgotten by most.

Maulana Hussain Ahmad Madani, head of the Deoband seminary, said Muslims were part of a united Indian nationhood, drawing criticism from Iqbal and Jinnah. In response, Madani wrote *Muttahida Qaumiyat Aur Islam* (*Composite Nationalism and Islam*), rejecting the Two-Nation Theory and the Muslim League's divisive politics. His stance had enormous symbolic importance – the League's claim that Muslims were a separate nation was being rejected by the head of Darul Uloom Deoband, India's most prestigious Islamic seminary.

Allah Bux Soomro in Sindh and the Khan Brothers in the NWFP also stood up for a united India. Soomro, Sindh's premier, organized an 'Azad Muslim Conference' in Delhi a month after the passage of the Lahore Resolution in 1940. The conference adopted a resolution, which asserted that India was 'the common homeland of all the citizens irrespective of race or religion'.[4] Khan Abdul Gaffar Khan (Badshah Khan) and his older brother Dr Khan Saheb led the fight for an independent and united India in the NWFP. Soomro was assassinated in 1943. Dr Khan won the 1946 elections, fought on the issue of a united India or Partition. Both Sindh and NWFP had overwhelmingly Muslim populations. The courageous stand of Soomro and the Khan Brothers showed that the League's demand for a separate Muslim homeland was not accepted even in Muslim-majority north-west India, where Iqbal had proposed it.

A striking contrast emerged between Maulana Madani, Soomro and the Khan Brothers on one hand and the Muslim League on the other. The League focused on communal issues, rarely mentioning independence until 1946, when British departure became inevitable. Soomro and the Khan Brothers fought for independence. The Azad Muslim Conference demanded that 'the future constitution of India should be framed by a Constituent Assembly elected on the basis of adult suffrage'.[5] In his 1940 speech, Jinnah rejected the idea of the Constituent Assembly deciding the country's fate.

The demand for Partition was opposed by the Momin Conference in 1943, which declared that 'the Momin community will not tolerate even the idea of Partition of India...'[6] The Majlis-e-Ahrar-e-Islam 'questioned the claim of the Muslim League that the latter represented the Muslims in India'.[7] Like the Azad Muslim Conference earlier, the Ahrars demanded adult franchise. This was significant. The League was a party of upper-class Muslims. Its dismal performance in the 1937 elections showed its lack of mass support, despite the separate electorate. Its sweeping victory in 1946 resulted from communal politics and an extremely limited franchise. The views of the vast majority of Muslims went unheard.

Maulana Madani

Maulana Madani said that Muslims belonged to a united Indian nation. This provoked Iqbal 'who made a scornful retort in poetry insisting that Muslims can have no nation except Islam'.[8]

Madani's treatise, *Muttahida Qaumiyat aur Islam*, was written in response to Iqbal's criticism. The message of unity irrespective of faith was significant, coming from a senior cleric well versed in Arabic and the Quran. The exchange occurred as the Muslim League shifted from viewing Muslims as a minority to claiming they were a separate 'nation'.

Iqbal composed a Persian poem in which he ridiculed Maulana Madani for claiming that *millat* is *watan*. The term *millat* describes people belonging to a common religion (Muslims in this case), while *watan* or country is a territorial concept. Iqbal believed that *millat* or the Muslim community transcended national borders, and thus went beyond *watan* or country. He saw identity in religious terms and therefore rejected nationalism rooted in territory. This also explains his leaning towards pan-Islamism. An exclusivist idea of state, which was co-terminus with religion, also ruled out the co-existence of Muslims and non-Muslims together in a country. Iqbal was rejecting the political pluralism underlying Madani's concept of composite nationalism.

The meaning of *millat* as implied by Iqbal was correct, though he had misrepresented Madani's position. He ridiculed Madani: 'You said from the pulpit that millat is from (based on) watan'. But Maulana Madani was referring to 'qaum'. He pointed out in his treatise, on the basis of Arabic usage and the Holy Quran, that 'qaum' means a group of people. It does not have a religious connotation; people of different faiths can be part of the same 'qaum'. I do not claim any expertise in theology, but Madani's use of the term 'qaum' is borne out by modern usage. The United Nations is called 'Aqwam Muttahida' in Arabic. Aqwam (nations) is the plural of Qaum (nation). The reference to 'nations' or 'aqaum' in the title of the world body does not have any religious connotation. Maulana Madani supported the secular connotation. Sir Syed Ahmad and Iqbal equated nation with religion; Jinnah endorsed this idea in his Lahore speech of 1940 though he spoke only in English.

Madani's political thought was very different from Iqbal's. He shared the nationalist belief in uniting Hindus and Muslims against the British to fight for freedom. He gave the historical context of British rule in India and the Middle East. He stated that when Indian trade and craftsmanship were strong, and Indian products were in demand in the English market, the British expounded the virtues of mercantilism and promoted it as if this were a universal theory.[9] But when the Indian crafts and trade weakened and British manufacturing became strong, they gave the slogan of free trade. Similarly, when Muslim power was strong, the view was put forward that Europe's map could not be changed, and the conqueror could not retain the land he had occupied. But when Muslim power weakened, the philosophy changed and it was said that a conqueror could not be deprived of his conquest.

Madani said Indians uniting as one country was dangerous for the English. If this sentiment grew and Indians realized they had the power to throw out the English and that it was shameful to collaborate with the foreign ruler, this would be the end of the British Crown's rule in India.[10] The West praised territorial nationalism as long as Islam and the Caliphate were strong in order to weaken the Ottoman Empire. But by the time Madani was writing, 'the same concept of territorial nationalism has become the worst thing in India next to Islam'.[11] He said that even if Wataniyat (territorial nationalism) was such a bad thing, since Europe had used it to weaken Muslim kings and the Ottoman Caliphate, the Muslims should use the same tool to weaken the British.[12] *This was a very perceptive remark.* Iqbal rejected 'nationalism' on the grounds that it weakened Islamic unity. In the contemporary geopolitical context, this only served the cause of the British Empire. During the First World War, the British used Arab nationalism to weaken the Ottoman Empire. However, they did not want the rise of nationalism to challenge their hold on the colonies.

Maulana Madani said the composite nationalism he desired was the same concept on which the Riyasat-e-Madina was founded by the Holy Prophet. This included Muslims as well as Jews.[13] He wrote, 'Prophet brought together Muslims and Jews to fight the enemy as one *qaum*.'[14] Maududi denied Madani's interpretation of the Quran and claimed that this was a 'military alliance between the Muslims and Jews, which did not last long', and 'Muslims exiled some Jews and killed some others'.[15] Madani stressed that inhabitants of India, regardless of their faith, should become united as Indians and form one nation to fight with the foreign nation which had damaged their common interests.[16] He maintained his courageous stand despite personal attacks by Iqbal and Maududi questioning even his faith.

Allah Bakhsh Soomro

Allah Bakhsh Soomro served as Sindh's premier from 1938 to 1940 and again from 1940 to 1942. He renounced British titles in 1942 to protest repression, was removed from office and assassinated in 1943.

Soomro had organized the All-India Azad Muslim Conference in April 1940, a month after the Muslim League session in Lahore. In his presidential address to the conference, he said,

> Whatever our faiths, we must live together in our country in an atmosphere of perfect amity and our relations should be the relations of the several brothers of a joint family, various members of which are free to profess the faith they like without any let or hindrance and all of whom enjoy equal benefits of their joint property.[17]

This countered Jinnah's Lahore speech, which asserted Hindus and Muslims were separate 'nations' and that a single state would lead to its destruction. The resolution adopted by the Azad Muslim Conference stated, 'India will have geographical and political boundaries of an indivisible whole and as such is the common homeland of all the citizens irrespective of race or religion who are joint owners of its resources.'[18]

This directly challenged the League's position enunciated at Lahore. Jinnah had said, 'It is a dream that the Hindus and Muslims can ever evolve a common nationality.' The Lahore Resolution had asked for a the carving out of 'Independent States'. Soomro was talking of a common homeland.

A key demand of the resolution of the Azad Muslim Conference was that the 'future constitution of India should be framed by a constituent assembly elected on the basis of adult suffrage'.[19] This demand for adult suffrage would have brought into the fold of electoral politics a vastly larger and different group of Muslims, other than the titled nawabs and members of the landed gentry. This is indeed the fundamental principle of democracy. The British favoured not only the minority, but a tiny section of that minority tied to the colonial masters by their interests. Soomro, as the premier of a Muslim-majority province, carried more weight than Jinnah or the Muslim League, who did not control a single province.

Khan Brothers

Khan Abdul Gaffar Khan (Badshah Khan) and his brother Dr Khan Saheb, the Congress premier of NWFP, played a heroic role in India's freedom struggle. Badshah Khan, known as the 'Frontier Gandhi', organized the Khudai Khidmatgar, who followed non-violence. They wanted NWFP to join India, supporting democratic pluralism despite facing hostility from the League and British officials. After Partition, Jinnah dismissed Dr Khan's ministry, despite its legislative majority. Badshah Khan spent years in Pakistani prisons or exile.

Badshah Khan, in his autobiography *My Life and Struggle*, has described the last days of British rule in NWFP. The British were supporting the Muslim League and its demand for Pakistan. Unlike his brother Dr Khan Saheb, Badshah Khan kept himself somewhat distant from practical politics. He wrote that he 'was not in favour of the elections of 1945–46'.[20] But when the elections were declared, he saw the British government throw its weight behind the Muslim League. Not only was the official machinery mobilized in favour of the League, but he saw 'British ladies going around canvassing too'. In a deeply conservative society, the ladies could enter houses to meet the womenfolk and exchange scarves (dupatta) as per the local custom. They would tell the Pathan ladies that the dupatta they wanted was their vote.

Badshah Khan writes: 'The issue at stake in this election of 1946 – the last general election in United India – was: India or Pakistan, Hindu or Muslim, Islam or Kufr, temple or mosque.' 'The Muslim League canvassers asked people: "Are you giving your vote to the mosque or to the temple?"'[21]

In July 1946, Badshah Khan and Maulana Azad were elected by the Khudai Khidmatgars and the Frontier Assembly to be members of the Central Assembly, the purpose of which was to give India a Constitution.[22] Joining the Constituent Assembly of united India was the key issue. This was part of the Cabinet Mission Plan but was rejected by the Muslim League, which was determined to press its demand for partition. The Khan Brothers had thrown in their lot with India.

Badshah Khan wrote that the victory of the Khudai Khidmatgars and the Congress in the elections of 1945–46, despite the British government aligning itself with the League in an election that was fought on the very clear issue of partition or united India, meant only one thing, 'that the majority of people in the country were behind us'. The Viceroy, however, decided on a referendum in the NWFP. This was a departure from the principle followed in other provinces, where the provincial legislature decided on joining either India or Pakistan. The Congress ministry under Dr Khan Saheb enjoyed the majority in the NWFP assembly, so the British decided to move the goalpost.

Badshah Khan wrote, 'It also hurt and grieved me deeply that even the Congress Working Committee did not lift a finger to help us, as we had hoped they would…' He added, 'The Congress, which was the representative body in India, not only deserted us but delivered us into the hands of our enemies.'[23]

Badshah Khan decided not to take part in the referendum, which was an unfair departure from the principle followed in all other provinces. This was perhaps not the best decision; his brother Dr Khan Saheb was ready to participate in the referendum. In the event, the abstention of the Khudai Khidmatgars from the referendum resulted in the Muslim League's victory by the barest of majorities. The Khan Brothers' demand for a referendum on the issue of 'Pakhtunistan or Pakistan' was turned down by Viceroy Mountbatten.

Mountbatten announced the partition plan on 3 June 1947, which was accepted by both the Congress and the Muslim League. The communal violence began in the NWFP. Dr Khan Saheb's ministry tried to protect Hindus and Sikhs. As Badshah Khan wrote, 'The Congress Government was a government in name only. The British government officials did not give Dr Khan Saheb the slightest bit of help or cooperation.'[24] He added, 'But for the Hindus the great blessing of this ministry was that the governor could not destroy them altogether, because Dr Khan Saheb stood in the way. The Governor was also a stumbling block in Dr Khan Saheb's way and he would not let the Doctor give the Hindus the complete protection he would have liked to give to them.'[25] The governor of NWFP at the time was Olaf Caroe, who was described by Badshah Khan as 'the enemy of the Hindus and the friend of the Muslim League'.[26]

Badshah Khan recounted that Hindus and Sikhs had locked themselves in Peshawar, fearing for their lives, until the Khudai Khidmatgars arrived. 'Ten thousand Khudai Khidmatgars, in their red uniforms, had arrived in Peshawar to protect the Hindus.' '…The Khudai Khidmatgars were on duty day and night and people only needed to get a glimpse of a red uniform to feel reassured and safe.'[27]

This chapter was nearing its end. Dr Khan Saheb's ministry was dismissed soon after Pakistan's formation. Briefly rehabilitated as Chief Minister of West Pakistan in the mid-1950s, he was assassinated in 1958. Badshah Khan spent years in Pakistani jails or in exile. He died in 1988.

Maulana Abdul Kalam Azad, Rafi Ahmed Kidwai, Soomro, Maulana Madani, and the Khan Brothers are some of the tallest Muslim personalities who opposed the Two-Nation Theory and the Partition of India. Indian academic Shamsul Islam has debated: Why did they fail? He has ascribed it to three reasons: a campaign of terror against the nationalist Muslims launched by the Muslim League; the Hindu right wing; and the Congress's mistake in negotiating with the Muslim League and Jinnah. There may be other views. But this leaves out the most important factor – the British.

The British controlled all levers of power. They cultivated a small Muslim elite with little mass following as a counterweight to Indian nationalism. The League and Jinnah played the spoiler's role but did not dictate British policy. The Hindu right wing was too weak; its dominant faction sought a united India (Akhand Bharat). The Congress made mistakes, but ultimately, Partition was a British decision. They could not bear losing the empire's crown jewel. The League wanted them to stay. The Congress wanted them out – so it had to be punished.

7

Jinnah's Speech of 11 August 1947

'I believe as a result of our farewell meeting Mr Jinnah took the earliest opportunity to bid goodbye to his two-nation theory in his speech on 11 August 1947 as the Governor-General designate of Pakistan and President of the Constituent Assembly of Pakistan.'

–Chaudhry Khaliquzzaman, President of Pakistan Muslim League, in his memoir, *Pathway to Pakistan*[1]

JINNAH MADE A FAMOUS speech in the Pakistan Constituent Assembly on 11 August 1947, which is considered by liberals in Pakistan as the gold standard from which the country has since fallen. It was a radical departure from the Two-Nation Theory on which the Muslim League had based its politics. The sudden shift after leading the demand for Partition on communal grounds has been a source of speculation. Jinnah did not live long enough to shape Pakistan's future and never repeated this theme. Six months later, at the Karachi Bar Association, he dismissed claims that Pakistan's Constitution would not be based on Shariat.

Chaudhry Khaliquzzaman, who seconded the Lahore Resolution and later became president of the Pakistan Muslim League, gave an account of the immediate background of Jinnah's speech. This chapter examines the speech from three perspectives: a dissenter, a supporter and the Pakistani establishment.

Jinnah said in his 11 August speech:

> If you change your past and work together in a spirit that every one of you, no matter what community he belongs to, no matter what his

> colour, caste or creed, is first, second, and last a citizen of this State, with equal rights, privileges and obligations, there will be no end to the progress you will make. I cannot emphasise it too much; we should begin to work in that spirit, and, in course of time, all these angularities of the majority and minority communities, the Hindu community and the Muslim community, because even as regards Muslims you have Pathans, Punjabis, Shias, Sunnis and so on and among the Hindus you have Brahmins, Vaishnavas, Khatris, also Bengalis, Madrasis and so on, will vanish.[2]

Jinnah added: 'You may be free to go to your temples, mosques or any other place of worship; you may belong to any religion or caste or creed, that has nothing to do with the business of the State...We are starting with the fundamental principle that we are all citizens and equal citizens of one State.'[3]

Jinnah's statement on equal citizenship for all regardless of difference in faith contrasts sharply with his 1940 Lahore speech, where he rejected Hindu-Muslim coexistence in a united India. He said, 'The Hindus and Muslims belong to two different religious philosophies, social customs, and literature[s].' Jinnah also said in the same speech, 'To yoke together two such nations under a single state' would lead to 'destruction of any fabric that may be so built up for the government of such a state'.[4] His speech seemed a reversal of his stance. Or did it?

Jinnah summed up his policy:

> ...Now, I think that we should keep that in front of us as our ideal and you will find that in course of time Hindus would cease to be Hindus and Muslims would cease to be Muslims not in the religious sense, because that is the personal faith of each individual, but in the political sense as citizens of the State.[5]

Jinnah's 11 August speech can be viewed from three perspectives: sceptics, who questioned his sudden shift after advocating Partition on a communal basis; admirers, who saw it as his true vision for Pakistan's future; and the Pakistani establishment, which largely ignores it. Wali Khan, leader of the NAP, represents the dissenting view in Pakistan. Son of Badshah Khan, he spent years in exile like his father. His credentials to comment on Jinnah's speech are strong – his father and uncle, Dr Khan Saheb, had practised the policies Jinnah belatedly embraced in this speech.

Justice Munir, in contrast, supported Jinnah's speech and used it to denounce the Nizam-e-Mustafa introduced by General Zia-ul-Haq in the 1980s. Munir, a Muslim League representative on the Boundary Commission headed by Sir Cyril Radcliffe, helped demarcate Pakistan's borders but had reservations about the country's ideological boundaries. As author of the Munir Commission report, he defended secularism in Zia's Pakistan and believed Jinnah envisioned a secular state.

The Pakistani establishment rarely acknowledges Jinnah's 11 August speech, preferring to highlight other statements. Among Jinnah's contemporaries, Maulana Shabbir Ahmad Usmani, the chief ideologue of the Muslim League, exemplified this view. Today, figures like Akbar S. Ahmed, a former civil servant aligned with the Pakistani state, echo this perspective. Prime Minister Imran Khan, addressing the Pakistan National Assembly on 6 August 2019 and the 'POK assembly' on 14 August 2019, said that it was *not* a 'secular' speech.

Jinnah's choice of words in this speech is intriguing. By asserting that minority and majority communities would cease to be distinct – not religiously, but 'in the political sense as citizens of the State' – he offered religious equality to minorities while denying them the very political rights he had previously championed for Muslim minorities in India. These rights had extended beyond religious freedom to separate electorates, ultimately leading to the demand for a separate state.

The Dissenter

Wali Khan discussed the significance of Jinnah's speech in his book *Facts Are Facts: The Untold Story of India's Partition*. He noted that the speech was not made in a press conference, 'but it was the official proclamation of the policy of the new State, made in the Constituent Assembly of Pakistan'.

The speech marked two significant departures from the ideology of Pakistan. Wali Khan wrote: 'First of all Jinnah uses the word "community" for the Hindus and the Muslims instead of "nations".

Second, while describing the Muslims, he mentions Pakhtoons and Punjabis along with the Shias and Sunnis. Similarly, while on the subject of Hindus, he mentions Bengalis and Madrasis along with Brahmins, Shudras, and Kshatriyas.'[6] Thus, Jinnah acknowledged that religion was not the only basis of identity, and that neither Hindus nor Muslims were homogenous groups.

Wali Khan posed the question: '...If this was Jinnah's declared ideology, what was the need to plunge the subcontinent into bloodshed and riots, and for what purpose were so many lives lost?'[7]

He also highlighted the paradox in the Muslim League's conception of Pakistan and its impact on minorities, which concerned both Maulana Maududi and nationalist Muslims who had stayed in India: 'We in the Frontier used to laugh at the antics of the Muslim League. It was often said that this was not the partition of India but the partition of Muslims. The League was prepared to desert crores of Muslims of India, without bothering to look back at their miserable plight.'[8]

Wali Khan also described the Muslim League's mutual hostage theory and its disastrous consequences for millions of refugees:

> The Muslim League leaders used to claim that the Hindus who would opt to stay back in Pakistan would be treated like hostages. If the Hindus in India committed excesses upon the Muslims, then the Pakistani Muslims would use Pakistani Hindus as political leverage. This was expected to maintain the balance. Having banished the Hindus from Pakistan, the question arose; What would happen to the helpless Muslims in India? How would they exert pressure and on whom? The one irrefutable truth was that no one was the least bit bothered about the Muslims who would be left behind in India.[9]

The Supporter

Justice Munir was a staunch believer in Jinnah's philosophy and provided the most sympathetic interpretation of it. As Chief Justice of Pakistan, he played a role in shaping its polity and ideology. He witnessed the transition from Jinnah to Liaquat Ali Khan and later served as a cabinet minister in Ayub Khan's government. He is remembered for authoring the Munir Commission report, which upheld an enlightened vision of Pakistan amid the anti-Ahmadiya movement of the 1950s. However, he also delivered the judgement validating the suspension of the Constituent Assembly by Governor-General Ghulam Mohammad based on the 'Doctrine of Necessity'. This opened the way for the military's dominance and was later used to justify coups.

Munir's book *From Jinnah to Zia* provides an overview of Pakistan's first four decades. He described Jinnah's 11 August speech as 'one of the clearest expositions of a secular state'.[10] However, as Prof. Ishtiaq Ahmad pointed out, Jinnah carefully avoided using the word 'secular'. This omission, though likely intentional, can be understood – such a statement would have been too radical a departure from the League's position. More difficult to ignore is that Jinnah was asking for religious differences to be set aside after making them the main plank of the League's demand for Pakistan.

After his 11 August speech, which was a departure from the Two-Nation Theory, Jinnah never revisited the idea. A single speech cannot signal a policy shift, or even intent to change the policy. Munir cited Jinnah's other speeches to argue that he wanted a secular Pakistan, but they suggest the opposite. Jinnah's broadcast to the United States stated that Pakistan's Constitution 'will be of democratic type embodying the essential principles of Islam. Today, they are as applicable in actual life as they were 1,300 years ago.'[11] A polity rooted in religion can hardly be described as a secular vision of Pakistan's future.

Munir strongly criticized the introduction of the Objectives Resolution by Liaquat Ali Khan. That resolution qualified 'the principles of democracy, freedom, equality, tolerance and social justice' by adding the caveat 'as enunciated by Islam'.[12] This caveat was also part of Liaquat Ai Khan's speech in the debate on the Objectives Resolution in the Constituent Assembly. Liaquat stated that 'all authority should be exercised in accordance with the standards laid down by Islam'. Munir wrote, 'the Objectives Resolution was a complete contradiction of his [Jinnah's] idea of a modern democratic secular state', and that Liaquat 'waited for six months' after Jinnah's death to move the resolution.[13]

Munir summed up his defence of Jinnah's 'secularism' by stating: 'He wanted a secular democratic government.' He added that in Jinnah's conception of Pakistan, 'religion would be an affair of the individual and [would] have nothing to do with the administration of the State'. Yet he also said that 'such government was to be based on Islamic principles and traditions'.[14] This directly contradicts the idea of secularism.

Munir also mentioned that Jinnah was 'opposed to a theocratic government' and 'he used the words Islam and socialism but they were used in their pragmatic sense, not in their doctrinaire sense'.[15] Theocracy denotes the rule of the clergy. Muslim League leaders kept political control but conceded the principle of politics based on religion. Not being theocratic does not mean being secular. The Muslim League used communal slogans in the 1946 elections. Seven decades later, Imran Khan attempted a similar approach by invoking the early history of Islam. His personal lifestyle was far removed from the ideals he espoused. The 'pragmatic' could be worse than the 'doctrinaire'.

The Establishment

The establishment does not refer to Jinnah's speech of 11 August 1947. It refers to his other speeches of the time which, in its view, represent Jinnah's vision. Maulana Shabbir Ahmad Usmani, one of the chief ideologues of the Muslim League, in the course of the debate on the Objectives Resolution in the Pakistan Constituent Assembly in 1949, stated: 'The Quaid-e-Azam too was referring to the basic principle of our Constitution when he observed in the course of his presidential address delivered at a Conference of the All-India Students Federation at Jullundur in 1943: "In my opinion, our system of Government was determined by the Quran some 1350 years ago."'[16]

Usmani cited Jinnah's letter to the Pir Sahib of Manki Sharif in November 1945, in which Jinnah assured that the 'Constituent Assembly', which would be 'predominantly Muslim' would 'enact laws for Muslims, not inconsistent with the Shariat laws'.[17]

Jinnah himself departed from the ideals of his 11 August speech within months. Addressing the Karachi Bar Association on 25 January 1948, he stated that Pakistan's Constitution would be based on the Shariat:

> Quaid-e-Azam Mohammad Ali Jinnah, Governor-General of Pakistan, speaking at a reception given to him in the Holy Prophecy's Birthday by the Bar Association, Karachi, said that he could not understand a section of the people who deliberately wanted to create mischief and

> made propaganda that the constitution of Pakistan would not be made on the basis of Shari'at. The Quaid-e-Azam said Islamic principles today are as applicable to life as they were 1300 years ago.[18]

Akbar S. Ahmed, in *Jinnah, Pakistan and Islamic Identity*, dismissed Jinnah's supposed secularism, citing his Karachi Bar Association speech as evidence of his true vision. Ahmed also highlighted Jinnah's rejection of Mountbatten's suggestion to use Akbar as a model for Pakistan, stating that the Prophet provided a more inspiring example.

Ahmed added, 'A few weeks later, Jinnah once again repeated the same theme using almost the same ideas and words: "It is my belief that our salvation lies in following the golden rules of conduct set for us by our great law giver, the Prophet of Islam. Let us lay the foundations of our democracy on the basis of truly Islamic ideals and principles."' (Darbar, 14 February 1948)[19]

Ahmed mentioned an interesting episode that gives an indication of Jinnah's thinking. 'In his formal speech to the Constituent Assembly of Pakistan on 14 August, Lord Mountbatten offered the example of Akbar the Great Mughal as the model of a tolerant Muslim ruler to Pakistan.'[20] Jinnah rejected the suggestion, he added. 'In a rebuttal which amounted to a public snub – Mountbatten was after all still the Viceroy of India – Jinnah presented an alternative model.'[21] Jinnah, in his reply, 'pointed out that Muslims had a more permanent and more inspiring model to follow, that of the holy Prophet'.[22]

Ahmed explained the reason behind Jinnah's reply:

> Of the six great Mughal emperors from Babar to Aurangzeb, Akbar is perhaps the one most self-avowedly neutral to Islam. To propose Akbar as an ideal ruler to a newly formed and self-consciously post-colonial Muslim nation was rather like suggesting to a convention of Muslim writers meeting in Iran or Pakistan in the 1990s that their literary model should be Salman Rushdie.[23]

Jinnah's speech rejecting Mountbatten's suggestion that Akbar should be the model for the new state came just three days after his 11 August address. Pakistan regards itself as the inheritor of Mughal rule over the subcontinent, yet Jinnah rejected the legacy of its greatest emperor, who had sought an inclusive society.

Ahmed noted that before his death in 1938, Iqbal described Jinnah as one of three 'shining heroes among Muslims', along with Aurangzeb and Mahmoud Ghazni. He said Iqbal 'refers to both Aurangzeb and Mahmoud as exemplary Muslim heroes in his poetry; in the letters he wrote to Jinnah just before he died, he addressed Jinnah as "the only Muslim" leader for the modern age.'[24]

Ahmed added, 'At Jinnah's death one of the most prominent clerics of Karachi, the Sheikh-ul-Islam, Allama Shabbir Ahmed Usmani, in his funeral oration described Jinnah as "the greatest Muslim after Aurangzeb".'[25]

Ayesha Siddiqa cites Jinnah's response to Egyptian cleric Hassan al-Banna, the founder of the Muslim Brotherhood, where he said: 'I have therefore decided to follow the advice you kindly gave me in your recent letter, that my government should assume a purely Islamic character and work in close cooperation with the other strong international Islamic organizations which are headed by your Ikhwan-al-Muslimun society [the Muslim Brotherhood].'[26]

Jinnah wrote this five months after his 11 August speech, presenting a very different vision of Pakistan. He was under no pressure to say something he did not believe in to a distant cleric. His letter to al-Banna was in line with what he had told domestic audience in his Karachi Bar speech.

Khaliquzzaman, in *Pathway to Pakistan*, gave an account of Jinnah's final meeting with Muslim members of the Indian Constituent Assembly before leaving for Pakistan. Khaliquzzaman has mentioned:

> Mr. Jinnah himself realized the grave dangers to Muslims who, after the partition were to be left in India. I remember that on 1 August 1947, a few days before his final departure for Karachi, Mr Jinnah called the Muslim members of the Constituent Assembly of India to his house at 10 Aurangzeb Road to bid farewell to them. Mr. Rizwanullah put some awkward questions concerning the position of Muslims who would be left over in India, their status, and their future. I had never before found Mr. Jinnah so disconcerted as on that occasion, probably because he was realizing quite vividly what was immediately in store for the Muslims.

> Finding the situation awkward, I asked my friends and colleagues to end the discussion. I believe as a result of our farewell meeting Mr. Jinnah took the earliest opportunity to bid goodbye to his two-nation theory in his speech on 11 August 1947 as the Governor-General designate of Pakistan and President of the Constituent Assembly of Pakistan.[27]

Khaliquzzaman's account suggests that Jinnah's promise of equal treatment for Hindus and Sikhs was a signal to India to protect its Muslim minority. But this does not explain everything. The Two-Nation Theory was not just Jinnah's idea – it was the League's policy. His 11 August speech came after Partition was already in motion, with mass riots and migration.

Khaliquzzaman carefully distanced himself from events he had helped shape. In his memoirs, he took credit for first suggesting partition to British Secretary of State Zetland in 1939, a year before Jinnah's Lahore speech. At the 1940 Lahore session, he seconded the resolution and invoked the mutual hostage theory, arguing that the fate of Hindus in Pakistan would ensure Muslim minorities' welfare in India. This theory was now being tested.

Prof. Ishtiaq Ahmad put it more bluntly in his monumental work on Jinnah: 'However, the main reason for the drastic deviation from the two-nation theory argument was to prevent the exodus of 35 million Muslims from India by assuring that in Pakistan Hindus and Sikhs would be treated as equal citizens.'[28]

It was not so much the welfare of Indian Muslims but the stability of the Pakistani State that had now forced Jinnah to temporarily go back on his pet theory. The consequences of Partition for the Indian Muslims was an acceptable cost in his calculus. He had earlier dismissed their concerns, saying in 1941 that in order to 'liberate' Muslims of Muslim-majority states, he was willing to let two crore Muslims of Muslim-minority states be 'smashed'.[29] A secular conception of the State was at best a temporary expedient to prevent the flight of Muslims to the promised "homeland".'

Farzana Shaikh cites R.J. Moore, who suggests that 'Jinnah at the time had been keen to retain a non-Muslim minority in Pakistan to serve as "hostages", in order to ensure fair treatment for Indian Muslims who chose to remain in India'.[30] This version is indeed closer to the Mutual Hostage Theory propounded by League stalwarts like Khaliquzzaman.

Jinnah's moderation, whether driven by concern for Indian Muslims or Pakistan's stability, was short-lived. By 25 January 1948, he retracted his 11 August speech, stating that Pakistan's Constitution would be based on Islamic law (Sharia) 'to make Pakistan a truly great Islamic State'.[31]

Khaliquzzaman stayed in India briefly after Partition and witnessed the widespread violence. He sought help from Congress leaders, including Patel and Sampurnanand (who later became chief minister of UP), to protect Muslim minorities. He later praised their efforts publicly, contradicting Pakistan's Foreign Minister Zafarullah Khan, who accused Congress leaders of abetting communal riots. This led to tensions with Jinnah when he visited Pakistan. Khaliquzzaman never returned to India.

Jinnah was unwilling to confront the consequences of Partition, which stemmed from the Muslim League's politics. The mutual hostage theory, which Khaliquzzaman himself had championed in 1940, collapsed in practice.

Perhaps those who favour the liberal interpretation of Jinnah's speech may reject Akbar S. Ahmed and Maulana Shabir Ahmed Usmani's views. But his own words left enough ambiguity. As Prof. C. Christine Fair, a noted American commentator, observes: 'Unfortunately, when it came to Islam's role in Pakistan's constitution and government structures, Jinnah often said different things to different audiences.'

A statesman's legacy has to be judged by his actions. There was no ambiguity about Jinnah's actions after 1940. He advocated divisive, communal politics, followed the British lead, and gave the call for Direct Action, which resulted in the massacre of thousands of innocents. Jinnah's recourse to religious idiom to broaden support for Pakistan inevitably strengthened the role of clergy in the new state. He returned to this again after his speech of 11 August 1947.

Jinnah passed away in September 1948. Six months later, Liaquat brought in the Objectives Resolution, which laid the foundation of an Islamic state. The Citizenship Act of 1951 closed the door for further immigration of Muslims to the promised homeland. Pakistan's subsequent evolution where religion casts a shadow on all aspects of the state and society is no accident of history.

PART 2

Faith, Politics and Interests

8

Divine Sovereignty

'The people of Pakistan, have the courage to believe firmly that all authority should be exercised in accordance with the standards laid down by Islam.'

–Prime Minister Liaquat Ali Khan
in the debate on the Objectives Resolution
in Pakistan Constituent Assembly, 1949[1]

THE OBJECTIVES RESOLUTION WAS adopted by the Pakistan Constituent Assembly in 1949. Prime Minister Liaquat Ali Khan introduced it six months after Jinnah's death. Jinnah did not define the nature of the state he had striven for. He never returned to the liberal vision of Pakistan he spelt out in his speech of 11 August 1947. If there was any ambiguity, it was removed by the Objectives Resolution and Liaquat's speech. Pakistan was to be an Islamic state.

The resolution laid down the objectives of the new state. Its preamble states: 'Sovereignty over the entire universe belongs to Allah Almighty alone and the authority which He has delegated to the State of Pakistan, through its people for being exercised within the limits prescribed by Him is a sacred trust.'[2] The preamble thus makes it clear that the powers of the state in Pakistan's Constitution are derived not from the people but the will of the divine. This limited the role of the elected legislature. Divine sovereignty covered both ecclesiastical and lay domains. There was to be no separation of religion, state and society. It circumscribed the minority rights, which were subjected to the religious injunctions of the faith of the majority community. This violated Article 19 of the Universal Declaration on

Human Rights, adopted by the United Nations General Assembly in December 1948, which states, 'Everyone has the right to freedom of thought conscience and religion', without attaching any caveats. The Objectives Resolution further stated authority delegated by the divine is to be 'exercised within the limits prescribed by Him'. This further constrained minority rights. It also had implications for the majority community. The Objectives Resolution asked for provisions to be made to enable Muslims to exercise their rights in accordance with the injunctions of the Holy Quran and Sunnah. Liaquat Ali Khan made an eloquent speech defending the Objectives Resolution. He described a 'polity where spiritual and ethical values should play no part in the governance of the people as a "Machiavellian idea"'. What he meant by 'spiritual and ethical values' were religious injunctions, which became clear from his next sentence. He said, 'The people of Pakistan have the courage to believe firmly that all authority should be exercised in accordance with the standards laid down by Islam.' He denied that there was 'any danger of establishment of theocracy', as such a system means 'Government by ordained priests' – an idea which is 'absolutely foreign to Islam'.[3] What was being substituted for governance by the priests was a Constitution where the source of legitimacy of laws of the state was religion, as interpreted by politicians. It was of little comfort to the minorities that the restrictions came from political masters rather than the clergy.

The Objectives Resolution contained two provisions about the protection of minority rights: '*Adequate* provision shall be made for the minorities to freely progress and practice their religions and develop their cultures' and 'adequate provisions shall be made to safeguard the *legitimate interests* of minorities and backward and depressed classes'.[4] [Emphases added] Both provisions were qualified by the preamble, which has made the Constitution subject to the 'sovereignty of Allah Almighty' and 'limits prescribed by Him'. The formulation that 'adequate' provisions were to be made for minority rights is open to interpretation. This ambiguity was compounded by reference to the 'legitimate' interests of minorities. The meanings of both these terms could vary widely. This was different from the 'adequate, effective and mandatory safeguards' mentioned in the Lahore Resolution. The makers of Pakistan's Constitution had also limited the import of these provisions to minorities practising 'their religions and develop their cultures'. This left out 'economic, political, administrative and other rights' mentioned in the Lahore Resolution. They had departed from their own chosen standard.

Liaquat Ai Khan added, 'Islam recognizes no distinctions based upon race, colour or birth.' Omitted from this formulation was a distinction based on religion. Pakistan's prime minister did not address the issue of religious discrimination, which the minorities feared. The nature of the state he had in mind became clear from his next observation. He said: 'The State will create such conditions as are conducive to the building up of a truly Islamic society, which means that the State will have to play a positive part in this effort.'[5]

What Liaquat Ali Khan was proposing was exactly what he had denied in the earlier part of his speech. The Pakistan of his conception was to be an Islamic state, where religion was to be the business of the state – contrary to the famous speech of Muhammad Ali Jinnah of 11 August 1947.

Justice Munir Ahmad wrote that if Liaquat had tried to introduce the Objectives Resolution in Jinnah's lifetime, 'the Quaid-i-Azam would never have given his assent to it'.[6] He writes further, 'After the Quaid-i-Azam's death, Liaquat Ali Khan waited for six months before he moved that Resolution which was unanimously passed by the Muslim members, the Hindu members having boycotted the session.'[7]

Justice Munir Ahmad's view is perhaps the minority view. Liaquat Ali Khan represented the establishment view, and he saw no contradiction between what he was proposing and what Jinnah had said. Indeed, he said this was in accordance with Jinnah's views. The prime minister said, 'You would remember, Sir, that the Quaid-i-Azam and other leaders of the Muslim League always made unequivocal declarations that the Muslim demand for Pakistan was based upon the fact that the Muslims had a way of life and a code of conduct…'[8]

On the face of it, what the Constitution said about the Muslims need not affect the non-Muslim minorities. Liaquat Ali Khan said, 'In our desire to build up an Islamic society we have not ignored the rights of the non-Muslims.' But his assurances were not part of the Constitution. The principles enunciated by the Objectives Resolution to guide the Constitution had an altogether different meaning.

Bhupendra Kumar Dutta of the Congress party moved an amendment to omit the preamble of the Objectives Resolution. He said, "'Politics" belongs to the domain of reason. But as you intermingle it with religion, as this Preamble to this nobly conceived Resolution does, you pass into the other sphere of faith.'[9] He appealed to the House not to 'bind those vast numbers, present and future, to our conceptions of perfection and happiness'. He urged the mover of the resolution, 'to agree to withdraw this Preamble which is not an essential part of the Resolution before the House'.[10]

There were some other notable speeches in the debate. Dr Ishtiaq Hussain Qureshi said politics and religion 'cannot be divorced from each other'. The Objectives Resolution qualified the principles of democracy, freedom, equality, tolerance and social justice by the phrase 'as enunciated by Islam'. Some opposition members had expressed apprehension about the effect of such a caveat on the scope of freedom to be enjoyed by the minorities. Qureshi was dismissive of such fears; he said the minorities should discard such fears and added that 'the real political safeguard for any minority is to win the affection and respect of the majority'.[11]

The Muslim League had insisted on a separate electorate, weighted representation, parity with the majority and eventually the creation of a separate state for Muslims in pre-Partition days. Post-Partition, its argument had shifted the onus onto minorities to win the respect of the majority.

Maulana Shabbir Ahmad Usmani, one of the chief ideologues of the Muslim League, stated, 'An Islamic State is not a State in its own right, with authority inherent in it. It is a State to which authority has been delegated.' 'The real sovereignty belongs to God.' 'Man is his vice-regent on Earth', and discharges his obligations 'within the limits prescribed by God'. His words make the inspiration behind the Objectives Resolution clear. He quoted Jinnah's presidential address to a conference of the All-India Students Federation at Jullundur in 1943, 'In my opinion our system of Government was determined by the Quran some 1350 years ago.'[12]

Usmani also quoted Jinnah's letter to the Pir Sahib of Manki Sharif in November 1945, in which he clearly stated: 'It is needless to emphasise that the Constituent Assembly which would be Predominantly Muslim in its composition, would be able to enact laws for Muslims, not inconsistent with the Shariat laws and the Muslims will no longer be obliged to abide by the Un-Islamic laws.'[13]

Maulana Shabbir Usmani reiterated that 'such statements were repeatedly made by the Quaid-i-Azam and other League leaders before the establishment of Pakistan. I cannot quote them at length for lack of time.'[14] Thus, an Islamic state and Constitution flowed from the logic of the Muslim League's position in pre-Partition India. This view challenges the claim that Jinnah was opposed to an Islamic state and wanted a secular, democratic Pakistan. The Maulana represented the clergy; Liaquat Ali Khan symbolized the state. It appears both agreed on the nature of the Pakistani state.

If Maulana Shabbir Ahmad Usmani represented the view of the conservative clergy, Mian Iftikharuddin was supposed to be a left-leaning intellectual. He dismissed the views of the Congress members that the wording of the preamble laid the foundations of a theocratic state. He said, 'Practically every country of the British Empire derives its authority through the agency of the king from God.' Mian Iftikharuddin went on to state, 'The God of the Muslims, the conception of Allah in the Muslim religion, is in no way less merciful than the conception of the Almighty in other religions.' He ignored the history of the British constitution, where religion had ceased to be a force in politics, as Jinnah had remarked in his 11 August speech. The nature of Islam was not the issue. What the minority members objected to was religion as the basis of politics. The Congress member had mentioned that politics and religion belonged to different domains.

Mian Iftikharuddin had casually dismissed the fears of the minority members about the state being based on religion. This, of course, had nothing to do with the nature of Islam, nor did the Congress member say so. Bhupendra Kumar Dutta was at pains to cast the debate in terms of reason and faith, avoiding any comment on religion. The minorities became the first victims of the philosophy underlying the Objectives Resolution. But it had implications for the majority as well, which became clear once the state began to lean progressively towards a conservative view of Islam.

Mian Iftikharuddin did, however, take exception to the wording of the preamble, which stated that the authority of the divine is delegated through the 'people' to the 'state'. The state was thus the ultimate recipient of the divine authority, not the people. He said this raised the danger that the state may arrogate to itself the right to decide what the limits 'prescribed by Him' were, within which the delegated authority would be exercised. This was indeed a fundamental question, which Liaquat Ali Khan had fudged by claiming that under the resolution, 'people' were the recipient of the authority delegated by the Almighty.

Iftikharuddin added, 'We know the final authority to decide about the limits, the final authority to interpret the rights of the people, is the people themselves. To bring in, therefore, the agency of the State is to confuse the issue.'[15]

As the number and percentage of minorities have dwindled to an insignificant level, the legacy of the Objectives Resolution now haunts the majority community. The primacy of the 'state' over the 'people' also weakens the foundations of democracy. This not only resulted from a series of military takeovers but was also built into the Objectives Resolution by the Muslim League politicians.

Delegates of Divine Power

The Objectives Resolution is now an integral part of the Constitution of the Islamic Republic of Pakistan. Under the Eighth Amendment adopted during Zia's regime in 1985, Article 2A was inserted into the Constitution, stating, 'The principle and provisions set out in the Objectives Resolution reproduced in the Annex are hereby made substantive part of the Constitution and shall have effect accordingly.' However, the resolution annexed to the Constitution omitted the word 'freely' to qualify the exercise of the rights by minorities, which was present in the original text. It took more than three decades to discover this omission and rectify it.

As part of Article 2A of the Constitution, the resolution qualifies and overrides fundamental rights. Its primacy over fundamental rights was affirmed by the Pakistan Supreme Court in its judgement in the case *Zahiruddin v The State and Others*. The Court stated that, 'Every man-made law must now conform to the injunctions of Islam.'

The import of the Objectives Resolution and its placement as Article 2A of the Constitution has had a major impact on the country's polity.

This time, the victim was not a minority member but the head of the ruling party in Pakistan. Nawaz Sharif was dismissed from the office of the prime minister in 2017 on the charge that he did not disclose the salary offered to him by his son's firm. The curious part of this episode was that the prime minister never received the salary he was accused of not disclosing.

The Pakistan Muslim League (Nawaz), responded by electing the deposed prime minister as the party chief. This required amending the Election Act of 2017 to drop a proviso that barred 'leaders from being elected to party offices'. The clause was originally inserted during Gen. Pervez Musharraf's tenure to bar Benazir Bhutto from being elected as leader of the Pakistan People's Party.[16] Nawaz Sharif's election as party head was challenged in the Supreme Court. The Court used the Objectives Resolution as the standard to strike down the legislation enacted by the Parliament. Chief Justice Saqib Nisar, in his judgement stated: 'in accordance with the Muslim faith, our democracy cannot be "in conflict with Islamic Principles".' He further added, 'only those people can enter the electoral process who fulfil the prerequisites and requirements spelt out in the Constitution itself *to be worthy delegates of Almighty Allah in order to exercise his powers in trust for Him* and for the welfare of the people of Pakistan by joining the political process.' [Emphasis added]

The Objectives Resolution has received judicial imprimatur. According to Justice Saquib Nisar, elected representatives are 'delegates' of the divine power and exercise 'his powers in trust for Him'. In democracies, elected representatives are accountable to the people, not God. The good judge was only giving expression to the resolution, which affects every aspect of the lives of both minorities and majorities in Pakistan. This also has a far-reaching impact on the future of democracy in Pakistan. It is another matter that democracy in Pakistan has elevated faith as the foundational principle of the Constitution.

9

The 'Other' Nation

'The resolution that was introduced at the Delhi Convention of the Muslim League "altered the Lahore Resolution in some ways." Mr Hashim and a few others objected when the word "States" of the previous resolution was replaced with "State" but they were overruled.'

–Sheikh Mujibur Rahman on Jinnah
altering the Lahore Resolution[1]

JINNAH IN HIS SPEECH in the Lahore session of the Muslim League in 1940 described Hindus and Muslims as two separate nationalities which could not be reconciled. After the birth of Pakistan, Bengalis became the 'other' nation. The Lahore Resolution had envisaged Muslim-majority 'states'. The plurality inherent in the concept of Pakistan reflected ethnic, linguistic and cultural diversities, not only between the two wings but also within West Pakistan. The Muslim League leadership sought to ignore these underlying differences. The Lahore Resolution was moved by A.K. Fazlul Haq, the chief minister of Bengal. After Partition, he became a champion of autonomy for East Pakistan.

Sheikh Mujibur Rahman was an enthusiastic Muslim League activist who ended up becoming a rebel against West Pakistan's domination over the majority eastern wing. His political autobiography, *The Unfinished Memoirs*, was compiled by his daughter Sheikh Hasina after his death. In this, Mujib described Bengali alienation which drove them to seek separate statehood. The process had begun before Partition with Jinnah's attempt to tamper with the Lahore Resolution, which envisaged sovereign, independent 'states' in the north-western and eastern zones of undivided India. The resolution that was introduced at the Delhi Convention of the Muslim League 'altered the Lahore Resolution in some ways', according to Mujib. 'Mr Hashim and a few others objected when the word "states" of the previous resolution was replaced with "state", but they were overruled…' Mujib went on to say, 'Scholars can perhaps decide whether the convention had the right to alter the terms of the resolution adopted in 1940.'[2]

In 1949, the Bengal Muslim League adopted a resolution demanding full provincial autonomy in all matters except defence and foreign affairs.[3] The demand for autonomy is usually voiced by the minority province or group. That it came from East Pakistan was unusual. It showed that despite its clear numerical majority, the eastern wing felt marginalized in the power structure of Pakistan, which was dominated by the Punjabi civil-military bureaucracy.

Successive constitutional schemes sought to create an artificial parity between the two wings of Pakistan in a bid to neutralize the numerical majority of the eastern wing. The first Constitution was adopted in 1956 only after the 'One Unit' system was accepted in 1955. This was designed to create a counterpoise to East Pakistan by welding together the four provinces of West Pakistan. Its victim was not only East Pakistan but also the smaller provinces of West Pakistan.

The treatment of the language issue brought home to the East Pakistanis that they were regarded by the Pakistani establishment as 'different', despite having sacrificed for Pakistan. Jinnah visited Dhaka in March 1948. In his address at the convocation hall of Dhaka University, he said, 'Make no mistake about it. There can be only one state language if the component parts of this state are to march forward in unison and that language, in my opinion, can only be Urdu.'[4]

Jinnah described Urdu as:

> a language that has been nurtured by a hundred million Muslims of this subcontinent, a language understood throughout the length and breadth of Pakistan and, above all, a language which, more than any other provincial language, embodies the best that is in Islamic culture and Muslim tradition and is nearest to the languages used in other Islamic countries.[5]

Jinnah was equating the Urdu language with 'Islamic culture and Muslim tradition'. It was being accorded a higher status because it was 'nearest to the languages used in other Islamic countries'. It was Urdu's proximity to languages 'in other Islamic countries' rather than synthesis with the local culture that recommended it to him to call it the only 'state language' of Pakistan.

Mujib described how there were protests against Jinnah's statement that 'Urdu will be the only state language of Pakistan'. 'Many of us raised our hands in protest and shouted, "No, no."' Speaking at a students' meeting, Mujib added, 'Bengali is the language spoken by 56 per cent of the people of Pakistan; it is a democratic country, and therefore the demand of the majority must be met.'[6] As he would realize much later, the foundational principles of the country were different. Pakistan was an ideological state.

Liaquat Ali Khan was even more emphatic in rejecting the demand to give Bengali an equal status with Urdu. He said, 'It is necessary for a nation to have one language and that language can only be Urdu and no other language.'[7] Jinnah passed away in September 1948, but Liaquat remained at the helm of affairs until his assassination in 1951. He would influence the direction of the nascent state even more profoundly.

The percentage of Bengali-speaking people in Pakistan went down in 1950 after communal violence in East Pakistan caused a large-scale exodus of the Hindu minority to India. Yet, the 1951 census in Pakistan showed that this percentage stood at 54.6, in contrast to 7.2 per cent Urdu speakers.[8]

While Jinnah and Liaquat favoured Urdu over Bengali, Ayub Khan betrayed a touch of racial superiority in his description of the people of the eastern wing. In his memoir, *Friends Not Masters*, he described Bengalis as belonging to 'the very original Indian races' who had never known any real freedom and showed 'all the inhibitions of downtrodden races'. He said they were 'under considerable Hindu cultural and linguistic influence'. On the other hand, he described the population of West Pakistan as a mixture of conquering races. He wrote, 'Lying on the gateways to the Indian subcontinent, it was inevitable that each successive conquering race should have left its traces here.'[9]

Language Riots

In January 1952, 'the Basic Principles Committee (BPC) of the Constituent Assembly of Pakistan submitted its recommendation for making Urdu as the only state language, which sparked off a wave of anger in East Pakistan and protests erupted'. On 21 February 1952, police opened fire on a procession of Dhaka University students protesting against the BPC recommendation, killing three students. The following day, further violence erupted when police fired on a mourners' procession, resulting in additional casualties.

To ease tensions over the language issue, Prime Minister Mohammad Ali Bogra agreed to make Bengali the second official language of Pakistan. The decision was made ahead of the 1954 elections for the provincial assembly of East Bengal.[10] Pakistan's first Constitution, adopted in 1956, recognized Bengali along with Urdu as the state language of Pakistan. Article 214(1) mentioned, 'The state language of Pakistan shall be Urdu and Bengali.'[11] However, this relief was short-lived. The first Constitution was hardly implemented. After his military coup in October 1958, General Ayub abrogated the Constitution and introduced a highly centralized system of administration which accentuated East Pakistan's marginalization. Pakistan's federal government made consistent effort to replace the Bengali script with Arabic script.

Minorities

The adoption of the Objectives Resolution in 1949 worsened the plight of minorities in Pakistan. This is discussed in detail in a later chapter on minorities. The 1950 killings of minority members in East Bengal resulted in the forced migration of Hindus to India on a large scale.

> In Dacca Hindus formed 59 per cent of the population and possessed 85 per cent of the properties in the city after the establishment of Pakistan. About 90 per cent of this Hindu population left for India after the 1950 holocaust, and the property holdings of Hindus fell to 12.7 per cent. About 90 per cent of the Hindu shops in Dacca were looted on 10 February 1950, and many were burnt down. Nearly

> fifty thousand Hindus in that city lost their houses on the same day. About ten thousand Hindus in the whole of East Bengal died during the February massacre.[12]

The killings of minorities in East Bengal formed the immediate background of the Nehru–Liaquat Pact of April 1950 on minority protection. This was followed by a tour by J.N. Mandal, the law minister in the Pakistan government, of the riot-affected areas. In his report to the prime minister in June 1950, Mandal detailed atrocities against the minorities. He also recommended disarming the Ansar militia involved in the killings, and recruiting police officers from among non-Muslims. None of these recommendations were ever implemented. Eventually, J.N. Mandal was forced to flee to India. In his resignation letter, he said, 'non-Muslims were oppressed daily', and faced a future 'darkened by the ominous shadow of conversion and liquidation'.[13]

The minorities issue became entangled in the wrangling over inter-regional parity. East Pakistan accounted for 56 per cent of Pakistan's population, and minorities formed a substantial chunk of the eastern wing's population. If they could be neutralized, this could help reduce the numerical majority the eastern wing enjoyed. This could be achieved either by means of forced migration or through a system of separate electorates. Both were attempted by the Pakistani leadership.

The Bengali delegation at the Pakistan Constituent Assembly had forty-four members; among them, four were non-Bengali nominees of Jinnah, while thirteen were Hindus.[14] The total strength of the first Constituent Assembly was sixty-nine in 1947. There was one Hindu member from Punjab. Thus, minority representation stood at 20 per cent of the total strength. This gives an indication of the salience of minorities in Pakistan, particularly in East Bengal, which the Pakistani leadership sought to neutralize.

West Pakistani politicians attempted to introduce a separate electorate for minorities to reduce East Pakistan's majority, where there was still a substantial minority population. This was also calculated to undermine the electoral base of East Pakistan parties. An attempt was made by introducing the Third Amendment bill. The Electorate Act of 1956 provided for a separate electorate in West Pakistan but a joint electorate in the eastern wing. As democracy was soon eclipsed in 1958, the nature of the electorate did not have much immediate impact.

'One Unit' System – 'Parity' with the Majority Province

Sardar Sherbaz Khan Mazari, a highly respected figure in Pakistan's politics, gave a dispassionate account of Pakistan's first four decades in his book *A Journey to Disillusionment*, and described political wrangling to negate East Pakistan's majority. He wrote, 'In the Constituent Assembly, the Bengali group was in a dominant position, having thirty-three out of sixty Muslim League members.'[15] He added, 'A federal Constitution with a Bengali majority in the legislature was an anathema to the bureaucratic-military establishment.'[16] They sought to neutralize the Bengali majority by devising the 'One Unit' system and voting procedure in the Parliament.

In September 1955, the Constituent Assembly approved the draft Constitution based on Chaudhry Muhammad Ali's formula for parliamentary representation. According to Sherbaz Mazari,

> It provided that the lower house was to consist of three hundred members elected on the basis of population, and the upper house would consist of fifty members equally divided among the five units, who would be elected by the legislatures of the units. East Bengal's majority in the lower house, on the basis of its population, would be balanced by the minority in the upper house.[17]

Thus, East Pakistan, with the majority population, was reduced to a minority in the upper house (ten out of fifty seats). It enjoyed a small edge in the lower house – 165 seats against 135 seats allotted to the West Pakistan provinces. But this was neutralized by the fact that both houses enjoyed equal powers, and in case of divergence between them, the issue was to be decided by a joint session, where a decision required the support of at least 30 per cent of the members of each wing. This, however, was soon overtaken by the 'One Unit' system. The 1956 Constitution had a unicameral legislature, where there was no upper house to represent provinces. This weakened the federal structure and strengthened the bias towards a unitary constitution.

The 'One Unit' system lumped together all four provinces of West Pakistan into one administrative unit to act as a counterpoise to East Pakistan. This forced merger also closed off the option for West Pakistan's smaller provinces to form an alliance with East Pakistan against Punjabi domination.

The legislative structure devised was perhaps an excessive precaution. The Punjabi coterie exercised its control through its dominance of civil-military bureaucracy, where East Pakistan was under-represented. Democratic decision-making, where the weight of East Pakistan's majority could have been felt, did not exist after Ayub's coup in 1958.

While the 'One Unit' system remained in existence till 1970, parliamentary elections under the 1956 Constitution never took place. They were pre-empted by Ayub Khan's coup in October 1958. The system of 'Basic Democracy' introduced by Ayub in 1960 was based on limited franchise. After the 1970 elections based on universal franchise, East Pakistan broke away, rendering the elaborate system of checks and balances against the eastern wing unnecessary.

Apart from the 'One Unit' system and the contrived constitutional scheme of parity between the two wings, the third element was squeezing out the minorities to reduce the numerical majority of East Pakistan. Most of the Hindu minority had already been driven out of West Pakistan by 1953. But there remained a substantial number in the eastern wing. To reduce their salience in politics, a separate electorate was pushed. This is covered in more detail in the chapter on minorities.

The wrangling over inter-regional parity in the Constitution had continued for more than six years from 1950 when the first report of the Basic Principles Committee was submitted by Prime Minister Liaquat Ali Khan, and in 1956 when Pakistan adopted its first Constitution based on the 'One Unit' system. The exercise showed deep suspicion between the two wings. The 'One Unit' system ensured that political parties would function along regional considerations. This accentuated differences between the two wings and made it difficult for the emergence of parties with a following on both sides of the divide. By the time this constitutional scheme was approved, the Muslim League had already suffered a massive defeat in the 1954 provincial elections in East Pakistan. It won only nine seats in a legislature of 310 members.[18]

Economic Disparity

While West Pakistan demanded and received parity in political representation with the numerically larger East Pakistan, it was not willing to concede parity in the economic sphere. The disparity between the two wings continued to grow. Though General Ayub, in his memoirs, maintained that there was no discrimination against East Pakistan, this is belied by the writings of his loyal aide, Altaf Gauhar. He has written in Ayub Khan's political biography, 'Under Ayub's highly centralized system, the people in the provinces never had the feeling of equality…' 'East Bengal, in particular, blamed and not without justification, the central government for exploiting the resources of the province and denying the people their fundamental rights. Ayub presided over a coalition of unequal and unwilling partners.'[19]

The process of exploitation of East Pakistan had begun much before Ayub Khan assumed power. In September 1949, Britain decided to devalue the pound sterling by nearly 30 per cent. Both India and Pakistan were part of the sterling area. India followed the British lead and devalued the Indian rupee; Pakistan refused to do so. Chaudhry Muhammad Ali in his memoir, *The Emergence of Pakistan*, has defended the decision by claiming that 'devaluation would not have promoted exports but would have raised the internal level of prices'.[20] He was then secretary general and later became the finance minister and prime minister of Pakistan. Devaluation generally has an inflationary effect on domestic prices. However, in this case, it was the British pound that had been devalued. Britain and India were Pakistan's main trading partners. An adjustment in the price of the Pakistani rupee in tandem with the devaluation of the pound and the Indian rupee would not have altered the relative exchange rate or affected domestic prices. By keeping the exchange rate artificially high, the Pakistan government created an overvalued currency.

Chaudhry Muhammad Ali wrote that the cabinet's decision to not devalue the currency 'startled the world by its demonstration of Pakistan's economic strength and independence of judgement'.[21] He added that Indians felt 'humiliated into the bargain; they had to accept that 100 Pakistani rupees were worth 144 Indian rupees'.[22]

Ghulam Muhammad, the finance minister at the time, had sent a telegram to Prime Minister Liaquat Ali Khan 'strongly urging devaluation pari passu with the sterling'. Thus, the decision of Liaquat Ali Khan's cabinet appears driven not by economic considerations, but by pride and prejudice. It rendered East Pakistan's jute exports uncompetitive in India, which was its main market.

Other than prestige, there could be two other explanations for the actions of the federal government, which defied economic logic. Devaluation would have made the import of capital goods, needed for the industrialization of West Pakistan, more expensive. Liaquat Ali Khan had no qualms about sacrificing the interests of the eastern wing in the process. An overvalued currency severed ties between East Bengal's jute producers and jute processing centres in India. This might not have been an entirely unintended consequence.

Chaudhry Muhammad Ali blamed the Indian government for the consequences of the actions of the Liaquat cabinet, which led to a 'disastrous fall in jute prices and financial ruin for millions of farmers in East Pakistan'.[23] In 1948–49, the Indian side was eager to enter into a twenty-five-year agreement with Pakistan for the purchase of jute.[24] The Indian jute processing industry, however, could not absorb a 40 per cent increase in the price of raw materials and had to look to domestic sources to grow jute. Eventually, Pakistan devalued its currency in 1952, when West Pakistan had completed the import of capital goods. The policy change was made when the interests of Pakistani industrialists demanded it; not those of the jute growers of East Pakistan.

Jayant a Kumar Ray states, 'According to the calculations of Mahbub ul Haq, the transfer of real resources from East to West Pakistan amounted to Rs 219 million per year in the period before 1955 (i.e. before the inauguration of the first Five Year Plan) and Rs 100 million per year in the period after 1955.'[25] Mahbub ul Haq declared, 'In respect of agriculture, transport, industry and other sectors, everywhere the position was in favour of East Pakistan in 1947 which has been reversed by 1964.' He termed it as 'a pure colonial practice', which involved 'transferring East Pakistan's surplus foreign exchange resources with which West Pakistan meets her consumption and capital goods requirements'.[26]

Autonomy

The Muslim League suffered a humiliating defeat in the 1954 East Bengal legislative elections at the hands of the United Front – a coalition of parties led by A.K. Fazlul Haq, who had moved the Lahore Resolution in 1940. Fazlul Haq formed the Krishak Sramik Party in 1953; his coalition partner was the Awami League of Maulana Bhashani, founded in 1949. The United Front fought and won the election on the basis of a twenty-one-point programme. 'This programme referred to the Lahore Resolution as it demanded autonomy for East Bengal in all fields except defence, foreign affairs and currency.'[27] The programme promised to make Bengali one of the state languages, industrialize East Bengal, and demand that the Pakistan Navy's headquarters be located in the eastern wing.

The movement for autonomy gained strength as a result of the 1965 war. East Pakistan felt vulnerable, as the Pakistan government made no effort in its defence. A direct result of this neglect was the six-point autonomy plan, which Mujib unveiled at a meeting at Chaudhry Muhammad Ali's house in February 1966 to present a unified front against Ayub's Tashkent Declaration with India. This was based on a federal Constitution for Pakistan where the central government was to be limited to defence and foreign affairs only.[28]

The plan reflected the bitter lessons of nearly two decades of exploitation by West Pakistan, in which the more populous eastern wing received a minority share in resources. Mujib was arrested in April 1966 and later implicated in the Agartala Conspiracy Case, which further aggravated the general feeling of discontent in the eastern wing.[29]

Ayub Khan's Exit

The unrest in both wings against Ayub's government continued to grow. While in West Pakistan, it had started with opposition to the Tashkent Declaration; in the eastern wing, it was fuelled by a sense of marginalization and demand for autonomy. In January 1969, the opposition parties formed a Democratic Alliance Committee (DAC) to coordinate their moves. Ayub announced that he would not seek re-election in the polls scheduled for 1970 and invited the opposition parties for a dialogue.

The round table conference with the opposition parties produced an agreement on direct elections on the basis of universal suffrage and a parliamentary form of government, 'but not on the question of parity between East and West Pakistan or the distribution of subjects between the centre and the provinces', as Ayub had noted.[30] Sheikh Mujib had disassociated himself from the negotiations 'because it had not supported East Pakistan's demand for autonomy'.[31] Zulfikar Ali Bhutto did not take part in the negotiations; he had 'entered into a secret understanding with the senior generals', according to Sherbaz Mazari.[32] President Ayub Khan was losing the support of the army, his primary constituency.

There is a revealing passage in Altaf Gauhar's biography of Ayub Khan which shows that the Punjab coterie was not willing to give up the idea of 'One Unit' even in the dying days of Ayub's presidency. Gauhar was sent to meet Chaudhry Muhammad Ali in March 1969 to drum up support for the beleaguered president. While Chaudhry Muhammad Ali and Maulana Maududi, the Amir of Jamaat-e-Islami, supported the agreement on election on the basis of universal suffrage and a parliamentary form of government, they remained opposed to any concession on the issue of regional autonomy. Muhammad Ali was also opposed to 'representation in the National Assembly on the basis of population', which 'would destroy the federal concept as it would disenfranchise the less populated regions'.[33] Representation based on share in the population is the basis of modern democracy.

In many countries, the federal structure allows for safeguards for smaller units. Under the US system, the Senate reflects the principle of parity between federating states, while the population principle is reflected in the election to the House of Representatives. The Pakistani system – before and after the emergence of Bangladesh – is remarkably different. The 'One Unit' system was not founded on parity between provinces; it was based on parity between the two wings. The smaller provinces of West Pakistan never had parity with Punjab. Democratic representation was completely absent till 1970. Ayub's coup d'état pre-empted elections under the 1956 Constitution. Under the 1973 Constitution, Punjab has not accepted equality with smaller provinces; it has preponderant weight in both the Senate and the National Assembly.

Unable to carry out the government in the face of the mounting demand for autonomy in the east wing, Ayub declared martial law on 20 March 1969. With the declaration of martial law, power slipped from his hand. This was a replay of Iskander Mirza's ouster by Ayub himself in 1958. Ayub handed over power to General Yahya Khan.

The Endgame

The general election of 1970 produced a sweeping victory for Sheikh Mujibur Rahman's Awami League in East Pakistan. 'The Awami League captured slightly over 75 per cent of the province's votes. It swept to a parliamentary majority by winning 160 out of 162 East Pakistani seats, which represented 53 percent of the total of 300 seats in the National Assembly.'[34] The Awami League had thus secured an absolute majority. 'In the western wing, the PPP managed to capture nearly 60 per cent of West Pakistan's seats in the National Assembly. The percentage of seats it won was much higher than the votes polled (38.89 per cent).[35] PPP won eighty-one seats.

The elections based on universal suffrage brought the old dilemma into sharper focus. The majority province could not be denied a share of power in a democratic set-up. Bhutto threw a spanner in the works. In December 1970, he announced that, 'Any constitutional arrangement which excluded him and his PPP would be doomed to failure.'[36] The Awami League's response was that it could frame the Constitution with or without the cooperation of any party.[37] Under the Legal Framework Order (LFO), 'the future Constitution could be determined by a simple majority of the new National Assembly'.[38]

The army had not expected a sweeping victory for Mujib. According to Mazari, with a view to diluting the Awami League's electoral chances, it had provided 'funds to parties such as the Muslim League and Nurul Amin's Pakistan Democratic Party'.[39] Mujib's massive victory posed a problem for it. His six-point programme had left only defence, foreign affairs and currency with the Centre. Even if the army were to accept this, the limited government required revenue to run it. Mazari wrote, 'Yahya Khan wanted the Awami League to make constitutional guarantees that the Centre would receive a fixed percentage of taxes raised by the provinces.'[40] He added that the Awami League was not willing to 'guarantee an allocation of funds to the future federal government'.[41] Nevertheless, Yahya announced in January 1971 that 'Sheikh Mujibur Rahman is going to be the future prime minister of the country'.[42]

Bhutto's *Idhar Hum, Udhar Tum* (We Are Here, You Are There)

Bhutto visited Dhaka on 27 January 1971 and held discussions with Sheikh Mujib on the six-point programme. According to General Gul Hassan Khan, commander-in-chief of the Pakistan Army from December 1971 to March 1972, Bhutto sought the portfolio of deputy prime minister or even foreign minister.[43] Sherbaz Mazari wrote that when Sheikh Mujib declined his demand, Bhutto 'threatened Mujibur Rahman with grave consequences'.[44]

Mujib was willing to compromise. He told a prominent West Pakistani politician, Shaukat Hayat that 'the Six Points were not sacrosanct'. But he wanted discussions with West Pakistani politicians other than Bhutto.[45] Akbar Bugti also described Mujib as 'extremely conciliatory towards West Pakistani politicians in general'.[46] Bhutto, however, sought to scuttle any understanding with Mujib. He had gained the support of General Hamid and General Peerzada, the two senior-most members of the junta after Yahya Khan. 'He threatened to "break the legs" of any Member of the National Assembly (MNA) from the West Wing who dared venture to Dhaka for the Assembly meeting.'[47]

As Bhutto ranted, 'Idhar hum, udhar tum (We are here and you are there)', Yahya Khan and his generals moved one step closer to the crisis.[48] The statement meant that Bhutto was not willing to let Mujib rule over West Pakistan. The leader of the minority party was unwilling to concede power to the majority party, instead favouring a break-up of the country.

A substantial agreement was reached by 19 March 1972. Martial law was to be lifted, and a central cabinet was to be formed with representatives from both East and West Pakistan. Though Sherbaz Mazari described both Mujib and Yahya as prisoners to the hard-liners in their camps, both had come a long way from their initial positions. Yahya had agreed to transfer power to Mujib. The latter, despite his majority in the National Assembly, had agreed to an equal position for the western wing in drafting the future Constitution.

The news of the settlement unnerved Bhutto. Though West Pakistan was to be allowed to decide its future on its own, this presented a problem to Bhutto. He had projected himself as the leader of West Pakistan on the strength of 39 per cent of votes polled. An exercise in working out 'special provisions and requirements of each province' could unravel his position. Mazari wrote, 'In the election, he had only won a majority in Punjab. In Sindh, he was three short of a majority. Balochistan and NWFP were out of his control altogether.'[49] As 'One Unit' had been dissolved, this arithmetic would have reduced him to the leader of only one province.

Bhutto, when he met Yahya Khan on 24 March, opposed the lifting of martial law, which the latter had agreed to. This was a strange demand, coming as it did from a civilian politician. Mazari was of the view that Bhutto may have been acting as a spoiler with the connivance of Yahya's generals who had decided on a crackdown.[50]

Mazari recounted that Ghaus Bakhsh Bizenjo, a senior opposition leader who had served as chief minister of Balochistan in the early 1970s, told him about his meeting with Mujib on 24 March, on what was to be the eve of the Pakistan Army's crackdown on East Pakistan. 'Mujib had finally agreed to the idea of forming his majority government without insisting upon the removal of Martial Law. This had become the serious constitutional sticking point between the two sides,' wrote Mazari.[51]

On the night of 25 March, the Pakistan Army launched Operation Searchlight and arrested the Awami League's top leadership. This was followed by the arrest of student leaders and intelligentsia. The Pakistan Army's actions were described in the 'Blood telegram' (named so after Archer Blood, the American Consul General in Dhaka) as 'genocide'.[52]

The operation triggered a mass exodus of Bengali refugees to India, and ultimately led to the Indian intervention and the liberation of Bangladesh. This was a repudiation of the Two-Nation Theory propounded by the Muslim League.

Five decades after Independence, Bangladesh leads Pakistan in terms of key indices of development. It had a gross domestic product (GDP) of $329.8 billion in 2019 as against Pakistan's $278.2 billion. Bangladesh's per capita income was $5,200 in purchasing power parity terms that year. The corresponding figure for Pakistan was $4,800. Bangladesh has a literacy rate of 86.3 per cent; Pakistan's is 59 per cent. An educated population is the greatest asset for a country's future.

East Pakistan was historically the poorer but more populated region of Pakistan. Its larger population was a source of concern and constant wrangling by West Pakistan to neutralize its salience at the federal level through various constitutional schemes. This equation has now been reversed. In 2020, Bangladesh's population stood at 164.7 million, whereas Pakistan's was 220.9 million. Although Sheikh Hasina's overthrow in 2024 has created a sense of uncertainty, Bangladesh's progress since breaking away from Pakistan cannot be denied.

Pakistan's Army Chief General Asim Munir, in an address to ulema (clergy) on 8 August 2024, asked, 'Where are those who used to say that we have drowned the Two-Nation Theory in the Bay of Bengal?'[53] The army, which launched Operation Searchlight against the people of East Pakistan in 1971, remains the ultimate custodian of the ideology of Pakistan. Bengalis were denied equal treatment, despite being mostly Muslim. Will they go back to the ideology Pakistan holds sacred? It is for the people of Bangladesh to decide their future.

10

Who Is a Muslim?

'Keeping in view the several definitions of a Muslim given by the Ulema, need we make any comment except that no two learned divines are agreed on this fundamental?

–Justice Munir on the definition of 'Muslim' in the report of the Munir Commission on anti-Ahmadiya riots[1]

As a member of the Viceroy's executive council, Sir Zafarullah Khan had a role in shaping the Lahore Resolution adopted by the Muslim League in 1940. After Partition, he argued Pakistan's case on the Kashmir issue in the United Nations Security Council. If he were alive today, he would be considered a non-Muslim in the country he helped create. He was an Ahmadiya.

Religious parties demanded in 1953 that Ahmadiyas be declared non-Muslim. This raised the question: Who is a 'Muslim?' Justice Munir, who headed the commission of inquiry into the causes of the anti-Ahmadiya riots, wrote a courageous report that postponed the debate. But the issue remained simmering. Ahmadiyas were declared non-Muslims under the Second Amendment to Pakistan's Constitution adopted in 1974. The state, under the Bhutto government, took it upon itself to define who was a Muslim.

The intolerance that led to the marginalization of religious minorities turned inward soon after the creation of the new state and began affecting the lives of the majority community. The Objectives Resolution adopted in 1949 declared that 'Muslims shall be enabled to order their lives in the individual and collective spheres in accord with the teachings and requirements of Islam'. Prime Minister Liaquat

Ali Khan, in his speech to the Constituent Assembly, said the state was not a 'neutral observer wherein the Muslims may be merely free to profess and practice their religion'. The 'enabling clause' extended the role of the state beyond law to religion and ethics.

Liaquat Ali Khan, in his speech in the Constituent Assembly introducing the Objectives Resolution, held out the assurance, 'The State will seek to create an *Islamic society free from dissensions*, but this does not mean that it would curb the freedom of any section of the Muslims in the matter of their beliefs.' [Emphasis added] He added, 'No sect, whether the majority or a minority, will be permitted to dictate to the others…'[2] The prime minister's assurance was belied when, within four years of the adoption of the Objectives Resolution, riots broke out in Punjab with the clergy demanding that Ahmadiyas be declared non-Muslims. The government had to hand over Lahore to the army to restore law and order. After the riots, a commission headed by Justice Munir was appointed to inquire into the cause of the disturbances. Munir has written in his memoir *From Jinnah to Zia* that the religious parties said they drew their inspiration from the Objectives Resolution. The resolution had curbed not only minority rights but the choice of believers belonging to the same faith, with the majority demanding the expulsion of one section.

Munir Commission Report

The anti-Ahmadiya riots raised the question of the definition of 'Muslim'. Justice Munir asked the ulema to give their views. The Munir Commission report expressed difficulty in arriving at an agreed definition of Muslim:

> Keeping in view the several definitions of a Muslim given by the Ulema, need we make any comment except that no two learned divines are agreed on this fundamental. If we attempt our own definition as each learned divine has done and that definition differs from that given by all others, we unanimously go out of the fold of Islam. And if we adopt the definition given by any one of the Ulama, we remain Muslims according to the view of that alim but kafirs according to the definition of every one else.[3]

Though the Munir Commission report had put a brake on the anti-Ahmadiya movement, the demand was revived and Ahmadiyas declared non-Muslims two decades later. This was not simply a religious edict but an amendment to the country's Constitution. The Ahmadiya issue remains alive even after the community was pushed out of the ambit of Islam by government legislation. In 2018, Imran Khan's government asked Princeton University economist Atif R. Mian to step down from the prime minister's Economic Advisory Council following 'mounting pressure from religio-political parties' against his appointment as he was an Ahmadi.[4]

Ahmadi places of worship continue to be attacked in Pakistan. They cannot be called 'mosques' under Pakistan's Constitution. The minaret of an Ahmadi place of worship in Gujranwala was removed in December 2022.[5] A historic building was demolished in Sialkot in May 2023 because it was an Ahmadiya place of worship.[6] The minaret of another Ahmadi place of worship was damaged in Karachi in July 2023.[7]

Repugnancy Clause

Justice Munir's courageous stand managed to stem the tide of anti-Ahmadiya violence in the 1950s. But Pakistan's lurch towards a greater role of religion in governance was already underway. The first Constitution adopted in 1956 included the Repugnancy Clause. It made legislation enacted by the national or provincial assemblies subordinate to religious injunctions. Article 227(1) states: 'All existing laws shall be brought in conformity with the Injunctions of Islam as laid down in the Holy Quran and Sunnah, in this Part referred to as the Injunctions of Islam, and no law shall be enacted which is repugnant to such Injunctions.'[8]

The Repugnancy Clause was also included in the third and current Constitution. This not only placed religion beyond the remit of the legislature but also made lay laws subject to religious injunctions. Pakistan never accepted secularism. But the state was making faith the guiding principle for law-making. Together with the Objectives Resolution, this laid the foundation of an Islamic state.

The Repugnancy Clause was made part of Pakistan's Constitution in 1956 when the Objectives Resolution was still only a statement of principles of policy in the preamble. The latter became a part of the Constitution in 1973. Both the Objectives Resolution and the Repugnancy Clause were adopted under civilian governments. There was no challenge to the authority of Liaquat Ali Khan or the Muslim League in 1949. Bhutto was at the height of his power in 1973, the military defeat of 1971 having temporarily removed the army from the power matrix. The claim that Pakistan's early rulers were a 'secularizing elite', which is often put forward by Pakistani commentators interpreting their country to the West, has no foundation.

The army gave an impetus to the process of Islamization. Unlike the civilian populations, the military did not have to pander to an electoral constituency. General Ayub appears moderate as compared to Zia. He focused on development. Pakistan's second Constitution, adopted under Ayub in 1962, initially referred to the country simply as the 'Republic of Pakistan'. In 1963, he gave in to the demands of the clergy and his Islamist allies and 'reinstated Pakistan as the Islamic Republic'.[9]

Under Zia, the Repugnancy Clause was given a boost. He created an implementation mechanism to give effect to it. He established Shariat courts at the provincial and federal levels to decide if the laws passed by the legislatures were in conformity with Islam's injunctions. This had the effect of creating a parallel judiciary outside the control of lay courts.

Who Is a Muslim?

Constitutions deal with citizenship. Pakistan's Constitution defines the faith of the majority community. The Munir Commission had posed the question of who a Muslim is to the ulema and made the determination that it was not possible to come to an agreed definition. This gave a reprieve to the Ahmadiya community. The task was attempted again under Bhutto. The Second Amendment to the 1973 Constitution included the definition of 'Muslim'. This is now Article 260 of the Constitution. The article also has a separate section defining who are 'non-Muslims'.

The difference between the rights and privileges of Muslim and non-Muslim citizens has made it necessary to define them as separate categories. This essentially amounts to grading citizens according to their faith. Non-Muslims are not only barred from holding the highest office in the land but are also effectively disenfranchised. This has been discussed separately in the chapter on minorities.

The definition of Muslims as well as non-Muslims in Pakistan's Constitution is as follows:

(a) 'Muslim' means a person who believes in the unity and oneness of Almighty Allah, in the absolute and unqualified finality of the Prophethood of Muhammad (peace be upon him), the last of the prophets, and does not believe in, or recognize as a prophet or religious reformer, any person who claimed or claims to be a prophet, in any sense of the word or of any description whatsoever, after Muhammad (peace be upon him); and
(b) 'non-Muslim' means a person who is not a Muslim and includes a person belonging to Christian, Hindus, Sikh, Buddhist or Parsi community, a person of the Qadiani group or the Lahori group (who call themselves 'Ahmadis' or by any other name), or a Bahai, and a person belonging to any of the scheduled castes.[10]

The above definition graduated Ahmadiyas out of the Muslim category and made them a religious minority. Zia followed a vigorous programme of Islamization. He issued decrees in 1979 replacing existing penal codes with the Hudud (punishment) Ordinances. These introduced punishment according to Islamic law. There was also increased stress on Shariatization. The liberals or the minorities did not react to this much, as they were too weak. The response was given by Shias, who are a minority within the Islamic fold. They were determined to resist the 'imposition of a Sunni programme of Islamization', according to Farzana Shaikh.[11] No Shia was included in the Federal Shariat Court. In protest, Shias refused to pay zakat (a religiously ordained tax) to the government.

The introduction of Sharia naturally raised the question: Whose version of Shariah? The Shias formed their own party Tehriq-e-Nifaz-e-Fiqh-e-Zafariya (TNFZ), which is roughly translated as 'movement to implement Shia thought'.

Zia's reliance on Sunni Madrassas furnishing recruits for Afghan Jehad led to state patronage of Sunni organizations. The sectarian divide continues to polarize the majority community between Sunni and Shias. Shias have suffered increasing attacks in different parts of Pakistan from Sunni extremist organizations.

11

Minority Rights

'As was then anticipated, western Pakistan was to include at least 26 p.c. of non-Muslims. They have now left and we have in West Pakistan a completely Muslim population. The percentage of non-Muslims in East Pakistan has also decreased.'

–Maulana Maududi, Jamaat-e-Islami founder in his testimony to the Munir Commission, 1953

THE ISSUE OF MINORITY rights is intensely political. For an objective understanding, it is necessary to detach it from the context of the divided legacy of the Indian subcontinent and see it in the light of United Nations norms.

The UN resolution on the subject is titled 'Rights of individuals belonging to national, ethnic, religious or linguistic minorities'. This does not admit group rights. This is a vital difference from the manner in which the British promoted the debate on the issue in India. By juxtaposing the minority as a group irrevocably opposed to the majority, they politicized the issue, making a constitutional settlement difficult and Partition inevitable.

During the inter-war period, the League of Nations dealt with the issue of minorities, but its Covenant did not include the right of self-determination. After the Second World War, the United Nations came into existence. Unlike the League, the UN Charter contained, in Article 2(7), a specific prohibition against intervention in the domestic jurisdiction of the member states. This ruled out intrusive monitoring of human rights by the world body.

At the time of India's independence, the body of human rights literature was still in its infancy. The Universal Declaration on Human

Rights (UDHR) was adopted by 1948. This has continued to provide the benchmark for the promotion and protection of human rights. It neither contained a provision on the right of self-determination nor minority rights. It certainly provided no validation to the dubious idea on which Pakistan was based – claiming minority rights to justify the creation of a separate state.

Article 1 of the UDHR states, 'All human beings are born free and equal in dignity and rights.' Article 18 mentions, 'Everyone has the right to freedom of thought, conscience and religion'. These are universal rights; they were not defined with reference to norms prescribed by any particular religion.

The makers of Pakistan's Constitution breached both principles of equality and freedom of religion in adopting the Objectives Resolution in 1949. The resolution made minority rights subject to precepts of a faith they did not belong to. Since then, the resolution has been incorporated in all three successive constitutions adopted by Pakistan – 1956, 1962 and 1973. Under Article 2A, the resolution now forms a substantive part of Pakistan's third and current Constitution. Ironically, the resolution, which was inherently discriminatory against the minorities, is used by Pakistan's Supreme Court as a benchmark to protect minority rights!

Social prejudices against religious minorities are found in most societies. What is remarkable in Pakistan's case is that these were embedded in the country's constitutions and laws. This amounted to a conscious policy adopted by the state. General Zia's regime is notorious for implementing Sharia laws, Hudud Ordinances and blasphemy laws. But the process began much earlier. The Objectives Resolution was adopted in 1949. Both civilian and military rulers have contributed to the Islamization of Pakistan. All three constitutions included the Objectives Resolution, which strengthened the role of Islam in the state and the society. While the 1956 and 1973 constitutions were adopted under civilian regimes, the 1962 Constitution was adopted under General Ayub. This trend was reinforced by the military, which encouraged religious parties to provide cheap cannon fodder for Jehad in Afghanistan and Kashmir. These parties and their military backers favoured a narrow interpretation of Islam, which fostered an atmosphere of intolerance and adversely affected minority rights. Persecution of religious minorities was followed by persecution of minority sects within Islam. This started with anti-Ahmadiya agitations and now includes Shia killings.

The rights of minorities defined the Muslim League's politics. This included the demand for a separate electorate, weighted representation and 'parity' with the Congress in any constitutional settlement. These had no equivalence in the international norms or constitutions of other countries. The Lahore Resolution, adopted in 1940, called for the establishment of 'Independent States' in the north-western and eastern zones of India where Muslims were in a majority. This posed the problem of minorities who would be left on either side of the divide. The resolution sought to solve this problem by calling for '*adequate, effective, and mandatory safeguards* should be specifically provided in the constitution for minorities in these units'. [Emphasis added] 'In other parts of India where Mussalmans are in a minority, adequate, effective and mandatory safeguards shall be specially provided in the constitution for them.' This was an expression of the 'mutual hostage theory', where the fate of the Hindu minority in a Muslim-majority area would guarantee the security of the Muslim minority in a Hindu-majority area, and vice versa. Khaliquzzaman, who was asked by Jinnah to second the Lahore Resolution, mentioned this in his speech. The hostage theory may not be the best expression of minority rights. The Objectives Resolution would dilute the standard of protection of minority rights further.

Those who support the thesis that Jinnah stood for a liberal conception of Pakistan, where minorities enjoyed equal rights, quote his speech of 11 August 1947 in Pakistan's Constituent Assembly. The speech has an ambivalence, which has been analysed in Chapter Seven. Jinnah himself never returned to this theme again. This fleeting recognition of minority rights was buried with the adoption of the Objectives Resolution by the Constituent Assembly in 1949. This defined a narrower vision, which circumscribed both the minority rights and the role of the elected legislature. This has become the constitutional norm since then.

Disappearing Minorities

While international attention has remained focused on Ahmadiyas and Christians in Pakistan, the worst victims of minority persecution are Hindus and Sikhs. Justice Munir has described the testimony of

Maulana Maududi, founder of Jamaat-e-Islami. He was questioned by Munir because Maududi had opposed the creation of Pakistan. In Justice Munir's words, 'In the "Tarjuman-ul-Quran" of February 1946 he had opposed Pakistan on the ground that if it was established, it will be a secular state and not an Islamic State.' In the course of the inquiry into the Punjab disturbances of 1953, he was questioned on this point. His answers to Justice Munir's questions are given below:

> A. I did express this opinion in the 'Tarjuman-ul-Quran' but that was on the basis of what was being presented to us then. Now the conditions are different and we can have a purely Islamic State.
>
> Q. How have the conditions changed?
> A. As was then anticipated, western Pakistan was to include at least 26 p.c. of non-Muslims. They have now left and we have in West Pakistan a completely Muslim population. The percentage of non-Muslims in East Pakistan has also decreased.[1]

Maududi gave his testimony to the Munir Commission in 1953. Within six years of Partition, non-Muslims, who were expected to comprise 26 per cent of the population of West Pakistan, had 'left'. As Maududi described it, 'We have in West Pakistan a completely Muslim population.' West Pakistan is now present-day Pakistan. This was ethnic cleansing before the term entered human rights vocabulary in the 1990s with the outbreak of civil war in the former Republic of Yugoslavia.

As against Maududi's estimate of 26 per cent, Justice Munir has put the percentage of minorities higher at 30 per cent in West Pakistan. But, his thrust was different. To him, the disappearance of minorities was not a matter of satisfaction. Munir said:

'If there had been no cross-migration and indiscriminate slaughter and the non-Muslims had stayed on in West Pakistan they would have had a percentage of 30, and there would have been no question of making them inferior citizens in a religious state. This view was supported by no less a person than Maulana Abul Ala-Maududi.'[2]

Maududi and Justice Munir viewed Pakistan's transformation differently. Maududi was pleased that non-Muslims had left, reinforcing his support for an Islamic state. Justice Munir, on the other hand, envisioned a Pakistan where minorities would be treated as equal citizens. The foundation for an exclusionary state, from which minorities would eventually be driven out, was laid in 1949 when Liaquat Ali Khan moved the Objectives Resolution. At that time, the Muslim League not only had a dominant majority in the Constituent Assembly but also held unquestioned sway over the people of the new state.

The Munir Commission also questioned Maududi about East Pakistan:

> Q. If East Pakistan were a separate State do you think you could have a purely Islamic Government in that region with the present Hindu population?
> A. There will be difficulties there, the percentage of non-Muslims there being about 25.
>
> Q. If East Pakistan is a necessary part of Pakistan, then how do you say that conditions have changed and that a purely Islamic Government can be formed for the whole of Pakistan?
> A. The difficulties have now lessened.[3]

The percentage of minorities was higher in East Pakistan than in West Pakistan. By 1953, the eastern wing still had a 25 per cent non-Muslim population according to Maududi. Maududi's views on Islam and Pakistan may appear anathema to the outside world. But he was more candid and logically consistent than the Muslim League. League leaders like Liaquat adopted the Objectives Resolution, which made minority rights subject to the faith of the majority but claimed that this would not affect the rights of the minorities.

According to the Census of Pakistan, 1951, the percentage of Muslims in West Pakistan,which is today's Pakistan, was 97.1. The Hindus were 1.6 per cent and Christians 1.3 per cent. The corresponding figure in East Pakistan was 76.8 per cent Muslims, 22 per cent Hindus, 0.3 per cent Christians and 0.9 per cent others.[4] Thus, the share of minorities had shrunk from 26–30 per cent at the time of Partition in West Pakistan to 3 per cent within four years of Partition.

1973 Constitution

Pakistan's present Constitution is the third the country has adopted. Adopted under the Bhutto regime, it was part of the post-1971 political compact. The emergence of Bangladesh demonstrated the futility of the Two-Nation Theory. PPP had come to power on the slogan of 'roti, kapda aur makaan' (bread, clothing and housing). The logical outcome of the change in the external environment and the socialist agenda which had catapulted it to power should have led to less emphasis on religion, which had failed to hold the country together. But Bhutto's priority was the consolidation of his power, and he was not averse to using religion for this purpose. He made the Objectives Resolution an integral part of the Constitution. A year later, in 1974, the Second Amendment to the Constitution declared Ahmadiyas as non-Muslims. Both developments took place when Bhutto was at the height of his power, with virtually no challenge to his authority.

Zia's military coup overthrowing the elected government was followed by an eight-year hiatus before 'party-less elections' were organized in 1985. The Eighth Amendment adopted the same year made the Objectives Resolution part of Article 2A of the Constitution. It was also given an overarching position qualifying fundamental rights, which followed in subsequent sections. Its immediate victims were minorities. But it also had a deep impact on the majority community.

As Prime Minister Liaquat Ali Khan had stated in the debate on the Objectives Resolution in the Constituent Assembly in 1949, 'the State will create such conditions as are conducive to the building up of a truly Islamic society'. Zia would now give effect to this by making Pakistan an Islamic state. The role of the state would extend to shaping the society and the private sphere of individual citizens belonging to the majority community.

While incorporating the Objectives Resolution in the Constitution under Article 2A in 1985, the word 'freely', which qualified the exercise of minority rights, was omitted. The original text of the Resolution contained the following provision regarding minorities: 'Whereas adequate provision shall be made for the minorities freely to profess and practice their religions and develop their cultures'.

The omission of the word *freely* was an amazing piece of skullduggery. A Parliament can always amend the Constitution or set aside a document.

However, it cannot change the wording of an existing document while reproducing it. This was done without acknowledging the amendment!

A study by a prestigious Pakistani academic institution, the Lahore University of Management Sciences (LUMS), taking into account the Zahiruddin case (a 1993 judgement in which the Pakistan Supreme Court upheld a law preventing Ahmadiyas from practising their faith as Muslims), has argued that 'the effect of Article 2A was such that laws now had to be in accordance with Islam and Article 2A was given an overarching effect in the context of religious minorities in Pakistan'.

Dropping the word 'freely' further restricted minority rights, which were already constricted by the preamble to the resolution. The Eighteenth Amendment to the Constitution, made in 2010, has re-inserted the word 'freely'. But this does not undo the host of restrictive provisions and laws that have come into effect in the intervening four decades.

The issue became a matter of judicial reference. Chief Justice Iftikhar Mohammad Chaudhary in his judgement on the Eighteenth Amendment, remarked, 'It is strange that not even a single member in the 1985 National Assembly noticed the mistake and allowed the 8th Amendment to pass just like that.'[5] He added, 'Nobody has the right to tamper with the basic document.'[6]

It had taken twenty-five years before the 'mistake' was rectified. Chief Justice Chaudhary stated, 'We have not disowned, but owned the Objectives Resolution and today the assembly has accepted it by rectifying the fault.'[7]

The correction of the mistake has thus left us with the original problem, where the legitimacy of the state was to be derived from the authority delegated by the divine, not the will of the people. The wording of the resolution, now an operative part of Pakistan's Constitution, also carried the injunction that the delegated authority will be 'exercised within the limits prescribed by Him'. This continues to affect not only the rights of minorities, whose strength has drastically dwindled, but also the majority community of that country.

Under Article 19 of the Pakistani Constitution, *freedom of speech* may be restricted 'in the interest of the glory of Islam or the integrity, security or defence of Pakistan or any part thereof, friendly relations with foreign States, public order, decency or morality....' While the restrictions apply to both majority and minority communities, the effect of the caveat 'in the interest of the glory of Islam' is discriminatory and injurious, particularly to the interests of religious minorities. The majority community may accept the precepts of their religion and restrictions flowing from them. Article 19 has extended these obligations to the minorities who belong to a different faith.

Under Article 20 of the Pakistani Constitution, the freedom to profess and practise religion is 'subject to law, public order and morality'. According to an article titled 'Constitutional Comparison and Analysis of Discrimination against Religious Minorities in Pakistan and India' by Marwa Khan, published in the LUMS Law Journal, 'the term "*subject to law*" *is vague*'. There can be three possible interpretations of this clause: 'law' here may refer to other provisions of the Pakistani Constitution; to the laws enacted by the legislature; or it may refer to both.[8] This ambiguity opens up scope for interpretation and possible misuse. 'Fundamental Rights, cannot be subjected to lower forms of laws.'[9] She added, 'Even if this view is accepted, there are multiple discriminatory provisions within the Pakistani Constitution which may be used for legitimizing restrictions on Article 20.'[10]

She stated that in comparison, the parallel 'Article 25 of the Indian Constitution does not employ such obtuse terminology since the grounds on which the freedom to profess and practice religion may be restricted have been expressly stated'.[11] The very basis of fundamental rights is completely different in the two constitutions. Under the Indian Constitution, the 'people' are sovereign and there is no reference to religious injunctions of the majority community governing minority rights. Under Pakistan's Constitution, 'Article 2 declares that Islam shall be the State religion of Pakistan', and Article 31 states it is the 'government's duty to foster the Islamic way of life'.[12]

Repugnancy Clause

As highlighted in the previous chapter, Article 227(1) of Pakistan's Constitution states, 'All existing laws shall be brought in conformity with the injunctions of Islam as laid down in the Holy Quran and Sunnah, and no law shall be enacted which is repugnant to such Injunctions.'[13]

Known as the 'Repugnancy Clause', this affects the status of minorities and has given a push for the Islamization of Pakistan. As a report by the International Federation for Human Rights (FIDH) and the Human Rights Commission of Pakistan (HRCP) stated, Zia's government 'spared no efforts to bring Pakistan's civil and criminal laws in line with Sharia law, thus creating legislation that limits the freedoms of non-Muslims'.[14] Hudud Ordinances were adopted in 1979, and religiously mandated punishments were adopted in 1980, which include 'hanging, amputation and other corporal punishments' for 'various violations under Sharia law, including drinking alcoholic beverages, theft, prostitution, adultery and bearing false witnesses'. 'In 1982 and 1986, the notorious blasphemy laws were adopted, and in 1984, the Law of Evidence (Qanun-e-Shahadat) was adopted, which discriminates against both non-Muslims and women with regards to evidence presented in court.'[15]

Zia not only changed the Constitution and the laws, but also 'decreed the establishment of a parallel legal system – the Sharia courts – to try cases under Islamic law'. As the FIDH-HRCP report mentioned, 'The Sharia Court system has effectively weakened the jurisdiction of the Superior Courts in Pakistan, and acts as a "super-legislature" as it can order immediate revision of national laws and its rulings are binding on high and lower courts.'[16]

Justice Dorab Patel, in his memoir *Testament of a Liberal*, has brought out that the Supreme Court's judgements not only did not check the encroachment on minority rights, but also undermined constitutional safeguards. In *Zahiruddin v The State and Others* (1993 SC MR 1718), the majority judgement delivered by Justice Chaudhary stated, 'The injunctions of Islam "are now the positive law" on account of Article 2 (A) of the Constitution.' It added, 'Therefore every man-made law must now conform to the injunctions of Islam…Therefore even the Fundamental Rights as given in the Constitution must not violate the norms of Islam.'[17]

This rendered Article 20 of the Constitution, guaranteeing freedom of religion to minorities, meaningless. The judgement avoided any reference to Article 25 of the Constitution guaranteeing the fundamental right of equality.

Separate Electorates

The impact of constitutional provisions discriminating against minorities is reinforced by the institution of separate electorates for both the majority and minority communities. Minority votes cannot influence the election of majority community candidates, which deprives them of political leverage. Their numbers have already been drastically reduced following forced migration.

The separate electorate for minorities was instituted after the Second Amendment declared Ahmadiyas as non-Muslims in 1974. In an article in the *Herald*, titled 'Problems with the Electoral Representation of Non-Muslims', journalist Asif Aqeel wrote, 'Six reserved seats were subsequently created for non-Muslims through the Fourth Constitutional Amendment in November 1975, making the National Assembly their electoral college.'[18] He continued, 'In September 1978, Zia amended election laws to create separate electoral rolls for Muslims and non-Muslims.'[19] Aqeel added, 'The general elections of 1985, 1988, 1990, 1993 and 1997 were all held under this system.'[20]

Voting for minority candidates was based on nationwide constituencies. The ostensible justification for such an arrangement was that minorities were thinly distributed over the entire country, and therefore local or regional constituencies were not possible. This meant that there was no lien between the elected and the electors, who may never have even seen or heard their representative.

Musharraf changed it to a system of *proportional representation* for minorities in 2002, while the candidates of the majority community were selected on the basis of First Past the Post system. The arrangement involved distributing ten minority seats among the political parties based on their performance in general constituencies. Against the minority seats allotted to different parties, the choice of candidate was part of a process of internal selection by the party bosses.

This system suffers from a democratic deficit on two counts. First, minorities have no say in deciding their political affiliation – the minority seats are allocated to the political parties based on their respective performance in the general category. This reduced the minorities to a politically neutral factor in the electoral arithmetic. This resulted in the paradox that the maximum number of minority seats could be awarded to the party least sensitive to their needs, as long as it won the largest number of seats in the general category. Second, minorities not only do not decide the political affiliation of their 'representatives', but they also do not choose them at all. The minority candidates are selected by the party leadership.

There were protests against the system, which has no parallel outside Pakistan. Musharraf initially agreed to revise it, but then a few months later, he reneged. Musharraf had cobbled up a coalition in the National Assembly, where the 'King's Party' – the PML(Q) was supported by an alliance of religious parties, Muttahida Majlis-e-Amal (MMA). Given his own inclination, Musharraf did not need much 'persuasion' from religious parties to continue with the arrangement which amounted to completely neutralizing minority votes.

A reference was made to the Court protesting against the inequity. A well-known Christian politician, Julius Salik, went to the Supreme Court against the proportional representation for minorities in 2010. 'In its verdict, issued in August 2015, the Supreme Court did not overturn the electoral system, but it did say that proportional representation for non-Muslims was against three principles laid down in the Objectives Resolution.'[21] The first such principle breached was that 'adequate provisions shall be made to safeguard the legitimate interests of minorities'. The second principle was 'The State shall exercise its powers and authority through the chosen representatives of the people.' The third was that 'the principles of democracy…shall be fully observed'.[22]

The Supreme Court, of course, had been very conservative in its judgement to treat the Objectives Resolution, which is restrictive of minority rights, as the benchmark. It is curious that the benchmark is not followed when it comes to protecting minority rights; it is to be used only to restrict them. Even after finding that a separate electorate breached an important article of the Constitution, the Supreme Court did not find it necessary to force the issue. The system continues unchanged even now.

The article in the *Herald* adds, 'Mainstream political parties and policymakers, too, do not seem to take non-Muslim legislators seriously. They were neither part of the political negotiations that lead to the passage of the 18 Constitutional Amendment in 2010. Nor were they invited to high-level meetings in early 2015 when the National Action Plan against extremism and terrorism was firmed up.'[23]

A report by FIDH/HRCP has noted, 'The representation of minorities in assemblies in Pakistan remains weak. While the National Assembly was reformed in 2002, increasing the total number of seats to 342, the number of seats reserved for minority representatives was not increased and remains at ten.' A proposal was mooted a decade later, in 2014, to increase reserved seats for minorities in the National Assembly. The government rejected it, 'claiming that such increase was not possible until a new population census was conducted'.[24]

Though Pakistan under Musharraf shifted back from a separate electorate to a joint electorate, the system of proportional representation devised for minorities alone seems calculated to disenfranchise them. As discussed above, they can neither choose their political affiliation nor elect the minority members in the National Assembly. Is this necessary to preserve the ideological frontiers of Pakistan? With around 3 per cent of the total population, minorities can pose no threat to the state or the ruling dispensation.

The Objectives Resolution adopted under Liaquat Ali Khan has proved to be the most durable feature of Pakistan's Constitution. The civilian parties came together to overthrow Zia's political legacy by adopting the Eighteenth Amendment in 2010. While they have deleted Article 58(2)(b) which allowed presidents to dismiss the elected assembly, they left untouched many other laws including the Hudud Ordinances, the Shariat Bill and blasphemy laws, which have increasingly fostered an atmosphere of intolerance and circumscribed minority rights.

There are few minorities left to exercise their rights. Though Partition affected minorities on both sides of the divide, the worst affected were Hindu and Sikh communities in Pakistan. Their share in the population of the area which is now called Pakistan came down from 26–30 per cent to less than 3 per cent within four years of Partition. Those remaining can take part in the voting, but their representatives are chosen for them by the majority parties in the convoluted electoral system devised by Musharraf.

PART 3

Nationality

12

Nationality, Language and Ideology

THE NATIONALITY ISSUE IN Pakistan is older than the creation of the country in 1947. It finds reflection in the Lahore Resolution, which called for 'independent states' in which the constituent units were to be 'autonomous and sovereign'. This was not a blueprint for a unitary State, which was a later construct Jinnah tried to put on it. Not only could there be two States in the 'North-western' and 'Eastern' zones, but the constituent units would also be 'autonomous' and 'sovereign'. Pakistan was to be a new State, but the provinces already existed. The resolution did not mention the nomenclature 'Pakistan'. East Bengal, Punjab, Sindh, NWFP, and Balochistan each already had a linguistic and ethnic identity. They were joined after Partition by a fifth group, the Muhajirs. The term refers to Muslims who migrated from Muslim-minority provinces in India. They were the original standard bearers of the Pakistani movement.

Khaliquzzaman, the first president of the Pakistan Muslim League, stated that Jinnah altered 'states' to 'state' in the League's 1946 convention. This denied national and linguistic identities, imposing a common 'Muslim' identity. The attempt to impose a homogeneous religious identity on an ethnically or linguistically diverse society continued after Partition when the rulers of Pakistan decided to create a 'One Unit' in West Pakistan. This was an attempt to deny the numerical majority of East Pakistan by creating an artificial parity with the Western wing. This also had the effect of reducing political space for the smaller provinces of West Pakistan. They lost their autonomy and were bundled together with Punjab. The capital of the new entity was Lahore. The demand for Pakhtunistan was raised before Partition. It was not preferred but was the fallback option for the Khudai Khidmatgar. Their preferred option under the Khan Brothers was to join India.

The language issue was raised by East Bengal in 1948. This was a reaction to Jinnah's speech in Dhaka University in 1948 when he said that Urdu can be the state language as it embodied the best in 'Muslim tradition'. Equating language with religion, and the latter as the basis of statehood, was part of the ideology of Pakistan. Bengalis felt cheated when, despite being the majority province, they were told to accept Urdu as the 'state language of Pakistan', which was spoken by only 4 per cent of Pakistan's population at the time. By the time of the 1951 census, this figure rose to 7.2 per cent with further immigration. This is treated in detail in the chapter on the other nation. The attempt to deny Bengali identity was to ultimately end in changing the name of the province from East Bengal to East Pakistan.

Sindhis became a minority in Karachi, which was made the national capital. Balochistan, with its distinct history and vast land, did not identify with Pakistan. The Khan of Kalat sought independence. Muhajirs were the strongest supporters of the idea of Pakistan but were to soon find out that they were considered outsiders in the promised land. Though Urdu was the state language in Pakistan in the 1970s, job reservations in Sindh reduced Muhajir dominance in the civil service. Their political hold had already declined after Jinnah's death in 1948 and Liaquat Ali Khan's assassination in 1951. Hindus, who made up around 25 per cent of the population at the time of Partition, were treated as foreigners in their homeland.

Aspirations of the people with widely differing ethnic, linguistic or religious backgrounds could have been accommodated in a federal set-up that provided political space to the provinces and was inclusive. This, however, the founding fathers of Pakistan were unwilling to concede. In their perception, the Mughal empire's decline was due to the weakening of the Centre after Aurangzeb's death. Muslim League leaders tried to build Pakistan into a strong unitary state, despite its nomenclature, which described it as a republic. They dubbed regional aspirations as 'parochial' or 'provincial' tendencies.

The ideology was reinforced by law. The Government of India Act of 1935 remained Pakistan's Constitution till 1956.[1] The act was conceived to concentrate all powers in British hands at the Centre. Jinnah adopted this as the basis of government in the new state and appointed himself the governor-general. This was a complete reversal of the Muslim League's position before Partition, when the party had consistently opposed the idea of a strong Centre.

The unitary bias of the new dispensation was reinforced by the changes made by the first prime minister of Pakistan. According to Justice Dorab Patel, an eminent jurist and a judge of Pakistan's Supreme Court, Mr Liaquat Ali Khan had 'got a major change made in the federal system of government by surreptitiously amending the Act of 1935'.[2] The amendment gave the prime minister the power to appoint or dismiss provincial cabinets. 'The amendment was made through an executive Order of the Governor General without the aid of the Constituent Assembly.' Dorab Patel wrote.[3] This was not made public. Both Jinnah and Liaquat were complicit in making the change which undermined the federal structure.

Justice Dorab Patel goes on to say, 'Mr Liaquat Ali Khan had dismissed the government of Dr Khan Sahib in the Frontier Province within the first week of independence on the ground that Dr Khan was not loyal to the country.' [4] He added, 'Not content with dismissing a non-League Government, Mr Liaquat Ali Khan also exercised his power under the Order of 1948 to dismiss Muslim League Governments in other provinces.' The Sindh Chief Minister Khuhro was dismissed immediately after the provincial assembly of Sindh had passed the budget, demonstrating its confidence in him. In Punjab, the Nawab of Mamdot was dismissed, and Daultana was appointed as chief minister in his place. After Jinnah's death, when Nazimuddin was appointed the Governor-General of Pakistan, Liaquat prevented Hamidul Haq Chowdhury from succeeding him as chief minister of East Bengal, even though he was the leader of the Muslim League party in the provincial legislature. Instead, Nurul Amin was appointed as the chief minister. The attempt to run the country as a unitary state left little political space to accommodate the ethnic or linguistic aspirations of people of different provinces.

1973 Constitution

The nationality issue persisted after East Pakistan's secession. West Pakistan – today's Pakistan – was never homogeneous. It comprised at least five ethnic groups: Punjabi, Pashtun, Sindhi, Muhajir and Baloch. Fearing fresh separatist movements, the 1973 Constitution sought to resurrect a unitary state under a federal guise.

Nilofer Afridi Qazi has given an account of the events. Her grandmother Jennifer Musa Qazi was the first member of the National Assembly from Balochistan and was one of the twenty-five members of the Constituent Committee and Assembly that signed the 1973 Constitution. Jennifer was Irish by origin and had married Qazi Musa. She represented the NAP, a socialist party. It was headed by Sardar Khair Bakhsh Marri, Sardar Jogazai and Wali Khan. The NAP demanded 'the recognition and protecting the interests of minority ethnonational groups', 'protecting their languages and cultures', a 'strong upper chamber in the federal legislature', and a 'Constitution-making process based on the equality of all four ethnonational groups from Punjab, Sindh, NWFP and Balochistan'. The demands were to ensure a more inclusive Pakistan. She added, 'Population alone could not determine the nature of our federation…'

Nilofer Afridid Qazi added, 'Out of the 400 amendments proposed by the opposition, only one was accepted.'[5] Thereafter, the opposition decided to boycott the constitution-making proceedings. By then, the assembly had only approved one-third of the provisions. PPP headed by Z.A. Bhutto enjoyed a brute majority in the Constituent Assembly. It drew its strength from Punjab and Sindh and rode roughshod over the demands of smaller provinces. It is an irony that his party has completely changed its position since and has become a votary of greater devolution of powers to the provinces. The experience of suppression of the Movement for the Restoration of Democracy (MRD) in the 1980s, where Sindh bore the brunt, may have played a part in this rethinking. The party is also aware that along with Balochistan, Sindh has the least representation in the army. The seventh National Finance Commission Award of 2009, during the PPP's term in office, allocated a larger share of resources to the provinces. During Asif Ali Zardari's presidency in 2010, the PPP pushed through the Eighteenth Amendment to the Constitution, which has provided more powers to the provinces. However, the nationality question remains alive.

Pakistan used Islam to suppress national and linguistic identities in Khyber Pakhtunkhwa and Balochistan, fuelling the rise of Islamist groups. The TTP in Khyber Pakhtunkhwa now challenges the state's authority. Regional parties, once advocating provincial aspirations, have been weakened. Zulfikar Ali Bhutto dismissed the NAP government in Balochistan, banning the party. Its successor, ANP, saw its activists killed systematically in NWFP/Khyber Pakhtunkhwa. The state equates regional identity demands with 'parochialism'.

While Islamabad suppressed tribal leadership in Balochistan, the province became home to the Quetta Shura of the Afghan Taliban in the wake of 9/11. This could not have been possible without the complicity of Pakistan's intelligence agencies. There was also an influx of Sunni extremist groups in the province. Religion is being used by Islamabad to suppress the Baloch national sentiment. This has only intensified the Baloch reaction as witnessed in the recent hijacking of a train on 11 March 2025.

Sindh's legacy remains divided. The 1972 language riots erupted when Urdu's status in Sindh was downgraded, sparking backlash from the Muhajirs, Pakistan's largest Urdu-speaking group. In 1992, the army launched Operation Clean-up against the MQM. The MQM–PPP rivalry persists, with the MQM facing state violence and army crackdowns. Muhajirs gave birth to Pakistan, but seven decades after its creation, remain immigrants in the promised 'homeland'. The military's dominance over the state structure in Pakistan has contributed to the centralizing impulse and made political accommodation of the nationality issue more difficult.

13

Khyber Pakhtunkhwa

'...the NAP and its leaders are not reconciled to Pakistan's existence, integrity, and sovereignty, that they have consistently been attempting to create doubts about people's belief in the Ideology of Pakistan with a view to destroying the very concept which formed the basis of the creation of this country...'

–Hamoodur Rahman, Chief Justice, Supreme Court of Pakistan, Pakistan v Abdul Wali Khan, MNA and others[1]

THE BRITISH CHOSE A geographical appellation to name the region North West Frontier Province (NWFP). The colonial power was concerned with the territory, not the people. The nomenclature was continued by Pakistan for more than half a century before it was changed to Khyber Pakhtunkhwa (land of the Pakhtuns or Pashtuns) in 2010.

While the British policy may have been based on indifference, the reluctance of Pakistan's rulers stemmed from the denial of national identities that made up the new state. In the case of NWFP, this was not simply a theoretical issue. At the time of Partition, the NWFP under the Khan Brothers did not want to join Pakistan. Their preference was to join India or have an independent Pakhtunistan. The philosophy of the Khudai Khidmatgars was a direct challenge to the Two-Nation Theory espoused by the Muslim League. Pakistan sought to counter Pashtun nationalism by promoting Islamic fundamentalism. It has succeeded brilliantly in this objective. Today, the province that opted for a secular India is a hotbed of extremist philosophy. However, the success of the Pakistani state has come at a price: the TTP is now challenging its writ. 'Independents' supported by Imran Khan's banned Pakistan

Tehreek-e-Insaf (PTI) secured an absolute majority in the provincial assembly elections in 2024. This may be, in no small measure, due to the close ideological affinity between the Taliban and Imran.

The NWFP always had a deeply conservative society. For Dr Khan Saheb and Badshah Khan, being a Muslim-majority province did not mean that it could not be a part of India. They opposed Partition. As Badshah Khan's son Wali Khan has written, 'We in the Frontier used to laugh at the antics of the Muslim League. It was often said that it was not a partition of India but partition of Muslims!'[2] That this view had popular support was clear from the resounding victory of the Congress, headed by Dr Khan Saheb, in the 1946 elections. While, in the case of other provinces, accession was decided on the basis of a majority in the assembly, in the case of NWFP, the British made a departure from this principle and held a referendum. The Khan Brothers demanded, that in such a case, the scope of the referendum should include the demand for Pakhtunistan. When this was rejected, Badshah Khan and his Khudai Khidmatgars decided to boycott the referendum. In the one-sided contest, the Muslim League won.

After Partition, Dr Khan Saheb's government in NWFP was dismissed, despite the majority it enjoyed in the provincial assembly. Pakistan's rulers had had little respect for the principle of democracy. Dr Khan Saheb was sacked because his loyalty to Pakistan was in doubt. That this was a political decision was clear when, a few years later, he was inducted into the central cabinet. He was also made chief minister of West Pakistan under the 'One Unit' system.

In 1957, the NAP was formed in Dhaka. This was a broad coalition of parties opposed to an overly centralized dispensation under the 'One Unit' system. Wali Khan, Badshah Khan's son, joined NAP. The founding members included, besides Wali Khan's father, Abdul Ghaffar Khan, the former Indian Muslim League member and socialist Mian Iftikharuddin, Sindhi nationalist G.M. Syed, Pashtun nationalist Abdul Samad Achakzai, Baloch nationalist Ghaus Bakhsh Bizenjo and the Bengali leftist and peasant leader, Maulana Bhashani.[3] The NAP under Wali Khan voiced the demand for provincial autonomy and socialist policies.

NAP took part in the elections of 1970. It emerged as the largest opposition party in the Pakistan National Assembly. It formed governments in Balochistan and the NWFP in 1971, in alliance with Jamiat Ulema-e-Islam (JUI). The party cooperated with the PPP in passing the 1973 Constitution.

'... However, this cooperation ended very soon, and as Mr. Bhutto dismissed the NAP government in Balochistan, the NAP government in the Frontier Province resigned in protest, and thereafter, according to the Government, NAP began a campaign of terrorism against the Government.'[4] Not content with driving the party out of power in two provinces, Bhutto dissolved the NAP in 1975. This was at a time when, according to Justice Dorab Patel, 'It was the major opposition party in the country, and its leader Wali Khan, was the Leader of the Opposition in the National Assembly. After dissolving the NAP, the Government referred its decision for approval to the Supreme Court, as required by the Political Parties Act.'[5]

Justice Dorab Patel mentioned that the government 'also alleged in its complaint that the NAP and its leaders were against the ideology of Pakistan. Mr Wali Khan and the other leaders of the NAP emphasized their loyalty to the country and pointed out that they had spent many years in jail because they were fighting for a democratic Pakistan....'[6] The Bhutto government used the issue of ideology to deny smaller provinces the political space they wanted in the federation.

Justice Patel has mentioned in his book, '*Further, according to Mr. Wali Khan, democratic states did not have official ideologies, and the alleged ideology of Pakistan had also not been defined in the constitution.* Finally Mr Wali Khan also specifically raised the plea that the policies of his party were supported by the historic speech made by Mr. Jinnah as Governor-General and President of the Constituent Assembly on 11 August 1947'.[7] [Emphasis added]

However, the Pakistan Supreme Court approved the Bhutto government's action. In summing up his conclusions in the reference, Patel observed:

> ...We find on the material produced before us no difficulty in upholding that the NAP and its leaders are not reconciled to Pakistan's existence, integrity, and sovereignty, that they have consistently been attempting to create doubts about people's belief in the Ideology of Pakistan with a view to destroying the very concept which formed the basis of the creation of this country, that they have always been preaching the doctrine of four/five nationalities/nations to prepare the ground for the ultimate secession of NWFP and Balochistan on the pretext of demanding the right of self-determination for different nationalities/nations inhabiting those Provinces.[8]

Pakistan was unwilling to accept the idea of 'nationalities' existing within a federal structure, even though Pashtun, Sindhi and Baloch were also Muslims. The judgement was delivered only four years after the separation of East Pakistan. The event pointed to the need for greater provincial autonomy. The Pakistani establishment, including the higher judiciary, had drawn a different lesson and strengthened centralized control. The dismissal of the Balochistan government was followed by the launch of a military operation in that province.

The judgement of the Supreme Court used the 'ideology of Pakistan' as the criterion for validating the dissolution of the NAP. Jinnah's speech of 11 August 1947, which Wali Khan had cited in his defence, was apparently not part of the ideology of Pakistan in the opinion of the country's top court. Justice Dorab Patel pointed out that the judgement never defined what that ideology was. He added, '…and there was a great force in Mr Wali Khan's plea that it was not for the Courts to decide whether Pakistan should have an official ideology, and, if so, what that ideology should be.'[9] Paradoxically, the Bhutto government's action in dissolving the NAP, and the Supreme Court's validation of its arbitrary decision, gave a fresh impulse to the idea of 'nationalities' after the party had agreed to work within the framework of the country's Constitution.

After the dissolution of the NAP, the Awami National Party was formed in 1986. The new party took up the Pashtun cause, earlier championed by NAP. It was also against military rule. However, the nationalist strand of Pashtun politics was weakened by the rise of jehadi organizations during the Afghan war. The arms and money that flowed to various Mujahideen groups in the 1980s had an impact on the politics of the province. This trend would be reinforced by the rise of the Taliban in Afghanistan in the 1990s. The growth of extremism was not a fallout of the Afghan Jehad. The problem originated in Pakistan. The Taliban cadre came from the madrassas in Pakistan. After the end of the Afghan war, the ANP allied itself alternately with the mainstream parties at the Centre – PPP and PML(N). The fact that the party that once dominated the province had to align with Pakistan's mainstream parties to survive in power showed its weakening base. According to French political scientist Christophe Jaffrelot, its coalition with the latter broke up in 1997 'when Nawaz Sharif opposed renaming the NWFP "Pakhtunkhwa"'.[10]

The rising trend of Islamic fundamentalism gained further momentum after the events of 9/11. The fall of the Taliban should have weakened the extremist movement and its offshoots in Pakistan. Instead, a group of religious parties called Muttahida Majlis-e-Amal (MMA) was allowed by Musharraf to form governments in NWFP and Balochistan after the 2002 elections. This was part of the bargain in which MMA supported Musharraf's government in the Pakistani Parliament. These were the parties that had opposed US military action in Afghanistan. The ANP had broken away from the anti-Musharraf coalition of opposition parties on the question of action against the Taliban and supported the US-led action. It was once again marginalized.

It is clear that MMA's victory was based on the army's support from the fact that in the subsequent elections in 2008, after Musharraf's exit, the alliance was wiped out. In the 2008 elections, the ANP 'won thirty-eight seats, enabling the party to take the lead of a ruling coalition including the PPP (twenty seats)'.[11] The ANP had hitherto defined itself as the voice of provincial autonomy. It now 'became a partner of the ruling coalition at the center'.[12]

According to Jaffrelot, the ANP supported 'counterinsurgency operations the Pakistan army led under pressure from the US in the FATA'.[13] Seen against the background of the ANP's opposition to the military, this may seem to be a change in its position. However, there was consistency in the party's position. It had opposed the communal policies of the Muslim League before Partition. It was now battling Islamic fundamentalism. What had changed was the army's position – it had earlier supported the jehadi groups not only during the Afghan War in the 1980s but also the Taliban in the 1990s. As America's partner in the war against terror, the Pakistan Army selectively took action against terrorist groups who were using the Federally Administered Tribal Area (FATA) region as a sanctuary. This change in the military's position would be short-lived.

The ANP won a symbolic victory when Article 1 of Pakistan's Constitution was amended in 2010 to rename the NWFP as 'Khyber Pakhtunkhwa'. However, the change in nomenclature came when the discourse in the province had begun to shift away from Pashtun nationalism to Islamic extremism. The weakening of the Pashtun identity was accompanied by the rise of the TTP. The ANP no longer sets the narrative in the province.

The Taliban occupied the province's Swat valley in 2007. Though they were repelled by the army, the episode showed their strength in the region. The TTP does not believe in parliamentary politics. Therefore, it is not possible to directly gauge the strength of the movement through election results. However, an index is provided by the success of Imran Khan's PTI. Imran opposed military action against the TTP and favoured dialogue with the militants at a time when the situation in the province was worsening.

There were also increased attacks on ANP leaders and workers on the eve of the 2013 elections. According to the Pak Institute for Peace Studies, the *New York Times* reported that 'a concerted campaign of Taliban attacks against the main secular party is violently reshaping the democratic landscape before parliamentary elections scheduled for May 11'.[14] 'BBC Urdu said that more than 700 ANP activists have been killed by snipers or suicide bombers during last four years, including a top party leader, Bashir Bilour.' Pakistan's *Express Tribune* newspaper reported on the eve of elections on 10 May that, 'ANP was the worst sufferer of terrorist attacks. Bashir Ahmed Bilour, a key ANP leader, was killed in a bomb blast ahead of ANP's election campaign in Peshawar.' The TTP declared the party 'un-Islamic'.[15]

An article in *Dawn*, also on 10 May 2013, said, 'The ANP seemed to be singled out by the TTP in Sindh, Balochistan and Khyber Pakhtunkhwa, being attacked almost on daily basis.'[16] The party's election campaign suffered as 'the first rank leadership of the party had already been put on virtual house arrest'. Threats were held out against the polling stations in areas where ANP was believed to enjoy the majority. A fatwa was issued urging the voters 'to abstain from voting for ANP as it was against Islam.'[17]

Imran Khan's PTI was a direct beneficiary of the campaign of targeted violence against the ANP. In the provincial assembly in Khyber Pakhtunkhwa, the PTI bagged 19.31 per cent votes and fifty-eight seats, ahead of the PML(N) with 15.9 per cent of votes and sixteen seats, and the ANP with only 10.34 per cent of votes and five seats. The PTI's rise was engineered by targeted violence against ANP leadership and its rank and file. The party gained the political space vacated by ANP in the elections. This heralded a shift of political balance towards the religious right.

The trend gained strength by the time of the 2018 elections. In Khyber Pakhtunkhwa, the PTI doubled its vote share to 34.09 per cent from 19.31 per cent in 2013. It won 34.09 per cent votes and eighty-five seats out of a total of 124 seats. The MMA, the coalition of religious parties, came second with 18.01 per cent votes and thirteen seats. The ANP finished third with 12.85 per cent votes and nine seats. The PML(N), with 10.47 per cent votes and six seats and PPP with 9.67 per cent votes and five seats, finished fourth and fifth respectively. The last three parties – ANP, PML(N) and PPP – together accounted for a vote share of 32.99 per cent with a seat tally of twenty. This was far behind the share of PTI alone in terms of votes (34.09 per cent) and seats (eighty-five). Together with the votes polled by MMA, the difference becomes even starker. The narrative in Khyber Pakhtunkhwa is now set by Imran Khan's version of Islamic ideology.

The Pashtun Tahafuz Movement (PTM), founded by Manzoor Pashteen from the south Waziristan district, calls itself a social movement for protecting Pashtun human rights. Its slogan is 'Ye jo dehshatgardi hai, iske peeche wardi hai (Military is behind this terrorism)'. The Pakistan Army made a series of compromises from 2006 onwards with the Taliban, who challenged the state's authority. However, it refuses to accept the PTM's demand for the protection of Pashtun rights within the framework of Pakistan's Constitution. The PTM previously had two members in the National Assembly but holds no seats in the current assembly elected in February 2024; the ANP won one seat. The party that once shaped the narrative in Khyber Pakhtunkhwa now stands marginalized.

The emergence of the Pashtun Tahafuz Movement in southern Waziristan shows that the secular strand of Pashtun politics is still alive, though much weaker. As the movement's nomenclature suggests, it stands for preserving Pashtun identity. The rise of a movement committed to non-violence in an area where the Pakistan Army was fighting a violent insurgency should have been welcomed by the Pakistani establishment. Instead, the PTM has received hostile treatment. An organization that seeks to revive Pashtun sentiment and looks up to Badshah Khan for inspiration invites suspicion and hostility.

Wali Khan had said: 'I have been a Pashtun for six thousand years, a Muslim for thirteen hundred years, and a Pakistani for twenty-five.'[18] His remarks reflected the secular ethics of the ANP. The army weakened a secular, Pashtun nationalist party like the ANP, and helped the rise of Imran Khan's PTI. Now, it will find it harder to counter the Taliban, who merely profess the ideology promoted by Pakistan's civil and military rulers over time. The TTP seeks to establish an Islamic emirate on the Pakistani side of the Durand Line.

14

Sindh

'During the public meetings, [Bhutto] insisted that the Sindh Assembly had acted reasonably in passing the language bill.'

–Sardar Sherbaz Khan Mazari[1]

SINDH HAS DEFINED INDIA'S identity. The word 'Hindu' comes from 'Sindhu' (Indus), the river that flows through the province. The ruins of Mohenjo-Daro stand as evidence of the Indus Valley civilization. In Pakistan's ideology, Sindh has a different meaning. The establishment calls it Bab-ul-Islam (Gateway of Islam), referring to the Arab invasion in the seventh century when Muhammad bin Qasim defeated Raja Dahir. Sindh also has immense economic significance. Karachi port is a crucial economic hub, with customs duties contributing significantly to federal revenues. It was Pakistan's first capital, but despite its historical and economic importance, Sindh has gained little.

There was little support for the Muslim League in Sindh in the 1937 elections. Even five years later, in early 1942, the pro-Congress Allah Baksh Soomro was the Sindh chief minister. According to Sherbaz Mazari, Soomro was asked by Governor Sir Hugh Dow to resign when he 'renounced the award of OBE and title of Khan Bahadur given to him by the British'.[2] This paved the way for a Muslim League government under Hidayatullah to assume power.

The Sindh assembly became the first provincial assembly in undivided India to adopt a resolution asking for a separate state for Muslims in 1943. A leading figure behind the move was G.M. Syed. He also played 'an instrumental role in mobilizing support for the Muslim League in Sindh from 1943 to 1945', according to political scientist Asma Faiz in her book *In Search of Lost Glory: Sindhi Nationalism in Pakistan*.[3] He was to eventually become a champion of Sindhi nationalism, demanding a separate Sindhu Desh. His political journey describes the meaning of Pakistan.

The PPP projects itself as the party of the federation at the national level, but in its home province, it articulates the voice of Sindhi nationalism. The ideology of Pakistan denied distinct national or ethnic identities of its constituent parts. Post-Partition, Sindh has struggled to assert its Sindhi identity.

New Province, Divided Legacy

After Napier's conquest of Sindh in 1843, it was made a part of the Bombay Presidency. The Sindhi language had Arabic, Devanagari and a local Khudawani script. According to Asma Faiz, 'The Arabic script was chosen by the British government for the official uses of the Sindhi language.'[4] The 1931 census brought out that Muslims were 70 per cent of the Sindh population, while Hindus were 28 per cent. However, Hindus were economically dominant. Economically marginalized Sindhi Muslims demanded the creation of a Sindh province. The new province of Sindh was created only in 1936. The British conceded a separate status for the province only in the last phase of their rule. They also played a role in shaping the linguistic identity based on Arabic script. This was an attempt to weaken the link with the indigenous tradition and create a rift.

Though Sindh was a Muslim-majority province, the Muslim League could not win a single seat in the Sindh assembly election in 1937. Allah Bakhsh Soomro, who was aligned with the Congress, was elected as the chief minister twice. In 1940, he organized a conference of nationalist Muslims in Delhi against the Lahore Resolution passed by the Muslim League. In the 1946 election, the Muslim League emerged as the largest party with twenty-seven seats, followed by the Congress with twenty-one seats in the sixty-member house.[5] Still, 'the governor's intervention was needed since the League and the opposition had equal numbers in the legislature'.[6]

Partition

The large influx of the immigrant population after Partition changed the demographic composition of Sindh. Soon, Sindhis became a minority in Karachi. They lost control of the city, which was elevated to the status of the national capital. Muhajirs were to be the beneficiaries of the new dispensation. But their advantage would be whittled away with time. They would discover that without a geography of their own, they were the most disadvantaged of Pakistan's five 'qaumein' (nationalities). Sindh is divided by both ideology and language.

Karachi was made the capital of the new state. The 'elevation' of Karachi to the status of the national capital was not without resistance. Sindh lost control of its principal town. According to Asma Faiz, the Sindh assembly 'put up a united front on the issue, unanimously passing a resolution on 22 February 1948 denouncing the conversion of Karachi into the federal capital. The move was declared a "flagrant contravention of the Lahore Resolution" as it would cripple Sindh economically and politically.'[7] Speaking in the Pakistan Constituent Assembly, on 22 May 1948, Muhammad Hashim Gazdar, a Sindhi representative, reminded the Liaquat Ali Khan government that 'Pakistan was established on a principle of autonomous provinces which was being openly violated'.[8] The Constituent Assembly, however, declared Karachi as the federal capital on the same day.

The city underwent radical demographic change within a few years. Asma Faiz wrote, 'On the eve of Partition, the population of Karachi was 450,000; it rose to 1,137,000 in 1951. In 1947, 61.2 per cent of Karachi's residents were Sindhi speakers. However, they were reduced to a meagre 8.6 per cent in 1951.' There was virtually no presence of Urdu speakers in the city in 1947. By 1950, they comprised half the population. Partition also altered the religious composition of the city. 'In 1947, 51 per cent of the city's population was Hindu, which reduced to 2 per cent in 1951.'[9]

The religious composition was changed by driving out the Hindu minority in the province, who were the majority within Karachi. According to US-based political observer Mohammad Ali Mahar, writing in the *Friday Times*, the Sindh riots of 1948 were not caused by 'a sudden provocation, but a planned effort, purely to deprive the rich minority of its wealth and property and drive them out of the city as well as frighten the rest'.[10] Mahar quoted Hamida Khuhro, 'her father, Muhammad Ayoub Khuhro, the then Chief Minister of Sindh, was threatened of dire consequences by the highest authority when he tried to stop the violence'.[11] The press fanned the communal violence. According to Asma Faiz, 'On 13 September 1947, the *Dawn* newspaper appealed to the Muslim National Guards to ensure that fleeing Hindus left Pakistan empty-handed.'[12]

Urdu was imposed on the province. 'The Sindhi language was banished from the city. According to one report, 1,600 Sindhi medium schools were shut down or converted to Urdu medium schools. Sindh University was made to move out of Karachi.'[13] City elders G.M. Syed, Hashim Gazdar and some Parsi leaders met the prime minister to complain of the attempt to artificially alter the culture of the city, Liaquat Ali Khan 'is on record as mockingly retorting "Do camel-herder have a culture?"'[14]

Pakistan clubbed together the four provinces of West Pakistan in 'One Unit' in 1955. The move was aimed at denying East Pakistan its numerical majority by creating an artificial parity between the two wings. But its victims were no less the smaller provinces of the west, which lost their distinct status. The move was opposed by the Sindh assembly. Sherbaz Mazari wrote,

> The Sindh Chief Minister Pirzada was able to produce a statement opposing the One Unit scheme signed by 74 out of the 110 members of the Sindh Assembly. He was abruptly dismissed and replaced by the Center by the ever-ruthless Ayub Khuro. Within a fortnight the very same Assembly cowardly reversed itself, and passed a resolution approving the One Unit by 100 votes to 4.[15]

The smaller provinces were now part of 'One Unit' where Punjab's position was preponderant. Sindh lost the provincial status it had struggled to achieve for nearly a century after Napier's conquest in the nineteenth century. The provincial status was restored only when 'One Unit' was dissolved by General Yahya Khan in 1970.

PPP: Federal Party or the Voice of Sindhi Nationalism?

The PPP, under Bhutto, emerged as the largest party in West Pakistan in the 1970 elections, winning eighty-one seats. A large part of its tally came from Punjab; it won sixty-two of the eighty-two seats in the province. Punjab had accepted a party led by a Sindhi. As Christophe Jaffrelot has remarked, this outcome 'attests to the determination of West Pakistan – still in search of parity – to unite forces against the Bengalis'.[16] Bhutto became president after East Pakistan broke away from Pakistan in 1971. He rose to power as the head of the largest party in Punjab. PPP had failed to win a majority in Sindh. Bhutto followed a centralizing impulse at the federal level. This was Punjab's agenda; it also suited his temperament for concentrating all powers in his hand. But in Sindh, he was to follow a different narrative.

PPP's success in forming the government in Islamabad post-1971 made Sindh a stakeholder in power at the federal level for the first time. This may have reduced the appeal of G.M. Syed's Jiye Sindh, but did not necessarily mean that the sentiment was dead. PPP had replaced Jiye Sindh as the main channel for the articulation of Sindhi nationalism. An expression of this strand of PPP's policy was the introduction and adoption of the Language Bill, declaring Sindhi the only official language of the province. Sherbaz Mazari, as an opposition member of the Pakistan National Assembly, has given a ringside view of the developments. He attributes Bhutto's support to Sindhi nationalism a result of a combination of racial memory and political manoeuvring. While the British described Punjabis, Pathans and Baloch as martial races, Sindhis were excluded from this category. Mazari says 'As a Sindhi, Bhutto was undoubtedly keen to redeem his racial heritage.'[17]

Tapping into Sindhi nationalism also made good politics. It was the dominant sentiment in rural Sindh. When the language riots forced Bhutto to retract his steps, he blamed Mumtaz Bhutto, his cousin and the chief minister of Sindh, in closed-door meetings. However, according to Mazari, 'During the public meetings, [Bhutto] insisted that the Sind Assembly had acted reasonably in passing the language bill.' 'He said that he commanded the power of the state and knew how to use it, and that he would crush those who conspired against his government.'[18]

Bhutto ushered in the Constitution of 1973, which reflected a centralizing tendency with limited provincial autonomy. He had ensured his supremacy, but in the process, placed Sindh, along with other provinces, under the tight control of Islamabad. In the garb of federation, Pakistan had reverted to a unitary status. The 1973 Constitution gave Pakistanis the right to settle anywhere in Pakistan. This was seen as a threat by Sindhis, who feared further ingress from the outside.

Bhutto's hanging left a deep impression on the Sindhi psyche and created a rift in perception. Sindh saw this as an attempt by the Punjab-dominated army to eliminate the first Sindhi who came to power at the federal level. Bhutto's trial produced a split verdict. The Punjabi judges on the bench voted for Bhutto's execution. Bhutto is called 'Shaheed Bhutto (Martyr Bhutto)' by PPP followers in Sindh. The slogan, however, does not have the same resonance in Punjab.

The MRD defined Sindh's identity in opposition to the army and Punjab. It also showed the fissures within the PPP. The Punjabi wing of the party largely remained neutral during the movement, while the brunt of the military action had to be borne by Sindh. Within the province, Jiye Sindh leader G.M. Syed remained neutral. Benazir showed ambivalence. In her autobiography, *Daughter of the East*, she mentioned that she was 'appalled' at the prospect of joining hands with members of the Pakistan National Alliance (PNA), who had led the agitation against her father in 1977. She described them in her book as 'murderers'. She was also concerned about the challenge to the Bhutto family from within the party by 'a PPP leader as powerful as Ghulam Mustafa Jatoi'. She added, 'Reluctantly, I agreed.'[19] Sardar Sherbaz Mazari, a senior member of the MRD, mentioned that Mrs Nusrat Bhutto was 'holding secret meetings with General Sadiq Abbasi, the Sindh governor, with a view to striking a deal with the regime'. He later learned in 1986 that 'not only did the Bhutto ladies reach a clandestine understanding with the regime in 1981, but that "Benazir kept her promise and secretly cooperated with the government by not issuing overly critical statements" right until her departure for London in January 1984'.[20]

Since the 1980s, the PPP has formed governments at the federal level thrice. Benazir formed the government twice in the early 1990s. After her assassination in 2007, the Zardari government served a full term from 2008 to 2013. While PPP has retained its vote bank in Sindh, its footprint across the country has increasingly shrunk. In the Sindh provincial assembly elections, the party secured 42.26 per cent of votes in 2008, 26.8 per cent in 2013 and 38.44 per cent in 2018. However, its vote share in other provinces has maintained a steady downward trajectory. In the Punjab provincial assembly elections, its vote share declined from 26.89 per cent in 2008 to 8.84 per cent in 2013 and further to 5.38 per cent in 2018. In NWFP/Khyber Pakhtunkhwa, the vote share dropped from 16.49 per cent in 2008 to 9.67 per cent in 2018. No less dramatic was the party's decline in Balochistan, where its vote share fell from 12.52 per cent in 2008 to 3.09 per cent in 2018.

In the 2024 elections, the PPP retained its hold at the provincial level and formed the government in Sindh. It has supported the federal government, headed by PML(N)'s Shehbaz Sharif, from the outside, while Zardari has returned as President. As its presence declines in other provinces, its continued dominance in Sindh will become increasingly important to the party.

Sindh faces growing threats from climate change and the construction of dams in the upper reaches of the Indus in Gilgit-Baltistan in POK. The 18th Amendment of Pakistan's Constitution, devolving more powers to provinces, was carried out during Zardari's presidency. This helps the cause of Sindh, though it is seen as weakening the federation by the Pakistani military establishment. The army is particularly unhappy, as this has reduced the Federal government's share of revenue from which the defence budget is drawn. PPP gives different messages to different constituencies. At the national level, it talks of a strong federation, while aligning with Sindhi nationalist sentiment at provincial level. Urdu may be the national language of Pakistan, but in Sindh, it is seen as the language of the community which has come from outside, deepening the divide between Sindhis and Muhajirs.

15

Balochistan

'The Government of Pakistan recognizes Kalat as an independent sovereign state in treaty relations with the British Government with a status different from that of Indian States.'

–Communiqué issued by Jinnah's office on 11 August 1947[1]

BALOCHISTAN, LIKE THE NWFP, rejected the ideology of Pakistan at birth. Pakistan initially recognized the princely state of Kalat as an independent, sovereign state.[2] Jinnah later forced its merger. In 1948, he sent the army to enforce it.

South Asia scholar Selig Harrison wrote that the attempt to impose a 'monolithic Pakistani nationalism' on the tribal structure 'constituted a frontal challenge to Baloch values'.[3] Baloch resistance brought retribution from the Pakistan state. They have suffered more than the Pathans; they have been the target of five military operations by the Pakistan Army, in 1948, 1958, 1962, 1973–77 and again in 2006.

Balochistan is home to the Sui gas reserves, which provide a large part of Pakistan's natural gas supply. Despite its vast natural resources, Balochistan remains Pakistan's most backward region. Its mineral wealth and strategic Arabian Sea location have tightened military control.

In the contemporary period, Balochistan has been in the news for three adverse reasons. First, Pakistan conducted its nuclear test in the province in 1998. The Baloch saw this as an expression of Islamabad's insensitivity. Their province was being treated as a wasteland by the Pakistani establishment. Second, in the wake of 9/11, the province became the seat of the 'Quetta Shura' of the Taliban. This transformed the tribal society into a hotbed of religious extremism. A corollary has been increasing attacks on Shias. However, the sectarian strife should not blind us to the origins of the problem – the denial of Baloch identity and state violence. Third, Gwadar Port has been leased to the Chinese. The Pakistani state has benefited from the geostrategic bargain without much economic gain or employment for the local people. This has brought outside presence and threatened the delicate ethnic balance of the region.

Pakistan's Recognition of Kalat's Independence

Before Partition, the region was divided into three distinct areas (British Balochistan, Kalat and the Marri-Bugti Tribal Area) and ruled by the agent of the governor-general. In a memorandum to the Cabinet Mission in 1946, the Khan of Kalat 'argued that the legal status of Nepal and Kalat was different from that of other princely states in the subcontinent'.[4] These two had a direct treaty relationship with Whitehall in London, while other Indian states were bound by treaties with the British Indian government in Delhi. The successor state or states could only claim the mandate of the latter.

Pakistan initially recognized Balochistan's independent status. A communiqué was issued from Jinnah's office on 11 August 1947, stating, 'The Government of Pakistan recognizes Kalat as an independent sovereign state in treaty relations with the British Government with a status different from that of Indian States.'[5]

The Khan of Kalat made a formal declaration of independence on 12 August. The ruler's position was supported by the fifty-two-member lower house of the Kalat assembly. Selig Harrison writes, 'Although most members clearly desired an alliance with Pakistan, an overwhelming consensus favoured independence as a precondition for such a relationship.'[6] Ghaus Bakhsh Bizenjo, the principal spokesman for the independence forces, said, 'We have a distinct culture like Afghanistan and Iran, and if the mere fact that we are Muslims requires us to amalgamate with Pakistan, then Afghanistan and Iran should also be amalgamated with Pakistan.'[7]

This confident assertion of the Baloch claim to a sovereign, independent status by Bizenjo, then twenty-nine years old, was a clear repudiation of the warped Two-Nation Theory. Much later, Bizenjo would become a member of the Pakistan National Assembly and take part in framing Pakistan's third and current Constitution. He would find that joining mainstream politics did not win a reprieve for the province. He would be dismissed as Balochistan's chief minister by the Bhutto regime.

Kalat's independence did not last long. According to Pervez Hoodbhoy, Viceroy Mountbatten cautioned Jinnah that 'an independent Balochistan might well become a security threat on Pakistan's western border'.[8] The British were concerned about stopping 'Soviet expansion into the warm waters of the Persian Gulf'.[9] Jinnah went back on his earlier promise and demanded that Kalat accede to Pakistan. 'The Baloch parliament, however, repeatedly rejected the merger', opting instead for an independent federation of Baloch feudatory states under Kalat.[10] The Khan of Kalat had 'employed Jinnah as his legal adviser in the past, and hoped to exercise some leverage'. He was to be disappointed. Jinnah sent in the army in 1948. The Khan eventually fell in and 'signed over Balochistan to Pakistan'. However, his brother Prince Karim continued to resist till 1949. Conflict with the Pakistani state had created Baloch resistance.

Frederic Grare, a Carnegie South Asia scholar, wrote in a report titled *Balochistan: The State Versus the Nation*, 'A few hundred ideologically motivated men assembled under the banner of Sher Mohammed Marri and the militant Baloch People's Liberation Front.'[11] Baloch leaders joined with Wali Khan to form the NAP in 1957, which voiced the demands of the smaller provinces – NWFP and Balochistan.

Bhutto Strikes

Baloch got the opportunity to cast their vote when the first elections under a universal franchise were held in Pakistan in 1970. The NAP won 60 per cent of the seats (twelve out of twenty) in the provincial assembly. As the largest opposition party in the National Assembly, the NAP cooperated with Bhutto in passing the Constitution Accord of 1972, which paved the way for the passage of Pakistan's third and current Constitution in 1973. This did not win a reprieve for the NAP government in Balochistan. Soon, it was dismissed and a military operation began. The operation was ordered by the civilian government under Bhutto.

On 10 February 1973, an arms cache was discovered during a raid on the Iraqi Embassy in Islamabad. 'The timing of the raid on the Iraqi Embassy coincided with the PPP government's actions to destabilize the government of Balochistan,' wrote Sherbaz Mazari. 'Bhutto decided to place the blame for smuggled arms on NAP leaders of Balochistan.'[12]

This was far-fetched; Iraq could not possibly have had any interest in the politics of distant Balochistan. Sardar Mazari writes 'The likely destination of weapons was Iran where Iraq was keen to incite insurgencies.'[13] 'Without a shred of evidence, the government instantly orchestrated a campaign accusing the Baloch NAP leaders of planning to arm insurgents in Balochistan with these weapons.'[14] The military operation in Balochistan was launched barely two years after the disastrous operation in East Pakistan. 'The needless brutality applied to the Bengali citizens of Pakistan was now being replicated on the Baloch citizens of Pakistan.'[15]

The arbitrary dismissal of an elected government on trumped-up charges and the launch of a military operation created an insurgency. Pakistan used air power against the Baloch. Initially, they used Chinook helicopters. Later, Iran sent thirty US-supplied Huey Cobra helicopters.[16] These turned the tide against the Baloch.

The military operation raised the profile of the army and undermined the Bhutto government. Bhutto could initiate it; he could not call it off. It ended only after Zia staged his coup and took back power. He 'freed the imprisoned Baluch leaders, Bizenjo, Mengal and Marri, and eventually reached an uneasy truce with them'.[17] Zia, however, refused to make any change in the 1973 Constitution that 'would rule out central intervention to dismiss an elected state regime'.[18] This had triggered the 1973 insurgency.

Regardless of their different political calculus, there was a continuity between the actions of Bhutto and Zia. Both upheld the unitary nature of the 1973 Constitution. Pashtun and Baloch leaders supported Pakistan's Constitution of 1973, because they believed it enshrined a federal structure where the provinces had more political space than before. The issue of ethnicity or nationality remained unresolved.

Unlike Bijenzo or Bugti, Nawab Marri did not accept working with the Pakistan state. He was based in Kabul. The fall of the Najibullah government in Kabul removed Afghanistan as a sanctuary for Baloch resistance. The uneasy peace lasted for more than two decades till it was disturbed after 9/11. The impetus for the resumption of violence again came from Islamabad. Balochistan was to be turned into a sanctuary for the Taliban and Al-Qaeda leaders fleeing Afghanistan.

Democracy, Nationalism and Ideology

The revival of democracy after Zia allowed Baloch national parties to participate in the electoral process. The results showed the strength of the nationalist parties. The Carnegie report by Grare stated, 'In the 1988 election, the combined vote for nationalist parties totalled 47.8 per cent. It reached 51.74 per cent in the 1990 election, and Baloch nationalist parties dominated the election again in 1997 and formed the government.'[19] Islamabad was to play an active part in reversing the process.

According to the Carnegie report, 'The equation changed with the 2002 elections, when the military rigged the elections and reinvigorated its long-standing alliance with the region's mullahs, helping the Muttahida Majlis-e-Amal (MMA) coalition of religious Islamic parties to gain power in Balochistan.'[20] Islamabad changed the eligibility criteria for candidates to require university degrees, but madrassa diplomas were considered equivalent. As a result, prominent nationalist leaders like Akbar Bugti, who had held the office of the governor of the province and was head of a major regional party, the Jamhoori Watan Party (JWP), could not participate in elections.

9/11

The Baloch had played no role in supporting the Taliban regime or the Al-Qaeda movement in Afghanistan in the 1990s. However, post-9/11, Balochistan emerged as the headquarters of the 'Quetta Shura', headed by Mullah Omar, the Supreme Leader of the Taliban. Was this an accident? Musharraf allowed MMA, a coalition of religious parties, to assume power in two provinces bordering Afghanistan – NWFP and Balochistan. These parties had supported the Taliban and furnished cadres to fight against the American forces in Afghanistan during Operation Enduring Freedom. Accommodating them in the government created a hospitable environment where the Taliban and Al-Qaeda could regroup.

Pakistan was using religious fundamentalism to suppress Baloch nationalism. This was a replay of what Islamabad had done in the NWFP to weaken the secular ANP. As an International Crisis Group report mentioned, the military was using Islamist parties '...in a bid to counter secular Baloch and moderate Pashtun forces'.[21] The report added, 'Using Balochistan as a base of operation and sanctuary and recruiting from JUI-F's extensive madrasa network, the Taliban and its Pakistani allies are undermining the state-building effort in Afghanistan.'[22]

Quetta Shura

There was rising alarm about the shift of Taliban and Al-Qaeda leadership to Balochistan. President George W. Bush signed anti-terrorism legislation on 3 August 2007, noting that 'the continued operation of the Taliban's Quetta Shura', called for progress 'to end the use of Pakistan as a safe haven for terrorist groups, including those associated with Al-Qaeda or the Taliban'.[23]

Though the Taliban maintained an office in Doha, the negotiations in 2010 with the US were directed by the Quetta Shura. It continued to do so well after the death of Mullah Omar in 2013, which was kept secret. The Pakistan Army suppressed Baloch nationalism but took no action against the Taliban and Al-Qaeda leadership based in Balochistan. Baloch nationalism challenged the ideology of Pakistan. The Taliban mindset was a product of madrassas in Pakistan.

The army's brutality increased alienation and gave renewed strength to Baloch nationalism, which is no longer rooted in the tribal structure. It has a wider base now and includes the urban middle class. This is reflected in the deployment of the security forces, which have shifted from tribal areas to urban centres in the south. According to the Carnegie report, 'The Frontier Corps, a paramilitary force that operates in Pakistan's border provinces, has apparently concentrated much of its 50,000-man strength in Balochistan in the southwestern areas of the province, mostly in the Panjgur, Turbat and Kech districts.'[24] The report further mentioned that the middle class is the main target of Pakistan's military, which 'seems to be an attempt to eradicate all manifestations of Baloch nationalism and to rule out the very possibility of its renaissance'.

The Pakistan Army's attempt to stifle nationalism by promoting religious fundamentalism has left its imprint on Balochistan's social fabric. There has been a marked rise in Shia killings. This is a new phenomenon; the province did not have a history of sectarian violence. A report by Human Rights Watch mentioned ninety-six Shia Hazaras were killed on 10 January 2013 in a suicide bombing. At least 150 were injured. In another bombing just over a month later on 17 February, at least eighty-four Hazaras were killed and 160 injured. The Lashkar-e-Taiba claimed responsibility for both attacks, the bloodiest sectarian violence in Pakistan since 1947.[25]

The Assassination of Akbar Bugti

In 2006, Akbar Bugti was killed in a cave in Balochistan by the Pakistan Army, which exulted 'we've got him'. His assassination was a watershed moment in the history of Balochistan. Musharraf claimed that only three out of seventy-seven sardars – Nawab Akbar Khan Bugti, Nawab Khair Bakhsh Marri and Sardar Ataullah Mengal – were 'anti-development and anti-democracy; they do not want democracy, rather they want to exercise their complete dictatorship and control in their areas'. Ruling out dialogue, he declared, 'We have to go for an operation to change this situation. We have to establish the writ of the government, and end the writ of [these] sardars.'[26]

The general's concern for democracy in an outlying province was indeed touching. He had come to power through a military coup. He virtually gave a public command for the killing of Bugti. The trigger for the military's action was Bugti's demand for a fairer share of the province's natural resources for its people.

The dispute, in Bugti's words, was about '… the natural rights of the Baloch ... and if the government accepted these rights there would be no dispute'. Bugti was resisting the appropriation of the region's wealth by Pakistan on unfair terms. A senior government official said, 'his death would open Kohlu district's untapped reserves for exploration'. These are estimated at 22 trillion cubic feet, with a potential commercial value of $110 billion over 100 years.[27]

During my stint in the Indian Consulate in Karachi, I had the privilege of being invited by Sardar Akbar Bugti to dinner during a visit to Quetta. He represented the secular tradition of Balochistan's tribal society and had invited many members of his tribe as well as a Hindu member of his party, Arjun Das Bugti, to meet me. The latter was a member of Bugti's JWP in the provincial assembly, who had been forced to resign on flimsy grounds. His name indicates that religion is not a factor in tribal affiliation. The Pakistani state allowed the Quetta Shura to flourish in Balochistan while assassinating Bugti, who stood up for Baloch rights and showed 'no tolerance for militant Islamists'.[28]

Riches and Poverty

Balochistan remains the poorest province in Pakistan, despite being rich in terms of natural resources. This dichotomy shows the ruthless exploitation by the state. According to a study by the Sustainable Development Policy Institute, Balochistan provides nearly 40 per cent of discovered natural gas reserves (19.3 trillion cubic feet out of 53 trillion cubic feet). However, it did not receive commensurate economic gains. 'The supply of gas to the major cities of Pakistan was started in 1964, but Balochistan's capital Quetta didn't receive gas until 1986 (and that too was supplied to meet the demands of the military cantonment); even today, most areas of Balochistan don't have a gas supply.'[29] According to a World Food Programme report, district Dera Bugti, which has supplied most of Pakistan's gas requirements, was the second-most food-insecure district of Pakistan, out of the then 120 districts.

The Seventh National Finance Commission (NFC) award in 2009 increased the share of provinces in the 'divisible pool' from 47.5 per cent to 57.5 per cent. There was also a slight increase in Balochistan's share from 7.17 per cent to 9.09 per cent.[30] However, the marginal improvement of 1.92 per cent in Balochistan's share of resources may not compensate for the low royalty for gas which is its chief economic resource. The royalty is calculated based on the wellhead price of gas rather than the market price. This results in a discriminatory pricing policy where Balochistan gets a much lower price for the same molecule of gas as compared to other provinces.

Sui gas from Dera Bugti was priced 'only at Rs 47 per unit versus Rs 171 of Dhodhak or Rs 122 of Badin, and Rs 240 of ZamZama', according to a report by the *Dawn*. Since a revision in 2009, the price has been raised to Rs 140 per unit, but 'remains low even now as compared to Rs 202 for Dhodhak, Rs 263 for Mari, and the median/average of around $4 per unit'.[31] The Balochistan government has demanded compensation for the underpayments of the past. It is worth noting that royalty payments are only a small part of the final gas price.

If the logic is based on production cost rather than the price the market will command, will Punjab accept a lower price for the food grain it produces? The dice are loaded against the numerically smallest province in the federation. Balochistan's total share, including excise duty and gas development surcharge, amounts to 25.33 per cent of the total price of Rs 140. Under this arrangement, Islamabad receives the bulk – almost 75 per cent – of the price of gas produced in Balochistan. This does not take into account that Baloch gas is priced at least 30 per cent lower than gas produced elsewhere. Hence, the actual share of Balochistan is only around 15 per cent, with Islamabad appropriating 85 per cent.

The last census in 2023 announced that the province's population was 14.89 million which came as a surprise. Till the final phase of the census process, the figure being reported was around 21.7 million. *Dawn* reported that according to a submission made before Pakistan's Supreme Court, former chief minister Mir Abdul Quddus Bizenjo 'was forced to approve the 2023 national census results'.[32] The lower census figure has a bearing on the province's quota in government jobs and its share in the NFC award. The original census figure would have also increased Balochistan's seats in the National Assembly by ten.

The new PPP-led coalition government in Balochistan presented the budget for the financial year (FY) 2024–25 in June 2024.[33] Out of the total receipt of Rs 955.60 billion, Rs 647 billion is the province's share in the federal divisible pool. The provincial receipts are only Rs 124.49 billion, or 13 per cent of total receipts. This makes the province completely dependent upon Islamabad. This is, of course, a result of the contrived situation, where the province has little control over its natural resources, with Islamabad appropriating 85 per cent as explained earlier.

The provincial budget also had a small surplus. Under the Pakistani system, provinces are exhorted to generate a surplus to compensate for the federal deficit. This effectively results in the poorest province subsidizing the national budget, which has allocated a staggering 26.83 per cent to defence expenditure in the current year's budget. This is discussed in detail in the chapter on economy.

The Old Order Changeth Not

Instead of attempting reform, the Pakistani military establishment seemed to have fallen back on old methods. In the 2018 elections, the newly formed Baloch Awami Party (BAP) secured 24.44 per cent of votes and twenty-four seats. It was followed by the MMA with 15.28 per cent votes and eleven seats. The PML(N) saw its fortunes diminishing. As against 10.28 per cent votes and twelve seats in 2013, its vote share fell to 1.56 per cent votes and one seat in the 2018 elections.

The 2024 elections saw PPP and PML(N), the two constituents of the Pakistan Democratic Movement (PDM) coalition at the federal level and considered close to the army, bagging eleven and ten seats respectively. The Jamiat Ulema-e-Islam Pakistan led by Maulana Fazal-ur-Rehman won ten seats. The BAP's seat share came down to five. After the PPP-led coalition formed the government in Balochistan, the province's Baloch National Parties have staged protests against what they have called 'massive rigging' in the general polls.[34]

The Shia pilgrims' groups going by land route from Balochistan to Shia shrines in Iran have been repeatedly attacked by Sunni extremist organizations. The border province has also been used by Jaish al-Adl to launch terror attacks inside the Sistan-Balochistan province of Iran. A day before the Pulwama attack in India, twenty-seven Iranian border guards were killed by a Pakistani suicide bomber in Sistan-Balochistan. In December 2023, eleven Iranian policemen were killed in an attack claimed by Jaish al-Adl. This led to Iranian retaliation on 17 January 2024 against Pakistan, and a Pakistani counterstrike the next day.

Pakistan's policy of using religious groups to suppress Baloch nationalism is drawing it into conflict with its Muslim neighbour to the west.

Gwadar

The Gwadar port is located in Balochistan. The port has given China a permanent base on the Indian Ocean, and shorter lines of communication to the Chinese mainland through Pakistan rather than the Strait of Malacca. Though Pakistan has reaped handsome dividends from the project, the people of Balochistan have not benefited. Most of the development work under the China–Pakistan Economic Corridor (CPEC) in the form of rail and road construction and power projects is taking place in Punjab. Balochistan has provided the port and suffered displacement of people.

Balochistan's trajectory since 1947 shows consistent denial of the national or ethnic aspirations of the Baloch people by the Pakistani state. The province rejected accession to Pakistan in 1947. Though Marri remained a rebel, eventually, Mengal, Bizenjo and Bugti agreed to work within its Constitution. Bizenjo had strong left leanings; Bugti was a tribal chief. Bizenjo, despite having forged a consensus on the adoption of Pakistan's 1973 Constitution, was sacked as governor of the province along with Chief Minister Mengal. Bugti, who took over as the province's governor after their dismissal, was considered close to Islamabad. He was killed by the Pakistan Army in 2006.

Pakistan has ruthlessly exploited Sui gas, most of which comes from Bugti lands. While East Pakistan could break away, given its small population and proximity to larger provinces, Balochistan cannot escape Pakistan's iron grip.

The Chinese presence in Gwadar has increased the strategic importance of the region in the Pakistan Army's calculus. Smaller provinces cannot expect fairness and equity in Pakistan, despite being predominantly Muslim. The hijacking of a train on 11 March 2025 in Balochistan by Baloch Liberation Army activists shows that the insurgency is no longer confined to tribes and has spread to the urban middle class from which the BLA cadre is drawn.

16

Muhajirs

'*Agey samandar hai* (The sea lies ahead).'

–Ayub Khan's warning to Muhajirs

THE URDU TERM 'QAUM' does not lend itself easily to translation in English. It is closer in meaning to 'nationality' rather than an ethnic group. Muhajirs who identified themselves with Pakistan before any other province accepted the idea have had to fall back on a narrower identity. But unlike other 'national' groups in Pakistan, Muhajirs cannot lay claim to a province. They have to share an uneasy coexistence with Sindhis, who have a prior claim on Sindh. Four decades later, they became targets of the Pakistan Army's Operation Clean-up in 1992. It was ironic that the torchbearers of the ideology of Pakistan became the victims of the State they created.

The word 'Muhajir' comes from the Arabic 'hijrah' and recalls the Prophet's migration from Mecca to Madina, giving it religious significance. Even seven decades after Partition, the term remains, reflecting their continued status as outsiders in the state they helped create. The community has clung to this identity, realizing that being Pakistani was not enough.

Muhajir identity has been shaped by state repression and ethnic conflict. The community organized as a political force through the Muhajir Qaumi Movement (MQM, later Muttahida Qaumi Movement) to defend its turf in urban Sindh but could not withstand army and ranger operations. Operation Clean-up, launched during Nawaz Sharif's first term, intensified under Benazir Bhutto. Its bloodiest phase was in 1994. The MQM split between Altaf Hussain's faction and MQM Haqeeqi, backed by state agencies.

After Altaf Hussain's statement in 2016 describing Pakistan as a 'cancer', the party split again. Now, there are three groups – a group under Farooq Sattar distanced itself from Altaf Hussain, who is based in London. It now calls itself MQM (Pakistan). The group owing allegiance to Altaf Hussain is called MQM (A); and MQM (Haqeeqi) continues.

Muhajirs were the biggest supporters of the idea of Pakistan. Post-Partition, the Muslim League dominated the new state, and the Muhajirs dominated the party. In the absence of elections at the federal level, the League was not only a political party but the electoral college from which all state functionaries and the ministers were 'selected'. Jinnah was the governor-general, president of the Constituent Assembly and president of the ruling party. After his death, Liaquat Ali Khan remained the prime minister, while Khaliquzzaman became the president of the Pakistan Muslim League. Under Khaliquzzaman, the League Working Committee was dominated by Muhajirs.[1]

After Liaquat Ali Khan's death, Muhajirs lost their political power. However, they retained their position in bureaucracy as they were better educated than their peers. This would change soon. After the Language Bill was enacted in Sindh in 1972, Muhajirs found that their position came under challenge even within Sindh. Though Urdu was eventually retained as one of the two state languages of Sindh, Muhajirs lost their dominance once job reservation based on language was introduced. This remains a major milestone in the evolution of a separate identity for Muhajirs; MQM as a political party emerged only in the 1980s. By 1992, they became the target of a military operation by the Pakistan Army.

Agey Samandar Hai (The Sea Lies Ahead)

After Partition, the Urdu-speaking Muhajirs were settled in Karachi. Punjab absorbed Punjabi-speaking immigrants; a common language helped assimilation. But despite producing noted Urdu poets like Iqbal and Faiz Ahmad Faiz, Punjab did not provide land to settle the Urdu-speaking Muhajirs. Even a cursory look at the map shows that Punjab, rather than Sindh, should have been the place for Muhajirs to settle down. It is much closer to the border and was indeed the first stop for refugees crossing over from India. During my stint at the Indian Consulate in Karachi, my Muhajir friends told me that a rumour was spread in Lahore that the Indian Army was about to attack. Its objective was to drive the Urdu-speaking immigrants out of Punjab.

Muhajirs dominated the Muslim League. But by the mid-1950s, the role of the party was eclipsed, and the civil-military bureaucracy had come to be dominated by Punjab. Malik Ghulam Mohammad became governor-general in 1951. Chaudhry Mohammad Ali became finance minister in 1951 and prime minister of Pakistan in 1955. Both Ghulam Mohammad and Mohammad Ali were former civil servants and Punjabis. Ayub Khan became defence minister in 1954, while still serving as the army chief.

Ayub's military coup in 1958 deprived Muhajirs of the influence they exercised through control of the main political party. Their representation in the army was low. Ayub was elected president in elections under the 'Basic Democracy' system in 1965. There was not a direct election; the president was to be elected by an electoral college of 80,000 Basic Democrats. His opponent was Fatima Jinnah, the sister of Pakistan's founder, who was supported by the Combined Opposition Parties (COP). Muhajirs identified themselves with Jinnah's legacy and opposed the Punjabi–Pashtun domination that Ayub represented. Though Ayub was elected by 65 per cent votes, he lost in Karachi, which was dominated by Muhajirs. Ayub also lost in Dhaka.

The outcome reflected the alienation of Muhajirs as well as Bengalis from Pakistan, the promised 'homeland' for Muslims of the subcontinent. Expressing his anger at the Muhajirs, Ayub Khan made his famous remark – 'Agey samandar hai (The sea lies ahead).' This menacing phrase conveyed that the Muhajirs had nowhere else to go. They would be thrown into the sea unless they accepted their fate. The statement lives on in the collective psyche of Muhajirs.

Urdu ka Janaaza Hai, Zara Dhoom se Nikley (This Is the Funeral Procession of Urdu; Let It Be Taken Out with Full Pomp)

Urdu was part of the ideology of Pakistan promoted by the leaders of the Muslim League. Urdu defined the Muhajir identity and assured their ascendancy in government jobs. According to Mohammad Ali

Mahar writing in the *Friday Times*, Liaquat Ali Khan introduced a 'highly lopsided' quota system in September 1948, 'where 42 per cent of jobs went to Bengal, 24 per cent to Punjab and 17 per cent to the rest of Pakistan, including Sindh, Balochistan, the NWFP and the State of Khairpur. The same percentage, a whopping 17 per cent – was set aside for the tiny population of migrants and Karachi (read, migrants)!'[2]

Muhajirs began with a disproportionate share in government jobs but lost their only leverage by the early 1970s. They had already lost political power and never had much representation in the army.

On 3 July 1972, the Sindh assembly passed the Language Bill, declaring Sindhi the province's only official language. This triggered widespread riots. Eventually, President Bhutto was forced to compromise, issuing an Ordinance on 16 July, making both Sindhi and Urdu official. The riots echoed East Pakistan's protests two decades earlier against Urdu's imposition. The issue extended beyond language – Muhajirs' share in government jobs remains subject to quotas, eroding their bureaucratic dominance.

The event has left a deep impression on the Muhajir psyche and shaped their ethnic identity. The Urdu daily *Jang* carried the banner headline *Urdu ka Janaaza hai, Zara Dhoom se Nikley*... (This is the funeral procession of Urdu; let it be taken out with full pomp). However, it is difficult to convey the rhythm of these words in English. The lines were written by Raees Amrohi. There is a mosque and a museum in memory of those killed in the language riots in the Liaquatabad area of Karachi.[3]

The bill was adopted at the provincial level in the Sindh assembly. Bhutto's cousin Mumtaz Bhutto was the chief minister. But a measure of such importance could not have been introduced without the consent of President Bhutto. Why did he allow the language controversy to be raised so soon after the majority province of East Pakistan had broken away?

The timing may not have been opportune, but there was a logic to it. Linguistic or national identities could not be denied in the name of religion. First East Pakistan, and now Sindh, was rejecting Jinnah's construct. Bhutto, of course, did not say so. He had denied political space to the Awami League, which led to Pakistan's break-up. He projected himself as Pakistan's saviour. Once in power at the federal level, he wanted to give Sindhi language primacy over Urdu, which Jinnah had described as embodying 'the best that is in Islamic culture'.

Bhutto symbolized commitment to *wifaq* (federation), which suited his ambition to cement authority at the Centre while supporting Sindhi nationalism at home. This duality remains central to PPP's policies. Muhajirs saw themselves as custodians of Pakistan's ideology, rejecting 'provincialism'. Now, they sought an identity based on Urdu, Pakistan's state language, which in Sindh had to struggle for equal recognition with Sindhi.

The language riots of 1972 deepened the divide between the 'old' and 'new' Sindhis. Over a period, this led to Muhajirs attempting to form a separate political grouping. It started with the formation of the All Pakistan Muhajir Students' Organization (APMSO) in 1978 and the MQM in 1984.[4] The MQM's opponents claim that the organization was created by Zia-ul-Haq to divide Sindh after the launch of the MRD movement in 1981. As scholar Vazira Fazila-Yacoobali writes, '...it is now widely accepted that the MQM, after its formal establishment in 1984, was supported and backed by the military dictatorship, in part to break the opposition to the military in the province of Sind.'[5] But the process of creating a separate identity had started much earlier.

The rise of the MQM in the 1980s was the result of the progressive marginalization of Muhajirs in Pakistan's power structure, forcing the community to fall back on its ethnic identity. The process was helped along by the Sindhi–Muhajir friction over the language and job reservation issues.

A major incident that shaped the Muhajir consciousness of being a separate group was the killing of college girl Bushra Zaidi in a road accident in 1985. The girl was a Muhajir; the driver of the bus that trampled her was a Pashtun. Pakistani-American lawyer and author Rafia Zakaria wrote in her book *The Upstairs Wife: An Intimate History of Pakistan*, 'It was the beginning of an ethnic war. In the day that followed, hundreds died, and from their blood, a fifth ethnicity emerged in Pakistan.'[6] The Muhajirs were not fighting for a separate country but for a fairer share in Pakistan's polity and economy.

The MQM won thirteen National Assembly seats in 1988 and allied with Benazir Bhutto's government. A key demand was the repatriation of 'Biharis' from Bangladesh – Muslims who migrated to East Pakistan in 1947 and sided with the Pakistan Army in 1971. Despite Bhutto's agreement with Mujibur Rahman to accept them, Pakistan never did. The PPP opposes their return, fearing they would bolster Muhajir ranks and upset Sindh's ethnic balance. Pakistan's refusal to accept them amounts to the state itself rejecting the ideology of Pakistan.

Pucca Qila

While Bushra Zaidi's killing triggered ethnic violence, the Pucca Qila incident pitted the Muhajirs against the state forces.

On 27 May 1990, the Sindh Police surrounded Pucca Qila, a Muhajir settlement in Hyderabad. The city is located in interior Sindh and has the second largest Muhajir population after Karachi. The police had arrived during the daytime when the menfolk were mostly away. The official version was that they were looking for a group of terrorists with a cache of illegal weapons.[7] The police ordered the women, who had shut themselves in their homes, to come out. Driven by hunger, they eventually emerged from their homes. The police opened fire on unarmed women who were carrying copies of the Holy Quran on their heads. 'According to some counts, more than eighty people died that day, most of them women and children.'[8] The incident marks a watershed in the collective memory of Muhajirs.

Operation Clean-up

After the 1990 elections, the MQM formed an alliance with the Islami Jamhoori Ittehad (IJI), led by Nawaz Sharif. Operation Clean-up was launched by the Pakistan Army against the MQM in May 1992. Muhajirs, who were the strongest supporters of the Pakistan movement before Partition, were now the target of the Pakistan military. The ideology of Pakistan did not spare those who championed it.

This was not a Sindhi–Muhajir conflict; it was an action by the army against Muhajirs. As Vazira Fazila-Yacoobali has noted, 'The discourse of ethnicity' shifts the focus away from the state. 'Thus the reliance on "ethnicity" as a causal factor of political violence and instability masks the repressive role of the state.'[9]

When Operation Clean-up was launched, the MQM was a partner in Nawaz Sharif's government in Islamabad. This did not save it from military action. This did not shield it from military action, highlighting the irrelevance of civilian parties in Pakistan's power structure. The army had struck against the prime minister's political ally. The operation was initiated shortly after the assassination of a senior army officer, though Altaf Hussain's rhetoric against class-dominated polity may have also played a role.[10] The official justification for the army's action was the worsening law-and-order situation in Sindh, affecting both urban centres and rural areas. I was serving in the Indian Consulate General in Karachi. The army's justification was a ruse; the operation targeted only urban Sindh, a Muhajir stronghold. According to Jaffrelot, 'In the course of this operation, 1,113 persons were killed by snipers in Karachi.'[11] The military withdrew from Karachi in 1994. However, violence continued. 'In 1995 the official death toll reached 2,095, most of the deaths occurring in the course of police operations,' Jaffrelot added.[12] The military operation continued regardless of the civilian parties in power.

The alliance secured them positions in both the Sindh and federal cabinets, along with the governorship of Sindh and the post of speaker of the provincial assembly. However, they were unable to get Nawaz Sharif to implement the three conditions he had agreed to: the repatriation of 'Biharis' from Bangladesh, an increase in the civil service quota for Muhajirs to 11.5 per cent, and the disarmament of MQM (Haqeeqi).[13]

The MQM was fully rehabilitated during the Musharraf period. Whether this was merely a coincidence or influenced by Musharraf's background is difficult to determine. Musharraf himself was a Muhajir. However, the interlude was short-lived.

'Pakistan Is a Cancer for the Entire World'

On 23 August 2016, the London-based Altaf Hussain, in a broadcast to his followers in Pakistan, said Pakistan was 'a cancer for entire world'.[14] He added, 'Pakistan is headache for the entire world. Pakistan is the epicentre of terrorism in the entire world. Who says *long live Pakistan… it's down with Pakistan.*' [Emphasis added] The statement was triggered by the mounting number of enforced disappearances and extrajudicial killings of workers.[15]

The statement was a repudiation of the ideology of Pakistan by the leader of the community which was the strongest supporter of the Pakistan movement. It triggered a sharp reaction from the establishment. The Farooq Sattar-led faction disowned Altaf Hussain and founded MQM (Pakistan). The Altaf-led group MQM (Altaf) dismissed Farooq Sattar from primary membership of the party which now has three sections, including MQM (Haqeeqi). The social engineering by the army has resulted in the erosion of the group's strength.

The MQM maintained its seat share in the National Assembly between the 2008 and 2013 elections. It won twenty-five seats in 2008, with a marginal decline to twenty-four in 2013. However, the party experienced a sharper drop in the Sindh assembly. In 2008, it secured fifty-one out of 132 seats, but this fell to forty-two in 2013.[16] Provincial assembly elections are crucial for the party to sustain its influence in urban Sindh.

The rise of Imran Khan's PTI may have been part of the reason for the erosion of the MQM voter base. According to Muhammad Feroz Iftikhar's 2017 thesis, titled *Legally Muhajir*, 'This party also claimed 10 per cent of the votes of the Sindh assembly, which gives a hint about where the MQM lost 4 per cent of its voters.'[17]

After Imran Khan's PTI turned against the army, the military establishment attempted to unite various MQM factions to counter PTI. In the 2024 elections, MQM-P regained some lost ground, securing twenty-eight seats in the Sindh assembly and seventeen in the National Assembly. This time, the MQM faction benefited from the Pakistan Army's crackdown on PTI.

Muhajirs have not been able to escape the minority complex. Before Partition, they saw themselves as a religious minority in need of a 'homeland'. Now, they are a permanent minority in Sindh. After the adoption of the Language Bill in 1972, the Urdu language no longer brings any privilege. Their share in government jobs is capped by a quota. They remain in a perennial quest for an identity.

PART 4

Ideologies, Strategies and Interests

17

Army

'The professional soldier in a Muslim army, pursuing the goals of a Muslim state, CANNOT become a "professional" if he does not take on "the colour of Allah" in all his activities.'

–General Zia-ul-Haq's foreword to Brigadier Malik's book *The Quranic Concept of War*[1]

In most countries, armies defend borders. Pakistan's Army also defends its ideological frontiers. Like so much else it has done, this is a self-assumed mandate. The army has played an outsized role in the country's politics. It has directly run the country for more than three decades and has acted as the most potent force shaping the country's policies behind the scenes, even when a civilian government has been in power. The army has appointed itself as the sole custodian of nuclear weapons. In Pakistan, the army is the state.

The Pakistan Army's philosophy is based on unremitting hostility to 'Hindu' India. This flows from the Two-Nation Theory advanced by the Muslim League in pre-Partition days. After Independence, this was projected in the external domain. The army's perception was coloured by ideology.

Religion became an idiom and a symbol for the Pakistan Army since its inception. The army used jehadi slogans during the 'tribal invasion' of Jammu and Kashmir in 1947–48. In 1965, it launched Operation Gibraltar, with infiltrating units named after Islamic heroes. Armed groups affiliated with the Jamaat-e-Islami were used to suppress the uprising in East Pakistan in 1971. Under Zia, the army spawned terror groups to advance Pakistan's strategic interests in Afghanistan and Jammu and Kashmir. Most of these groups were inspired by an extremist philosophy nurtured by the military. The army was not only the guardian of ideological frontiers but it also took an active role in shaping them.

The Pakistan Army enjoyed the proximity to the British and American defence establishments. However, it departed from the central axiom followed by them – neutrality in domestic politics. With General Ayub Khan's coup, the army took over the role of running the country. The path for the army's takeover was paved by the Muslim League, which delayed national elections. Ayub blamed political parties for the chaos, but he struck when they had reached an agreement on the election under the 1956 Constitution. This feat would be repeated in 1977 by Zia. The third coup was staged by Musharraf in 1999.

The army intervened in domestic politics even when it did not take over power directly. It eased out Nawaz Sharif in 2017 for not declaring the money he had not received. Saving the country from its elected representatives is an onerous task; the army undertook it enthusiastically. The military's repeated intervention in politics not only weakened democracy but strengthened religious fundamentalism.

British strategists projected Pakistan as a moderating, pro-Western force in the Arab and Muslim world. It was considered a bulwark against communism. Many Western commentators fondly believed that the army would check the rise of Islamic fundamentalism within Pakistan. Each of these three assumptions has been proved wrong. General Mirza Aslam Beg, as the serving army chief, gave a call for 'strategic defiance' of the West when the pro-West Gulf states were facing an existential threat from the Iraqi invasion of Kuwait in 1991. Pakistan developed the Sino-Pakistan axis in 1963 when it was receiving American military aid to fight communism. The army's tacit alliance with religious groups has strengthened these groups within Pakistan.

Pakistan has enjoyed close relations with Turkey, but their armies followed different models. The Turkish Army tried to preserve the secular legacy of the country. This brought it into conflict with Erdogan's Islamist policies. The Pakistan Army, on the other hand, has promoted religion. Of course the problem goes deeper – the Muslim League's ideology was the opposite of the world view of modern Turkey's founder, Mustafa Kemal Ataturk.

In most countries, nuclear weapons are controlled by the top civilian leadership. In Pakistan, they are the exclusive preserve of the Pakistan

Army. Nawaz Sharif visited the Kahuta nuclear plant during his first term as prime minister in 1990–93. At the time, I was serving at the Indian Consulate in Karachi. The media reported that Sharif was the first prime minister permitted to visit the enrichment facility. The clear hint was that his predecessor Benazir Bhutto never received this honour. It did not strike his media managers how incongruous it looked to the outside world that the prime minister of the country had to get permission from the military to visit a nuclear facility.

The acquisition of nuclear capability did not encourage more responsible behaviour. Pakistan proliferated nuclear technology in Iran, Libya and North Korea. Though nuclear physicist Abdul Qadeer Khan was made the scapegoat, the nuclear programme was tightly controlled by the military, and proliferation could not have taken place without the approval of its top leadership.

During Zia's period, as Pakistan's nuclear weapons capacity was not declared, it resorted to the doctrine of deterrence through uncertainty. Since then, it has progressed to developing tactical nuclear weapons as a war-fighting instrument. Pakistan has a First Use policy, which is inherently destabilizing. The nuclear strike is to be launched before the enemy does so. Even worse is that Pakistan's nuclear doctrine includes the threat to use nuclear weapons against India's conventional response, which amounts to lowering the threshold for the use of nuclear weapons. This could lead to a rapid escalation of the conflict to the nuclear level. Pakistan's actions are driven by its aspiration to assert dominance over its larger neighbour, even at the risk of catastrophic consequences. Operationally, the Pakistan Army has moved beyond mere deterrence, incorporating nuclear weapons into its defence doctrine. This aspect is explored in greater detail in the chapter on nuclear deterrence.

Conventional armies fight wars with unified command and control. Pakistan was keen to maintain deniability for its support of the terror campaign in Jammu and Kashmir and the Afghan jehad. This necessarily means relying upon religious groups to provide a cadre. Multiple points of decision-making increase the risk of escalation. With the development of nuclear weapons, the Pakistan Army stepped up covert activities. The Kargil war in 1999, a year after the nuclear tests in South Asia, saw the infiltration of regular troops as well as mujahideen across the LOC. C. Christine Fair has termed it as, 'Jehad under the nuclear umbrella'.[2]

According to Pakistani diplomat Husain Haqqani's book *Pakistan: Between Mosque And Military*, under Jinnah, the country allocated '70 per cent of its projected expenditure in its first year's budget for defence'.[3] This was justified as a 'forced' decision in view of 'an ongoing war in Kashmir and the need to maintain the military that had come to Pakistan's share'.[4] There is a vast amount of literature available to show that the war in Kashmir in 1947 was initiated by Pakistan. It was a war of choice. Since then, disproportionate defence expenditure has remained a feature of the Pakistani economy.

Pakistan's military spending or defence budget in 2023 was 2.802 per cent of the GDP.[5] The corresponding figure for Bangladesh was 1.023 per cent and India was at 2.443 per cent. Most NATO countries had a defence budget below 2 per cent of the GDP until recently.

After 1971, Pakistan's frontiers shrank with the secession of the eastern wing. This should have led to a substantial reduction in the defence budget. However, after a slight dip for two years, by 1975, the country's defence expenditure ($0.77 billion) had exceeded the level ($0.74 billion) in 1971. The increase happened under a civilian government, headed by Zulfikar Ali Bhutto. For more than three decades (1965–99), Pakistan's military expenditure remained above 5 per cent of the GDP, reaching nearly 7 per cent of GDP during the Zia period.

Jammu and Kashmir

Colonel (later Major General) Akbar Khan, who led the tribal invasion of Jammu and Kashmir under the pseudonym of General Tariq in 1947, described the sight of the invading tribesmen in his memoir *Raiders in Kashmir*: 'The spectacle before us was like a page out of old history. Memory flashed back many, many centuries. This, one felt, is what it might have been like when our forefathers had poured in through the mountain passes of the Frontier.'[6]

After more than a millennium of Islam in the subcontinent, Akbar Khan viewed the newly created country as the successor to foreign invaders. He was not alone in embracing this imagery; it was a widely held perspective among the Muslim League leadership. Even the pseudonym adopted by Akbar Khan carried historical significance – Tariq ibn Ziyad, the Muslim conqueror of Spain in the eighth century CE.

The Pakistan Army has vacillated between two opposing views of its role, based on ideology and interests. On the Jammu and Kashmir issue, these have converged and reinforced each other. While Akbar Khan represented the ideological view, Jinnah described Kashmir as the 'jugular vein of Pakistan' – a view based on a cold calculation of Pakistan's interests and strategy. Pakistan's claim on Kashmir is based on the ideological grounds that it is a Muslim-majority state. It bartered away part of the territory to Communist China and has appropriated hydropower resources of POK – the part of Kashmir Pakistan occupied illegally. Its actions are based on its perception of interests.

During Operation Gibraltar in 1965, Pakistan launched regular troops across the ceasefire line. According to Altaf Gauhar's books *Ayub Khan: Pakistan's First Military Ruler*, the operation 'was entrusted to five forces, Tariq, Qasim, Khalid, Salahuddin and Ghaznavi, all named after legendary Muslim conquerors'.[7] The army had fallen back on Islamic history to find inspiration, despite the ostensibly westernized outlook of Ayub and then-foreign minister Bhutto. The operation proved to be a failure. The local Kashmiris, instead of rising in support of their 'saviours', reported them to the Indian security forces.

The tendency to fall back on Islam in defence of the country's territorial interests became stronger in 1971. The army went beyond the use of icons from Islamic history to tie up with religious parties to suppress Bengali ethnicity. Farzana Shaikh has written, '... in 1971 it had worked closely with the armed wings of pro-Islamic parties, notably the Jamaat-i-Islami, to secure religious sanction for its brutal campaign against the "enemies of Islam" among Bengalis in East Pakistan.'[8] It used volunteers from the Jamaat-e-Islami to act as an auxiliary force in executing Operation Searchlight in East Pakistan. The irony that Islam was being used against Muslims escaped Pakistan's Army.

Pakistan's defeat in the 1971 war and the loss of its eastern wing created an identity crisis in the country and within the army. The Muslim majority had broken away from the state created as the 'homeland for Muslims of the subcontinent'. There was no serious introspection about government policy, which denied the Bengali majority its due share in Pakistan's polity. Instead, there was a twofold reaction. In the external sphere, there was a conscious attempt to move closer to the Arab world. At home, the role of Islam in providing ideological underpinning to the state deepened. Both were initiated by Bhutto, much before Zia's coup.

The lurch towards Islam did not save Bhutto. He could not tolerate a government run by the opposition party in Balochistan. He sent the army to pacify the province after the dismissal of the NAP government headed by Bizenjo. This paved the way for the army's return to domestic politics.

Zia, Afghanistan and Transnational Islam

The Afghan jehad strengthened the ties between the army and religious parties. It also increased the accent on transnational Islam. The Pakistan Army was not only defending territory but also acting as the vanguard of an Islamic civilization. There was a difference between Ayub and Zia. Ayub used Islam as an ideology but did not want to share political space with religious parties. Zia accommodated political Islam. He incorporated the Objectives Resolution in the Constitution and gave it overriding legal force. He also created the Council of Islamic Ideology. However, his contribution to the Islamization of Pakistan went beyond constitutional changes and embedding it in the state structure, important as they were. He forged a tacit alliance with the Jamaat-e-Islami initially. This meant a move towards the Deobandi school of thought. The Deobandi school leaned heavily towards an austere, puritanical version of Islam. The army was laying down the religious doctrine which should be followed by the society. It was not simply following but shaping the ideology of Pakistan.

Zia was a shrewd tactician. He believed in a 'big tent' which accommodated religious parties of various persuasions. Only political parties were left out of the tent. He had come to power by overthrowing the nascent political order which had brought a civilian government to power. The 1985 elections were 'party-less' and were boycotted by the PPP. Zia broadened his alliance with religious parties beyond Jamaat-e-Islami. Farzana Shaikh writes that he used the Jamiat Ulema-e-Islam (JUI) 'in containing ethnic discontent in Balochistan', and used the rhetoric of Islam 'in curbing Pashtun sub-nationalism in NWFP'.[9]

One of the chief architects of the Afghan jehad was Lt General Akhtar Abdur Rahman, the chief of Pakistan's Inter-Services Intelligence (ISI) in the Zia regime. Brigadier Mohammad Yousaf has written his political biography. The title is revealing: *Silent Soldier: The Man Behind the Afghan Jehad General Akhtar Abdur Rahman Shaheed (martyr).*

When Zia inquired about his 'appreciation' of the military situation, General Akhtar said, 'his recommendation was that Pakistan should support the jehad'. More than the Soviet threat to Balochistan, the ISI chief was concerned about the threat to Islam from the advance of communism. He said, 'Further, and of equal, if not greater significance, Islam was under attack.'[10]

Given the asymmetry in the power equation between Pakistan and the USSR, Pakistan's Afghan policy carried an enormous risk that defied military logic. It could only be justified in terms of ideology. Brigadier Yousaf wrote 'For General Akhtar the key to victory was Kabul'. Yousaf adds 'His favourite expression when addressing the Mujahideen leaders was, "Kabul must burn".'[11]

Yousaf has described the reasons for keeping Americans out of operational control of Mujahideen activities. He said, '…to do so would have meant giving truth to Soviet propaganda that the war was not a jehad, but an extension of US foreign policy, with Afghans fighting Afghans on behalf of the two superpowers'.[12] Was it simply a matter of managing perceptions? Lt Gen. Akhtar was keen to maintain the ideological purity of jehad. The tactical objective of maintaining Pakistan's control of Mujahideen activities blended well with ideological justification.

Brig. Yousaf has written that the Americans were uneasy that the ISI favoured Islamic fundamentalist parties. He defends General Akhtar's conduct of a covert operation, saying, 'Certainly, Akhtar sought to win the war in order to see an Islamist government replace the communist one.'[13] The victory was being defined in ideological terms – the establishment of an Islamic government in Kabul.

After the end of the Afghan war, Lieutenant Generals Hamid Gul and Javed Nasir, the ISI chiefs tried to export Pakistan's ideology to Central Asia and even supported Muslims in Xinjiang province in China.[14]

Strategic Defiance of the West

At the height of the Gulf War, on 1 February 1991, Pakistan Army Chief General Mirza Aslam Beg gave a call for strategic defiance of the West.[15] The statement was surprising, given the context. Pakistan had historically aligned itself with conservative Gulf monarchies rather than radical regimes. Zia had served in Jordan and played a pivotal role in crushing the Palestinian uprising against King Hussein in 1970. There were large Pakistan Army contingents posted to Saudi Arabia in the 1980s. Pakistan had little interest in Iraq. Now, when Kuwait had been overrun by Saddam Hussein, and the Saudi kingdom faced an existential threat, the Pakistan Army chief had given a call for defying the West, on which Gulf monarchies depended for their survival.

After decades of collaboration with the US, and receiving military and financial assistance, Pakistan had switched to the anti-US position. The Gulf War involved not only America's strategic interests but an existential threat to the Saudi kingdom, which was a fellow Muslim country. General Beg said he believed that 'the Western powers provoked the Iraqi intervention in Kuwait'.[16] He added, 'The war is undermining the unity of the Muslims, and may end up enacting the tragedy of Karbala.'[17] He said, 'Saddam Hussain is now viewed by Muslims all over the world as a great defender of the Faith.'[18]

General Hamid Gul, the former ISI chief, opposed Pakistan's support of American intervention. Najam Sethi wrote in the *Friday Times*, 'In 1991, during the first Iraq war, he articulated the theory that US forces would be defeated by Saddam Hussain's army and the war would be long drawn out and leave a trail of body bags as in Vietnam.'[19] Gul's view did not necessarily reflect sympathy for Saddam Hussein, whose Ba'ath party had a socialist, secular orientation. The Pakistan Army had served conservative Gulf monarchies. It reflected a deep-seated antipathy to the United States and a pan-Islamic world view.

Terror

Prof. Ishtiaq Ahmed has noted that one of the recommended readings for officers at the Staff College, Quetta, was Brig. S.K. Malik's book *The Quranic Concept of War*. Written in the early 1980s, the book emerged at a time when the Pakistan Army had already gained considerable experience in sponsoring terrorism. It offers an ideological justification for this approach, with a foreword penned by General Zia himself. The book states: 'The Quranic military activity thus enjoins us to prepare ourselves for war to the utmost in order to strike terror into the hearts of the enemies …' 'Terror struck into the hearts of the enemies is not only a means, it is the end in itself.'[20]

Malik added: 'Terror is not means of imposing decision upon the enemy; it is the decision we wish to impose on him.' Zia commended the book and wrote in the foreword:

> This book brings out with simplicity, clarity and precision, the Quranic philosophy on the application of military force, within the context of the totality that is JEHAD. The professional soldier in a Muslim army, pursuing the goals of a Muslim state, CANNOT become a 'professional' if he does not take on 'the colour of Allah' in all his activities.[21]

Zia had erased the distinction between a professional soldier and a jehadi. He emphasized that a soldier's professionalism was contingent on taking on the 'colour of Allah'. His vision extended beyond the Pakistan Army; he spoke of a 'Muslim' army. Its objective was not merely the defence of the state's frontiers but the establishment of a Muslim state.

Nuclear Doctrine

Stephen Philip Cohen, in his book *The Pakistan Army*, has mentioned his discussion with an unnamed Pakistan Army officer. The officer stated:

> Islam provides for conditions and criteria which will make it impossible to launch nuclear weapons without a just cause. Nuclear weapons are modern terror weapons, and Islam enjoins us to strike terror into the heart of the enemy, it provides moral guidance, a set of principles for going to war – such a decision would not be irresponsible![22]

The unnamed officer's statement gives an indication about the mindset of Pakistan's military. Islamic precepts provide 'moral guidance' for use of nuclear weapons. The contention that 'Islam enjoins us to strike terror into the heart of the enemy' is not deterrence, as it is normally understood.[23] Nor is it a proportional response. Cohen wrote the book *The Pakistan Army* in the 1980s and updated it in 1998. The passage quoted above was present even in the earlier version, when Pakistan was not a declared nuclear weapons state. Though stated in crude terms, the use or threat of use of nuclear weapons to strike terror expresses the core of Pakistan's nuclear doctrine.

Pakistan has continued the low-intensity warfare even after both India and Pakistan went nuclear in 1998. Underlying this is the belief that fear of escalation to the nuclear level will prevent India from retaliating. This was the assumption behind Pakistan's Kargil adventure.

Jehad Within

Cohen in his book has also analysed the orientation of Pakistan Army officers in terms of their social backgrounds. He divided them into 'British', 'American' and 'post-1971' generations. The last group, he said, are representatives of the wider society in class origin.[24] He said this group is more exposed to Islamization. This does not quite capture the problem. Zia belonged to the pre-1971 generation. Yet, he gave the strongest push towards Islamization.

The Afghan war not only radicalized Pakistan society, but also the military. Khaled Ahmed, a noted Pakistani commentator, states that the army, which was the main handler of the Afghan Jehad, 'itself was not immune to the influence of radicalism'.[25] He cites further, 'Several army officers had pledged their allegiance (bayat) to different Jihadi spiritual leaders…'

Farzana Shaikh has described the transformation in the Pakistan Army during the Zia period. Zia encouraged the spread of Tabligi ideas in Pakistan society and within the ranks of the army. The Tabligi movement stresses the growth of 'Umma consciousness' or 'global Muslim unity'. This provided a convenient justification for extending Pakistan's reach 'beyond the frontiers of the nation-state, whether in Afghanistan or Kashmir'.[26] This came at a time when the breaking away of the eastern wing of the country had shaken the certitude of young officers in the claim that Pakistan was the 'homeland' to Muslims of the subcontinent. East Pakistan was not only overwhelmingly Muslim but constituted the majority in undivided Pakistan. To this generation, 'Zia's image of the Pakistan Army as an "army of Islam" entrusted to protect "the territorial and ideological frontiers of the state" had an inherent appeal.'[27]

Zia's support to the Tabligi movement contributed to radicalization within the army. Zia had a domestic agenda in promoting the Tabligi movement. It helped him diversify the religious basis of his regime. Zia 'grew increasingly wary' of the Jamaat-e-Islami (JI), which hitherto provided the doctrinal prop to the state.[28] The JI competed for political space; the Tabligi Jamaat confined itself to the religious sphere. It was also easier for serving army officers to join a seemingly 'non-political' organization like the Tabligi Jamaat rather than Jamaat-e-Islami, which had emerged as a political party.

The problem has become much worse since the Afghan jehad. There was an attempted coup by Major General Zahirul Islam Abbasi in September 1995. Abbasi had written a paper 'The Quranic Concept of Leadership: Its Adoption and Application in the Pakistan Army'.[29] Though the officers involved were arrested before the coup was ever launched, the incident underlined the danger within.

General Musharraf's decision to join the US-led coalition against terror brought a reaction from within the ranks of the armed forces. According to Khaled Ahmed, 'After he ordered the jihad in Kashmir closed in 2003, General Musharraf was attacked not only by the jihadi organizations but officers and employees from within the military.'[30]

Since then, there have been three major incidents on Pakistani military installations. Pakistan Army GHQ in Rawalpindi was attacked by terrorists in October 2009, who managed to break inside the heavily defended complex, 'taking dozens of people hostage in a day-long siege'.[31] The attackers also killed a brigadier. In May 2011, 'a small group of fighters managed to storm the heavily defended *Mehran naval air base* in retaliation for the killing of Osama bin Laden by US Navy Seals three weeks earlier'. [Emphasis added][32] In August 2012, militants attacked Kamra Airbase, 75 kilometres north-west of Islamabad. The TTP claimed responsibility for the assault and dedicated the attack to Al-Qaeda leader Osama bin Laden. Nine attackers were killed by the security forces, while the militants claimed they had killed twelve soldiers and destroyed three aircraft.[33]

Khaled Ahmed has cited Riaz Mohammad Khan, former foreign secretary of Pakistan. He writes:

> Khan knew that ISI's support of the 'charismatic' mujahideen was based not on any strategic analysis but on 'reverse indoctrination', something that haunts the GHQ in Rawalpindi where the army chief may at times be scared of his own officers. *Soon, the army chiefs of Pakistan became convinced that if they tried to get rid of the non-state actors turned terrorists they could get killed.* [Emphasis added][34]

As the army tried to do a course-correction and fight the TTP, it seemed to be losing the support of the religious parties who have long been its partners in promoting terrorism. Jamaat-e-Islami chief Dr Syed Munawwar Hasan declared on TV: '….since the Pakistan army was fighting against those fighting the enemy of Allah, they could not be called martyrs.'[35] Inter-Services Public Relations (ISPR), the media and PR wing of the military, described the JI chief's statement as 'an insult to the thousands of Pakistani civilians and soldiers killed and needs to be recanted'. The party tried to distance itself from the statement by describing it as the personal views of its chief. The episode showed deep ambivalence in Pakistan about countering the TTP even though the latter had begun to attack the Pakistan Army.

General Qamar Javed Bajwa, the former Pakistan Army chief from 2016 to 2022, in his last interview before retirement stated that the military had decided not to interfere in any political matter. 'In my opinion, the reason for this is the constant meddling by the army in politics for the last 70 years, which is unconstitutional.' He said, 'That is why, since February last year, the military has decided they will not interfere in any political matter.'

General Bajwa's avowal of a non-partisan role came rather late. He was responsible for easing out Prime Minister Nawaz Sharif in 2017 and bringing Imran Khan to power in 2018. He found his protégé, Imran Khan, challenging his 'neutrality' and calling him 'Mir Qasim' – a byword for a traitor in the lexicon of the subcontinent. This was unprecedented in Pakistan's history. Civilian prime ministers cannot challenge the army chief while in power. Once removed, they either face exile or threats to their lives. Imran Khan is an exception.

After Imran Khan's arrest on 9 May 2023, there were attacks by his supporters on the army headquarters as well as the Lahore Corps commander's residence. This was previously unimaginable. The ISPR's statement left no doubt about who was responsible. As Raza Rumi's editorial in the *Friday Times* observed, 'Alongside the rioting and plunder of military installations, a group of men was hoping that there would be a mutiny of sorts in the army, resulting in the exit of General Asim Munir. Despite all his denials, Imran Khan had most certainly placed all his bets on this outcome.'[36] He added that the Lahore Corps commander has been fired, and 'internal purges are underway'.[37]

The fact that the mob could enter these two highest-security places raises some disturbing questions. According to the army's version, this was the result of 'restraint' on their part, without even bothering about its own *saakh* (prestige). Non-violent resistance is not part of the Pakistan Army tradition. Were the soldiers refusing to obey orders? Was this to avoid civilian casualties? If this was the meltdown of army command and control, this points to a greater danger. Pakistan claims that it has robust arrangements in place for the safety of its nuclear arsenal. But there is no safeguard if the soldiers and officers are radicalized. The army's cohesion is being tested.

The loss of prestige invites new challenges. The army's self-assumed mantle of the custodian of the ideology of Pakistan is being challenged. Nawaz Sharif and Asif Ali Zardari have been accused in the past of defaming the army abroad. But criticizing it at home is a much more serious matter. Video clips of the Lahore Corps commander's residence doing the rounds on social media showed the opulent lifestyle of the army leadership. This clubbed the generals with the corrupt political parties who are accused of looting national wealth.

General Asim Munir is considered as 'Hafiz-e-Quran', one who has memorized the holy book. The Pakistan Army considers piety a virtue in a professional soldier. Under Munir, the army has resumed its role of interfering in domestic politics with gusto. Its role in the economy has been institutionalized by creating the Special Investment Facilitation Council. The body, headed by the prime minister, includes the army chief. The army, together with the higher judiciary, has ensured that Imran Khan remains mired in legal trouble. They, however, could not prevent 'Independents' supported by his PTI from winning the largest number of seats in the National Assembly in the February 2024 elections.

The stress on transnational Islam by Zia neatly tied up with Pakistan's strategy of expanding its influence in Afghanistan and Jammu and Kashmir in the 1980s. It was also used in the new millennium to restore the Taliban to power in Kabul. It has, however, created a major predicament for the Pakistan Army. The Taliban, and their ideological kin TTP, have a philosophy that does not recognize the borders of the nation state. The challenge is not simply to the Durand Line; the TTP wants to establish an Islamic emirate in Pakistan.

General Asim Munir, in a convention of the clergy on 8 August 2024, warned against the use of social media for spreading chaos. He dubbed it as 'fitna' (heretical treachery) on behalf of the 'Khawarjin'. Khawarjin means those who have gone outside the fold of Islam. The terms were chosen from Islam's early history for greater legitimacy. The army chief's message had multiple targets. He mentioned the situation in Afghanistan and Khyber Pakhtunkhwa. This was a veiled warning against supporting the TTP. The statement came against the backdrop of the events in Bangladesh, where Sheikh Hasina was overthrown from power. He was cautioning that this cannot be repeated in Pakistan.

General Munir's words had a third target closer to home. A post on Imran Khan's X handle had urged his followers to study the Hamoodur Rahman Commission report on the events leading up to the separation of East Pakistan.[38] Imran was reminding Pakistanis of the army's role in the country's break-up.

It was no coincidence that the army chief chose the clerics as his audience – they shape the world view of the TTP as well as the Pakistani electorate. In Pakistan's troubled history, street agitations led by clerics have been used to oust Zulfikar Ali Bhutto in 1977 and Nawaz Sharif in 2017. General Munir was telling them not to try it again.

Former ISI chief Lt General Faiz Hameed's arrest may have been calculated to pressure him to implicate Imran Khan in the events of 9 May 2023. However, it has also brought out the rift within the army ranks, including the highest echelons. This is not simply an intra-personal conflict between General Munir and the former ISI chief; Imran has a following within the army. General Munir is presiding over a divided house.

Pakistan is sometimes described as a 'garrison state'. The description seems apt for a country run by the army. But the Pakistan Army does not believe in the austerity that is usually associated with the conception of such a state. The high levels of defence expenditure have left few resources for socio-economic development. The imagined threat from India and investing the army with a role in jehad, have made it difficult to address the country's pressing needs. Pakistan is at odds with both of its Muslim neighbours to the west, Afghanistan and Iran. The army has clashed with the same Taliban it brought to power in Kabul in 2021. It also conducted an exchange of missile attacks with Iran's Islamic Revolutionary Guard Corps in January 2024. Have these twin developments dented its certitude about the strategy and ideology it has followed? Or does it still cling to the transnational identity of Pakistan and its self-assumed role of defending Pakistan's ideological frontiers?

Ideologies do not respect state borders, as the TTP has shown. The Pakistan Army has succeeded brilliantly in undermining whatever chances the country had of emerging as a normal state and sowed the seeds of chaos.

18

Afghanistan

'...General Ahmad had a message for Mullah Omar quite different from the one that Washington had pressed his government to convey.'

–ISI chief's mission to Kandahar after 9/11

9/11 HAS BEEN THE defining moment of the twenty-first century. More than two decades later, Afghanistan remains in turmoil. The US-led Operation Enduring Freedom resulted in the downfall of the Taliban regime. However, Al-Qaeda leaders managed to escape. It was only in 2011 that US Special Forces killed Osama bin Laden. He was found to be living in Abbottabad, 70 kilometres from Islamabad.

Following the American withdrawal and collapse of the Ashraf Ghani government in 2021, the Taliban are back in power in Afghanistan. The American withdrawal and the capture of Kabul by the Taliban were described by Prime Minister Imran Khan as 'removing the shackles of slavery'. Pakistan had undermined American policy in Afghanistan by giving sanctuary to the Taliban for over two decades. In doing so, it not only risked its relationship with the US, but ignored the threat posed by the TTP to its domestic peace and security. What impels Pakistan to take such a risk? Is this in quest of achieving 'strategic depth' against India? Or ideology? The political costs of the policy go beyond any definition of interests.

Pakistan justifies its Afghanistan policy in terms of seeking strategic depth against India. This implies either seeking domination over its smaller neighbour or changing the frontiers. The strategic depth is not sought in terms of a cooperative relationship with Afghanistan. Pakistan is unmindful of that country's wishes in the matter. Afghanistan seeks friendly relations with India; it sees Pakistan as a threat. Currently, the regime in Kabul is at loggerheads with Islamabad. The Afghan Taliban have refused to hand over TTP members to Islamabad. The Taliban and Pakistan are divided by a shared ideology. Pakistan supports the philosophy underlying an Islamic emirate in Afghanistan but does not accept it at home. This dichotomy in Pakistan's policy is at the root of the conflict with the Afghan Taliban over TTP.

More significant than the foreign policy issues are the domestic changes in the two countries which resulted from Pakistan's Afghanistan policy. These often mirror each other. The Taliban regime in Kabul has proclaimed an 'Islamic emirate'; they reject both democracy and pluralism. Pakistan is undergoing increasing Islamization. The TTP advanced to Swat in 2006. The Lal Masjid (Red Mosque) incident in 2007 challenged the writ of the state in Pakistan's national capital. The radicalization of Army ranks is reflected in the advice of the then ISI chief Lt General Mahmud Ahmad to Mullah Omar to resist American pressure to hand over or expel Osama bin Laden. Imran Khan has emerged as the most popular leader in Pakistan. He is known to be a Taliban sympathizer.

Since their return to Kabul, the Taliban regime has demonstrated that it is unwilling to share power with other stakeholders. The Taliban have imposed a puritanical order with restrictions on women's education and work. They have not accepted the Afghan Constitution. Taliban 2.0 look much like the Taliban of the 1990s.

The Taliban's return to power raises uncomfortable questions which may have a bearing on Afghanistan's future. Do the Taliban represent Pashtun nationalism or Islamic fundamentalism? Are the Taliban reconciled to a revolution in one country? Would they keep their promise of not supporting terrorism? Does this commitment only include America or other countries too? What lesson have they learned from their experience over the last two decades?

Afghanistan voted against Pakistan's admission to the United Nations. It stated that in the 1947 referendum conducted by the British in NWFP, the Pashtun region not only ought to have been given the choice to join India or Pakistan, 'but also should have been offered the additional options of becoming an independent state or joining with Afghanistan'.[1] Afghanistan completely repudiated the Durand Line. This demand was also voiced by Dr Khan Saheb in the last phase of negotiations with the

British. Mountbatten turned it down. The Muslim League leadership, and certainly their British patrons, could not have been unaware of the strength of the feeling of Pashtun nationalism. Pakistan was a new creation with no history behind it. The new entity needed settled borders.

The declaration of the Durand Line as the international boundary partially resolved the external problem, though this was not accepted by Afghanistan. But the internal problem remained. The Durand Line has divided the Pashtun community living in the area. The NWFP was, at best, a geographical appellation coined by the colonial power to mark the frontiers of its imperial possession, unmindful of the sensitivities of the people of the area. Pakistan's rulers did not wish to give recognition in any way to Pashtun nationalism. It would take almost five decades before Islamabad would countenance accepting the Pashtun demand to change the nomenclature of their province to Khyber Pakhtunkhwa or Pakhtun homeland. Pakistan was reluctant to even remotely hint at accepting the idea of Pashtun nationalism, which it champions on the other side of the Durand Line.

Ideology: Pashtun Nationalism or Islam?

Pakistan's narrative on Afghanistan has two strands. The Taliban are projected as representing Pashtun nationalism. It sought to appropriate Pashtun nationalism in Afghanistan while suppressing it at home. Since its creation, Pakistan consistently tried to erode the influence of the National Awami Party and its successor, the ANP, by promoting religious parties. The second strand of Pakistan's narrative is ideological. The Taliban aim to establish a pure Islamic state in Afghanistan. This is tinged with a preference for a Wahabi conception of Islam.

There is an inherent contradiction in these two themes. A narrative of Pashtun nationalism is based on a territorial concept of state. An emirate demanded by the Taliban is based on the concept of a Muslim *ummah*, which cannot be confined to a geographical construct. As far as their Pakistani mentors were concerned, these contradictory strands served their purpose. They created an ethnic division in Afghan society, making it easier for Islamabad to play favourites. The Taliban received their ideological orientation from madrassas based in Pakistan. Mullah Omar himself was a product of the Binori mosque in Karachi.

There were other contradictions inherent in Pakistan's narrative. Though Afghanistan has had Pashtun rulers, Pashtuns were merely the largest minority. An International Crisis Group report on 'The Problem of Pashtun Alienation' mentioned:

> While the last census, in 1976, was never completed, estimates used by the United Nations put Pashtuns at 38 per cent of the population, making them the largest single ethnic group. The Dari (Persian)-speaking, Sunni Tajiks are the second largest ethnic group, accounting for roughly 25 per cent of the population. Shia Hazaras in the central highlands account for 19 per cent of the population.[2]

The attempt to impose a homogeneous order was based on the denial of Afghanistan's diversity.

Afghanistan and Pakistan: Contrasting Beginnings

Afghanistan and Pakistan were founded on different principles. Afghanistan was a tribal society, predominantly Muslim, but religion was not the foundational principle of the state. The demand for Pakistan was based on religion.

The Afghan kings in the late nineteenth and early twentieth centuries opposed British imperialism. Muslim League leaders tried to ingratiate themselves with the British rulers. The two developments were nearly coterminous. Sir Syed Ahmad Khan founded the Aligarh Muslim University around the time the Afghan kings were trying to resist the British advance. There were three Anglo-Afghan wars in 1839–42, 1878–80 and 1919. Though Sir Syed Ahmad – like the Afghan rulers – stressed the need for Western education, his political orientation was completely different.

Afghanistan took its first steps towards modernity under the monarchy. The process was slow and halting. The drive for modernization is often associated with Amanullah Khan, whose reforms brought a reaction and overthrow of the monarchy by Habibullah Kalakani, known as Bacha-e Saqao. However, it was initiated much earlier by Habibullah Khan, Amanullah's father. On a state visit to India in 1907, he addressed the students at Aligarh, 'There is, I am told, a violent prejudice among many Indian Muhammedans against that particular kind of education which we call European education. What folly is this! Listen to me, I stand here as the advocate of Western learning.'[3]

Habibullah Khan was not advocating a secular society. He was trying to reconcile tradition with modernity. Habibullah was followed by Amanullah Khan as the ruler of Afghanistan. Amanullah tried to accelerate the pace of reform and invited the hostility of the clergy. He was overthrown by Bacha-e Saqao. The British haste in recognizing Bacha-e Saqao, who represented an extremist philosophy, sealed the fate of the Amanullah regime.

Six decades later, Pakistan would follow the British policy of encouraging religious extremism to suppress Afghan nationalism. While Afghan emirs battled the conservative impulse of Afghan society, the Taliban, aided by their Pakistani mentors, would reinforce it.

Durand Line and the Search for Strategic Depth

Frontiers have waxed and waned depending upon the dictates of geopolitics and the ambitions of states. The Durand Line was the product of the Anglo-Russian rivalry over Afghanistan and Central Asia. The British sought to check the Russian empire's advance as well as Afghan influence in the border regions of their empire. The Afghan King capitulated under British pressure and signed the Durand agreement. According to the book *The Emergence of Modern Afghanistan* by Vartan Gregorian, the famous Armenian-American historian and president of the Carnegie Corporation, 'The Durand Line divided the allegiance of many tribes, without regard to the ethnography of the region.'[4] The line strengthened British control in the border region. 'It gave the British control of the border passes and thus the power to prevent Afghan nomads from entering India or re-entering Afghanistan.'[5]

The British, in drawing up the Durand Line, were marking the limit of their sphere of influence. The line served to check Russian or Afghan claims and safeguard Britain's Indian empire. Farzana Shaikh noted, 'The intention behind the establishment of the Line was not to annex territory or to extend sovereignty,' but as Denis Fitzpatrick, the then Lt Governor of Punjab, stated, 'obviate the need or necessity for effective occupation as a bar to annexation or encroachment by a competing state'.[6]

Though Pakistan claims it inherited the frontiers drawn by the British, it has made a subtle change in policy. Having drawn the Durand Line and signed the Anglo-Russian Convention of 1907, which established Afghanistan as a buffer state, the British were content to consolidate their hold on their Indian colony. Pakistan initially declared the Durand Line as the international boundary. This changed three decades later. An ambitious Zia, sensing Soviet withdrawal from Afghanistan had opened up space for Pakistan's expansion, sought to create a sphere of influence in the name of Islam extending beyond Afghanistan to Central Asia. This policy required fluid borders to allow interference in the neighbouring states.

Pakistani journalist and author Ahmed Rashid cites Sahebzada Yaqub Khan, Pakistan's foreign minister during the 1980s, as saying, 'the military deliberately never asked for Afghan recognition of the Line'.[7] The reason for the Pakistani military's reticence was that a defined border with Afghanistan restricted its reach to extend its influence in Afghanistan and beyond in Central Asia. 'A defined border would have entailed recognizing international law and obligations and the sovereignty of Afghanistan. As long as there was no recognized border there was also no international law to break if Pakistan forces were to support surrogate Afghan regimes such as the Taliban.'[8]

Pakistan sought a pan-Islamic bloc extending to Central Asia. An unintended consequence of maintaining fluid borders was that the TTP has now secured a base in Afghanistan for its attacks on Pakistan. This is probably the reason that Pakistan has built a fence along its border with Afghanistan. There are reports that the fence has been pushed into Afghan territory. It is ironic, though, that Pakistan has been forced to build the fence after installing a government of its choice in Afghanistan.

The policy of seeking strategic depth in Afghanistan makes little military sense. Most of Pakistan's civilian centres lie in the east, near the Indian border. In case of conflict with India, Pakistan's military assets have to be deployed on the border with India, rather than withdrawn into Afghanistan. During the 1965 war it was the Shah's Iran, not Afghanistan, which provided the strategic depth to Pakistan by providing sanctuary to Pakistan Air Force planes.

The policy of seeking strategic depth in Afghanistan may have become redundant with Pakistan acquiring nuclear weapons capacity.

Pakistan needs to either revise its Afghan strategy, or it does not believe in the credibility of its nuclear deterrent. Admittedly, Pakistan lacks the depth to survive a nuclear exchange. But does it mean that it plans to disperse its nuclear assets in Afghanistan's unsettled landscape?

Withdrawal of Great Powers: Pakistan Emerges as Power Broker

Following the Geneva Accords of 1988, Soviet forces withdrew from Afghanistan. The US lost interest in the region with the diminishing of the Soviet threat and the dissolution of the Soviet Union by 1992. Its attention was focused on the Gulf War. Iran hosted more than 2 million Afghan refugees and was an interested party. But it had a weak hand. It was just emerging from the Iran–Iraq war, and its focus was on internal consolidation. Thus, Pakistan emerged as the sole power broker in war-torn Afghanistan. Pakistan used the opportunity to promote Islamist parties based in Peshawar.

The Geneva Accords covered the withdrawal of Soviet troops from Afghanistan, but did not include an agreement on the future government of Afghanistan. While the UN initiated the process of forming a broad-based interim government, Pakistan stepped up pressure to impose a government of its choice by military means. The Najibullah government withstood the Jalalabad offensive supported by the ISI in 1989. However, after the dissolution of the Soviet Union in December 1991 and the cut-off of fuel supply and financial support, Najibullah's position became untenable. American political scientist Barnett Rubin, in his book *The Search for Peace in Afghanistan: From Buffer State to Failed State*, wrote, 'Najibullah offered to hand over power to Zahir Shah or to a neutral force, but not to a fragmented resistance that had not defeated him and that offered no united alternative.'[9]

The UN Secretary-General Perez de Cuellar asked all parties to submit a list of candidates from whom a committee would summon 'a nationwide meeting to decide on an interim government and the holding of elections'.[10] The UN appointed Benon Sevan as a mediator. His offer to Pakistan to take the lead in putting together a list of 'neutral personalities' to whom power could be transferred was in contrast with the UN's approach, which had asked different stakeholders to submit their lists to the UN. Instead of a solution based on a broad consensus emerging from within Afghanistan, Benon Sevan surrendered this role to Pakistan. The Afghan conflict had at least four parties, which included monarchists, Najibullah and the People's Democratic Party (PDP), the Communist party elements, Peshawar-based parties and Iran-based mujahideen groups. Pakistan narrowed the choice down to Peshawar-based parties.

No agreement was reached among the Peshawar-based parties. A month later, Nawaz Sharif convened a second meeting in April. Benon Sevan was invited to wait in a separate room at the prime minister's house. Riaz Mohammad Khan wrote, 'The meeting ended inconclusively and a deeply disappointed Javed Nasir wistfully remarked: "*The only person who proved worthy of his word this evening was a non-Muslim.*"' [Emphasis added][11] The fulsome tribute to Benon Sevan by the then ISI chief is a commentary on the partisan role played by the UN mediator, whose actions eventually cost Najibullah his life. He had pressurized Najibullah to announce his resignation the previous month. The resignation was, of course, to take place 'once the United Nations had established an interim government'. But events in a rugged country that had witnessed more than a decade of war do not always follow the script. In the power vacuum created by the announcement of Najibullah's impending resignation, his own generals deserted him. On 16 April 1992, Najibullah moved to the UN compound, his flight out of the country having been blocked by Abdul Rashid Dostum's men, who controlled the airport.

Rise of the Taliban

The Taliban are sometimes equated with the mujahideen who took part in the Afghan jehad against the Soviet intervention. This view vests them with a degree of legitimacy. This is, however, a misperception. As an organization, the Taliban were created in 1994, six years after the Soviet Union completed its withdrawal from Afghanistan in 1988 and two years after the collapse of the Soviet Union. Their cadres were too young to have fought in the war against the Soviet Union. The Peshawar Accord brokered by Pakistan in 1992 to decide the power-sharing between the eight mujahideen groups did not include the Taliban. Taliban were not included because they did not exist at the time.

The view that seems to credit the rise of the Taliban movement to a series of unrelated events does not give the full picture. It is too simplistic to suggest that the brave students (Taliban) advanced to Kandahar and onwards to Kabul in one grand sweep. They took over Kandahar in November 1994; they entered Kabul in September 1996. Their military advance in a protracted struggle needed considerable logistical support from Pakistan. Their victory was based on mobility and air power which other groups lacked. The Taliban convoys of Toyota pick-up vans needed petrol. This could not have come from Shia Iran, or the northern border, which was still manned by Russian troops. This support came from the Pakistani establishment. As Barnett Rubin writes further: 'Pakistan's policy now replaced cooperation of the ISI, the Jamaat-e-Islami, Hikmatyar, and eastern Pashtuns with an axis based on Babar's Interior Ministry, the JUI, the Taliban, and the southern Pashtuns.'[12]

After Nawaz Sharif was forced out of power, Benazir formed her second government in 1993. Benazir's coalition partner was Jamiat Ulema-e-Islam (Fazal-ur-Rehman). Hekmatyar was backed by the Jamaat-e-Islami, which was Nawaz Sharif's coalition partner. With the change of principals, the agents in the field also had to change. Hekmatyar was replaced by students (Taliban) from madrassas run by the JUI. Hekmatyar had become a liability; he was unacceptable to both the US and the Saudis, two of Pakistan's principal patrons. The move was supported by the military establishment.

The Taliban, having been brought up in Afghan refugee camps in Pakistan, were not part of Afghanistan's tribal society. Mullah Omar, who headed the organization, had preached in the Binori mosque in Karachi for nineteen years. Pakistan supported the Taliban not because they represented Pashtun nationalism, but because they embodied Islamic fundamentalism. It has sought to use religious fundamentalism to suppress Pashtun nationalism on its side of the Durand Line. The Taliban made no attempt at power-sharing, contrary to the UN's call for a broad-based government.

Al-Qaeda

There are two events that bring out the nature of the Taliban regime and its integral relationship with Pakistan. The first was the Taliban's refusal to extradite Al-Qaeda leader Osama bin Laden despite Saudi intervention in 1998. Saudis viewed Al-Qaeda's leadership as a threat to their country; there was also increased pressure to extradite Osama after the attack on the US embassies in Kenya and Tanzania. The Taliban could not have withstood the combined pressure of the US and Saudi Arabia without Pakistan's tacit support. The second was the destruction of the Bamiyan Buddhas in March 2001. On both occasions, Pakistan did not use the enormous leverage it had over the Taliban regime. The Taliban, in turn, remained steadfast in their allegiance to Al-Qaeda.

Prince Turki bin Faisal al Saud, the Saudi intelligence chief at the time, made two visits to Afghanistan in July and September 1998 to meet Mullah Omar to persuade him to either expel bin Laden or hand him over to the Saudis. Omar refused both options. What was the consideration that overrode Pakistan's interest in relations with two of its key benefactors? It had discovered in Afghanistan an ideal place to train mujahideen for jehad in Jammu and Kashmir. Locating the camps in Afghanistan provided Pakistan with deniability. But the relationship went beyond logistics. Maulana Masood Azhar, as well as Khalil ur-Rahman, who were involved in terrorist activities in India, were close disciples of Osama bin Laden.

Following the bombings of the US embassies in Kenya and Tanzania, US President Bill Clinton ordered missile strikes on Osama bin Laden's camp in Afghanistan in August 1998. Pakistan not only did not help Saudi Arabia and America to extradite bin Laden, it leaked the news of the impending American strike to him. American journalist Steve Coll writes, 'Former ISI Chief Hamid Gul later said that he provided the Taliban with advanced warning of the American attack, according to reports that circulated inside the US government.'[13]

Bamiyan Buddhas

On 26 February 2001, the Taliban issued an edict, ordering the destruction of all statues and non-Islamic shrines in Afghanistan. Chief among them were two Buddha statues at Bamiyan, which were part of Afghanistan's heritage.

Afghanistan's official seat at the UN was not held by the Taliban regime, which was not recognized. The Afghan official delegation to the UN stated, 'The main responsibility for the damage and plundering of Afghan cultural property lay with the military junta of Pakistan, which was directly involved in the actual fighting in Afghanistan and was the main source of religious extremism in that part of the world.'[14]

Despite appeals from the international community, the Taliban destroyed the Bamiyan Buddhas.

9/11 and Operation Enduring Freedom

After 9/11, ISI chief Lt General Mahmud Ahmed was asked to go to Kandahar to tell Mullah Omar either to hand over Osama bin Laden or be prepared for an American attack. Khalid Ahmed, a Pakistani commentator, quoted Canadian journalist Kathy Gannon, who was attacked and wounded while reporting from Afghanistan, as saying, 'The General was a religious zealot, very much like Mullah Omar. A hawk with pan-Islamic visions, he had been a staunch supporter of jihadists both from Pakistan and elsewhere.' Gannon further writes that General Ahmed 'took the slow-talking leader aside and urged him to resist the United States. He told Mullah Omar not to give up bin Laden. General Ahmed travelled several times to Kandahar, and on each visit, he gave Mullah Omar information about the likely next move by the United States.'[15]

General Mahmud Ahmed was relieved of his duties by General Musharraf. Having bought his peace with the Americans and the promise of military and economic support, Musharraf proceeded with the MMA deal. A coalition of religious parties in Pakistan, it consisted of the same groups who had supported the Taliban against the American military operation in Afghanistan. Musharraf allowed them to form governments in two provinces bordering Afghanistan – NWFP and Balochistan. This provided the Taliban with a conducive environment to regroup before launching their operations against coalition forces in Afghanistan.

The policy of accommodating jehadi groups only emboldened them. By 2004, the militancy had gained ground in the NWFP and FATA. Soon, the jehadi elements were challenging the writ of the state. The Pakistan Army sought to placate militia groups by signing agreements with them, which gave them more respectability. The high-profile but controversial Shakai Peace Agreement was signed in 2004. This emboldened the religious groups. Riaz Mohammad Khan, the former foreign secretary of Pakistan, wrote, 'More than 200 Maliks were slaughtered in places where the army withdrew after military action.'[16]

A peace agreement in northern Waziristan was signed on 5 September 2006 between the Pakistan government and the militants. The accord was brokered by Maulana Fazlur Rahman of the JUI (F). The government had capitulated. It had agreed to stop ground and air operations, release the militants, demolish the check posts, compensate the militants for their losses and return the weapons to them.[17]

Riaz Mohammad Khan has criticized the accord as conferring legitimacy on the rebel groups, which elevated tribes to the level of 'qaums'. Pakistan had made a separate deal with the militants, while the US was battling them in Afghanistan. This was a repeat of the 1980s, when sanctuaries provided by Pakistan to jehadi groups kept the insurgency alive in Afghanistan. Only this time, instead of Soviet troops, the Americans were on the receiving end.

Pakistan's duplicity had a cost in terms of creating the TTP, which challenged the writ of the state at home. While formally launching TTP, Baitullah Mehsud declared 'an autonomous Emirate of Waziristan' and openly professed alliance with Al-Qaeda and Mullah Omar, whom he regarded as Amir-ul-Momineen (commander of the faithful).[18] He was killed in August 2009 in a drone attack. His statement points out how artificial is the distinction between the 'good' and the 'bad' Taliban maintained by Pakistan, and the Taliban's link with Al-Qaeda.

The killing of Osama bin Laden by US Marines inside Pakistani territory evoked a strong reaction from the Pakistani government. The official statement described it as a violation of Pakistan's sovereignty. The argument side-stepped the question of how the presence of the Al-Qaeda leader, living with his family close to the Pakistan Military Academy, went undetected for so long.

The popular reaction to the killing of Osama was a spontaneous outpouring of grief for the death of the Al-Qaeda leader. This was not simply the reaction of Pakistan's streets. In June 2021, Foreign Minister Shah Mahmood Qureshi evaded answering the question of whether bin Laden was a terrorist or a martyr.[19] This ambivalence reflected the widespread belief among Pakistanis that 'the war on terror is not our war'.

Return of the Taliban to Power

There was a triumphal mood in Pakistan at the Taliban's return to power in Afghanistan in 2021. However, intra-Taliban differences delayed the formation of the new government in Kabul. The issue was resolved only with ISI Chief Lt General Faiz Hameed's visit to Kabul. When the new cabinet was announced on 7 September 2021, the thirty-three-member administration did not include women, minorities and other political groups. Mullah Baradar, who negotiated the Doha agreement with the US, was sidelined as deputy to Mullah Mohammad Hasan Akhund, the new acting prime minister.

Sirajuddin Haqqani, who has an American bounty of up to $10 million on his head and is the scion of the Haqqani network, was appointed acting interior minister.[20] Admiral Mike Mullen, the then chairman of the US Joint Chiefs of Staff Committee, in a testimony to the US Senate Armed Forces Committee, had described the Haqqani network as the 'veritable arm of the ISI' and that Pakistan was 'exporting violence' to Afghanistan.[21] Mohammed Yaqoob, the acting defence minister, is the son of Mullah Omar, the first supreme leader of the Taliban.[22]

The Islamic Emirate of Afghanistan of 2022 appears no different from the regime the Taliban established in their first innings two decades ago. Girls have been barred from secondary education. Attacks on Hazara minorities have started. Afghan rulers a century ago had tried to move the country towards modernity, though they were unsuccessful. The Taliban, supported by Pakistan, reversed the progress the country made since the Bonn conference in 2001.

Pakistan has brilliantly succeeded in achieving its goal of installing a government of its choice in Kabul. Has it achieved the 'strategic depth' the Pakistani generals sought? Would the Taliban oblige Pakistan by recognizing the Durand Line?

Instead, there has been a dramatic deterioration of relations between the two countries. Pakistan has pushed back Afghan refugees into Afghanistan and closed the border. The Taliban regime has refused to hand over TTP elements to Pakistan. There have been armed clashes between the two countries with Pakistan carrying out strikes inside Afghanistan. Pakistan wanted a porous border through which its influence could travel to Kabul and Central Asia. It has now built a fence. Pakistani generals and strategists have handed Pakistan its biggest diplomatic debacle in decades. Instead of achieving strategic depth, they have created a source of instability on their country's western front.

Was the turn of events entirely unexpected? The Taliban are ideologically driven cadres and have refused to sacrifice the TTP, which shares the same philosophy. The TTP aims to establish an Islamic emirate in Pakistan, as the Taliban have done in Afghanistan. Pakistan supported the establishment of an Islamic emirate in Afghanistan but is not willing to concede it at home. What compounds the problem for Islamabad is the ambivalence in Pakistan's strategic community. There are sections within the army and the clergy who share the Taliban ideology. After all, the Taliban came from madrassas in Pakistan.

Pakistani intervention has moved Afghan society towards obscurantism. Under Zahir Shah, Afghanistan was a monarchy. Its 1964 Constitution gave all citizens equal rights. Article 25 of the Constitution said, 'The people of Afghanistan, without any discrimination or preference, have equal rights and obligations before the law.' Article 34 said, 'Education is the right of every Afghan and shall be provided free of charge by the State and the citizens of Afghanistan.'

Najibullah's communist regime accelerated social changes, though its methods were authoritarian. Under the Taliban regime, women are denied education and work opportunities. Shia Hazaras and other minorities are persecuted.

Pakistan supported the Taliban at the expense of its relationship with America. This was an ideological choice, not a security imperative – India did not have a military presence in Afghanistan. The Islamic Emirate of Afghanistan has an appeal inside Pakistan. This is no longer confined to Khyber Pakhtunkhwa, where the Pakistani establishment sought to use religion to suppress Pashtun nationalism. Punjab has become the breeding ground of extremist philosophies. The province accounts for 62 per cent of Pakistan's population. The Tehreek-e-Labbaik Pakistan (TLP) arose in Punjab, the province which brought Imran Khan to power.

Today, Imran Khan is in jail, and General Faiz has been court-martialled. But it will not be easy to turn the clock back. Radicalization has increased in the country, and within the ranks of the army while it continues to advance Pakistan's ideological frontiers.

19

Jammu and Kashmir

'One of our activists, Ali Mohammad Tariq asked Jinnah if the future of Kashmir would be decided by the people of Kashmir. Pat came the reply, "Let the people go to hell". When people learned about this they were quite hurt.'

–Sheikh Abdullah on Jinnah's 1944 visit to Kashmir[1]

JINNAH VISITED KASHMIR IN June 1944 where he met Sheikh Abdullah, leader of the National Conference. Sheikh Abdullah has described an exchange between Jinnah and one of the National Conference workers quoted earlier. As Jinnah's response showed, there is no place for the wishes of the people in Pakistan's matrix.

Jinnah described Kashmir as the jugular vein of Pakistan. This was based on a cold calculation of interests. Pakistan depends upon waters from the Indus, which rises in Tibet and flows into POK from Jammu and Kashmir. It cites this in support of its claim on Kashmir. A similar case can be made for many other geographies divided by politics. This is, however, no argument for trying to change frontiers by force and deception, as Pakistan has done in 1947–48, 1965 and 1999 in Kashmir.

The Kashmir issue is described as an 'unfinished agenda' of Partition. This is a reference to the Two-Nation Theory of statehood based on religion. According to this viewpoint, Kashmir belongs to Pakistan as most of its population is Muslim. Linking the issue to religion adds an element of inflexibility in the conduct of policy. It is possible to compromise on territorial issues. Faith is not negotiable.

The debate on the Simla Agreement in Pakistan's National Assembly in July 1972 produced an interesting exchange. Bizenjo, a member of

NAP, from Balochistan asked, 'Should we go on thinking aimlessly as to what will be the fate of 50 lakh Kashmiri Muslims? There are five crore Muslims in India as well. Do Kashmiri Muslims bear more value than five crores Indian Muslims?'[2]

Bizenjo's comments capture the essence of the Kashmir issue, which Pakistani leaders consciously avoid. The welfare of Muslims in the rest of India needs a plural society. The secession of Kashmir on grounds of religion will undermine this principle. Interestingly, Pakistan had shut its doors to the immigration of Indian Muslims by 1951, with the adoption of the Pakistan Citizenship Act. A state created as a 'homeland' for Indian Muslims refuses to accept those in whose name the country was created. Since then, it has refused to accept 'Bihari' Muslims, despite the commitment given to Bangladesh. Their return to the country of their choice will not bring land. Pakistan's enthusiasm for the Kashmir 'cause' is rooted in the promise of territorial acquisition.

Over time, Pakistan's policymakers have trapped themselves in a dogma of their own making. Kashmir was part of Rahmat Ali's map, but did not form part of the Lahore Resolution. The map, published in 1933, was a student's fancy, but the Lahore Resolution was a formally adopted position of the party. Pakistan has erected what was not even mentioned in the country's foundational document, as the central issue in India–Pakistan relations. Without settling this, the relations cannot be normalized. Jinnah mentioned that relations between Hindus and Muslims are irreconcilable. After Partition, Pakistan carried this narrative into inter-state relations.

Bhutto talked about a thousand-year war between the two countries in his speech at the United Nations in December 1971. A lost war and breaking away of Muslim East Pakistan did not change his perception. He repeated this during his speech on the Simla Agreement in the Pakistan National Assembly in July 1972. Pakistan's policy of sponsoring terrorism in the name of religion has reinforced this strand. Invoking religion to support its claim to Kashmir may have been an ideological justification for a policy decided for other reasons. It has now become a defining feature of Pakistan's policy.

Pakistan raises the Kashmir issue in every international forum. It remains silent on its treatment of the people of POK and the Northern Areas, since renamed Gilgit-Baltistan. Kashmir is not simply a foreign policy issue. To understand Pakistan's Kashmir policy, one must also take into account its actions within POK and Gilgit-Baltistan. Do the people of the territory have azadi (freedom) to decide their fate? Do the governing structures that Pakistan has created in the territories reflect the wishes of the people? Are the Muslims of POK treated on par with the Muslims of Pakistan?

Pakistan's ideology is shaped as much by the religious groups that provide cadres to wage jehad in Kashmir as the calculations of the military. This is based on a narrow creed. It does not respect the notions of equality and respect for diversity, which are the cornerstones of the modern concept of human rights. The plethora of terror outfits – Harkat ul-Ansar, Hizbul Mujahideen, Al-Badr, Jaish-e-Mohammed and Lashkar-e-Taiba – have Arabic names. The Arabic nomenclature chosen by these groups betrays their foreign inspiration and origins. Arabic is not the language spoken by the people of Jammu and Kashmir. A 'freedom struggle' depends for its success upon identification with the local people. These groups use a different idiom. In their view, Kashmiris are part of Pakistan, not by choice, but by faith.

Invasion (1947–48)

Col. Akbar Khan led the 'tribal' invasion of Jammu and Kashmir in 1947. He has described that the invasion was approved in a meeting chaired by Prime Minister Liaquat Ali Khan.[3] Muhammad Yusuf Saraf, a Muslim Conference activist, has mentioned that 'no Kashmiri-speaking leader or worker was taken into confidence', even though senior Muslim Conference leaders were present in Lahore. Even Sardar Ibrahim Khan, who was to later become the first president of POK, was not invited to the prime minister's meeting.[4]

Akbar Khan justified the invasion in terms of territorial and economic gains for Pakistan, instead of the aspirations of the Kashmiri people. He said Pakistan's military security would be seriously jeopardized if Indian troops came to be stationed along Kashmir's western border. He added, 'Our agricultural economy was particularly dependent upon the rivers coming out of Kashmir. The Mangla Headworks were actually in Kashmir.'[5]

Even Saraf, a Kashmiri himself, who eventually became Chief Justice of the POK Supreme Judicial Council has justified the invasion in terms of Pakistan's territorial and strategic interests rather than Kashmiri aspirations. He said 'the foremost gain' was the capture of '4,144 square miles of territory, now known as Azad Kashmir'. 'Yet another positive gain' was the capture of '29,814 square miles in the strategically vital Northern regions that have linked it directly with the People's Republic of China and thus enabled it to influence the geopolitical course of history in Asia'.[6] This was a very perceptive comment. Without Pakistan's control of Northern Areas, now called Gilgit-Baltistan, there would have been no CPEC.

United Nations Dynamics

The United Nations Commission for India and Pakistan (UNCIP) resolution of August 1948 had asked Pakistan to withdraw 'all' the forces under its control from the territory occupied by it, while India was asked to withdraw only the 'bulk' of its forces. The difference in obligations of the two countries was a recognition that India had a de jure position on Jammu and Kashmir; Pakistan had none.

Pakistan's refusal to withdraw from the territory illegally occupied by it was indeed a violation of the UNCIP resolution of 1948. This is the reason why Pakistani diplomats are very reticent about mentioning it. Ironically, the POK Constitution mentions the resolution. It states that Pakistan's control of foreign policy, defence and currency of the territory is part of its responsibility under the UNCIP resolution. This is a complete travesty of truth. The resolution which asked Pakistan to withdraw all of its forces cannot be cited as the basis for extending Pakistan's occupation of the territory indefinitely.

Pakistan and its apologists base the country's continued occupation of the territory on a reference to 'local authority' in the text of the UNCIP resolution. Read in context, this interpretation is completely illogical. Not only Pakistan was asked to withdraw 'all' forces under its control, but the resolution specifically mentioned that the 'local authority' was to function under the UN's surveillance, rather than Pakistani control, as that country claims.

Withdrawal of 'all' forces under Pakistan's control was to be followed by a plebiscite. Pakistan's refusal to withdraw frustrated that objective. This sequence is not only a matter of interpretation. It was part of the 'Principles of Plebiscite' prepared by the UNCIP and accepted by both countries. India accepted it on 23 December 1948; Pakistan accepted it on 25 December 1948.

Since then, Pakistani diplomats have moved the goalpost. Instead of the UNCIP resolution of August 1948, they mention United Nations Security Council (UNSC) resolution 98 of 1952. India did not accept the latter. Being a Chapter VI resolution, its application requires the consent of the parties. Its chief attraction for Pakistan is that it dropped the demand for the withdrawal of 'all' the forces under Pakistan's control. Interestingly, it also omitted the demand for a plebiscite from the operative part of the resolution. This probably is an added reason why it has become popular with Pakistan in retrospect. Pakistan has shied away from plebiscite whenever a formal proposal was made, as the following section brings out.

Plebiscite

If Kashmir is central to Pakistan's foreign policy, the plebiscite is central to Pakistan's narrative on Kashmir. Contrary to its official stance, Pakistan carefully avoided holding a plebiscite and turned down specific proposals to do so on at least three different occasions. A plebiscite under the UN's auspices was suggested by Mountbatten to Jinnah in his meeting on 2 November 1947. Jinnah did not accept the offer.

The second time Pakistan rejected the plebiscite was in 1950, when the UN mediator Owen Dixon suggested it. Owen Dixon mentioned that a single plebiscite in the entire state would leave pockets of minorities on either side of the divide, leading to mass migration. He, therefore, suggested regional plebiscites and narrowed the scope to the Kashmir Valley. He wrote in his report to the UN that India was willing to consider it, but Pakistan rejected it on the grounds that this was a departure from the principle of a single plebiscite. He added that Pakistan, however, was willing to accept a partition of the state, provided it got the Valley. Thus, Pakistan was willing to make a departure from the principle of a single plebiscite as long as it got the Valley without a vote. Pakistan's insistence on a 'single plebiscite' was only a pretext.

The third time Pakistan rejected the plebiscite was in 1953. This was the most significant occasion when Pakistan shied away from the plebiscite. Sheikh Abdullah was arrested in 1953. Pakistan, sensing an opportunity, immediately proposed bilateral talks. Pakistani Prime Minister Mohammad Ali Bogra came to Delhi. A joint communiqué was issued after the Nehru–Bogra talks, committing both countries to a plebiscite. Bogra went back to Pakistan and wrote a letter to Nehru on 1 December 1953, going back on the offer of plebiscite. The reason cited was the same as in 1950 – a regional plebiscite was different from the principle of a single plebiscite. We have seen earlier that this was only an excuse. Pakistan was willing to abandon the single plebiscite in 1950 provided it got the Valley without a vote.

Why was Pakistan averse to risking plebiscite, which was its stated position? The answer lies in the internal situation in POK. Pakistan dismissed Sardar Ibrahim, the POK president, in April 1950, a month before Owen Dixon arrived in the subcontinent in May. This was the beginning of the Sudhan revolt, which lasted till the late 1950s. The Pakistan Army launched a military operation to quell the revolt. The Muslim Conference submitted a Memorandum to the Pakistan Constituent Assembly in 1955, complaining of en masse torture, detention and rape.[7] The disturbed situation on the ground explains Pakistan's reluctance to agree to the plebiscite. It was unsure of winning the vote even on its side of the ceasefire line. The issue is discussed in more detail in my book *Forgotten Kashmir: The Other Side of the Line of Control.*

Accession to Pakistan

Though Pakistan has maintained the fiction of POK's distinct status as a separate territory, 'Azad Kashmir' (Free Kashmir), the only option allowed under Pakistan's Constitution, is POK's accession to it. Article 203 of Pakistan's first Constitution, adopted in 1956, mentioned, 'When the people of the State of Jammu and Kashmir decide to accede to Pakistan, the relationship between Pakistan and the said State shall be determined in accordance with the wishes of the people of that State.'[8]

The article makes a priori assumption that the people of the state of Jammu and Kashmir will decide to accede to Pakistan. The Pakistani Constitution does not allow them any other option, making a mockery of the plebiscite. Once they have acceded, determining their wishes would be irrelevant! Interestingly, this choice was made by the Pakistan Constituent Assembly in which the people of POK had no representation! India followed the democratic method, where the Constituent Assembly of the state of Jammu and Kashmir in 1957 made the decision. Given the context of the Cold War, India's choice was criticized by the UNSC, which adopted a resolution against India. Pakistan's blatant action taken a year before went unnoticed by the international community.

Since the adoption of Pakistan's first Constitution in 1956, this clause has been retained. The third and current Constitution included it as Article 257. There have been twenty-six amendments to Pakistan's Constitution since 1973, but this article has remained unchanged. This shows the continuity in Pakistan's Kashmir policy. It pays lip service to the idea of plebiscite but closed this option way back in the 1950s.

Northern Areas or Gilgit-Baltistan

The Northern Areas account for 85 per cent of the territory of POK. It has tremendous strategic importance as it borders Afghanistan and China. Without waiting for the plebiscite, Pakistan took over administrative control of this area. It has since been renamed Gilgit-Baltistan to erase historical links of this region with Jammu and Kashmir and disguise its steady integration in Pakistan contrary to Pakistan's stated position of respecting the UNSC resolutions.

The Pakistani version of history keeps changing. According to the current narrative, this change in the status of the territory was made under the Karachi Agreement of 1949. Pakistan took this over in 1947 itself. British Major William A. Brown, who staged a coup against Maharaja Hari Singh's administration in Gilgit on 1 November 1947, recorded in his memoir that he handed over the territory to Pakistan's political agent Mohammad Alam on 17 November 1947. Why wasn't the territory, which was part of Jammu and Kashmir, handed over to the provisional government, which had been declared three weeks earlier on 24 October? Instead, it was placed under Pakistan's agent. In effect, Pakistan took over administrative control of the Northern Areas in November 1947, much before the Karachi Agreement of 1949.

The so-called Karachi Agreement of 1949 was signed by Nawab Mushtaq Ahmed Gurmani, Minister for Kashmir Affairs, on Pakistan's behalf, while Sardar Ibrahim and Chaudhry Ghulam Abbas signed it on behalf of POK. The former was the POK president, and the latter was the Muslim Conference chairman. The agreement was kept secret because Pakistan had changed the territorial status quo without plebiscite. It came to light in a judgement of the POK High Court in 1993. The plaint was filed jointly by all the political parties of the territory, including the Muslim Conference, who wanted the Northern Areas to be restored to POK. The High Court described the separation of the Northern Areas as a *violation of the UNSC resolution* and asked for the territory to be returned to POK. The judgement was deeply embarrassing to Islamabad, which went to appeal to the POK Supreme Court. The Supreme Court reversed the High Court's judgement on the purely procedural issue of jurisdiction.

Pakistan's actions showed that neither the 'wishes of the people' of Kashmir nor ideology mattered when Pakistan's core interests are involved. In his later years, Sardar Ibrahim, who was supposed to have ceded the Northern Areas to Pakistan, denied ever having signed the Karachi Agreement. According to political science scholar Dr Javaid Hayat, 'However, Sardar Ibrahim in various public meetings rejected that he ever signed an agreement known as the Karachi Agreement.'[9] This casts doubt over the authenticity of the so-called Karachi Agreement.

1965 War and Tashkent Declaration

Pakistan launched Operation Gibraltar in 1965 on the assumption that the people of Jammu and Kashmir would rise up in support of the infiltrators. This did not happen. When India decided to open a second front by crossing the international border to attack Lahore, Ayub and Bhutto made a secret visit to Beijing to enlist Chinese support. They met the Chinese premier, Chou Enlai, who advised Ayub to prepare to wage a long-drawn war with India, even if it meant losing some major towns. Ayub was not prepared to lose Lahore.[10] Pragmatism had triumphed over ideology.

Neither the UNSC resolution 211, adopted after the 1965 war, nor the Tashkent Declaration mentioned previous Security Council resolutions or the 'Kashmiris' right of self-determination'. Both documents were accepted by Pakistan.

1971 War and the Simla Agreement

The emergence of Bangladesh in 1971 demonstrated the futility of the Two-Nation Theory, which defined the ideology of Pakistan. A common religion was not sufficient glue to bind the two wings. Bhutto, who had played a major role in the break-up of Pakistan by blocking the transfer of power to Mujibur Rahman's Awami League, instead chose to blame India. In his speech at the UN, he talked of a thousand-year war.

He repeated this rhetoric during the debate on the Simla Agreement in the Pakistan National Assembly. He labelled the opposition leaders who challenged his vision of the thousand-year war as 'defeated people'. He stated, 'I can look down the vista of years and see the vision of victory after a 1000 years and not at the defeat of today as they do.' Bhutto's conclusion was, 'Thus the validity of the concept of confrontation is not lost by the defeat of Pakistan.'[11] He had decided to keep the Kashmir issue alive despite having signed the Simla Agreement. Pakistan's interest lay in a cooperative relationship with India in order to focus on rebuilding the country. But, Bhutto was not willing to give up the ideology of 'confrontation'.

POK's 'Interim Constitution Act, 1974'

Bhutto had a free hand to shape Pakistan's Kashmir policy in the immediate aftermath of the 1971 war. Pakistan's defeat curtailed the role of the military in decision-making. Bhutto's PPP was the largest political party in what was left of Pakistan. During his term, POK got its first Constitution in 1974. However, it was termed as an 'interim' Constitution. Did this denote that the final status of the territory was yet to be settled in a plebiscite? Pakistan had taken over direct control of the Northern Areas in 1947, and ceded part of POK to China in 1963, without waiting for the plebiscite.

There is nothing 'interim' about Pakistan's control over POK. Pakistan has exercised absolute power over the territory and its people. Article 31 of the POK's Constitution vested all the legislative and executive powers in the council headed by Pakistan's prime minister, rather than the elected assembly. This essentially meant rule by proxy. The Constitution plays down the Kashmiri identity while defining 'Who is a Muslim'. The definition of

Muslim in the Constitution only served to make Ahmadiyas non-Muslims in POK. Pakistan offered the people of POK ideology instead of azadi.

Self-Determination

Pakistan uses the slogan of self-determination. Does it allow it in POK? Article 4(7)(ii) in POK's Constitution forbids questioning the 'ideology of accession to Pakistan'. This makes the outcome of any plebiscite predetermined in favour of accession to Pakistan. Political parties which do not accept this condition are not allowed to participate in elections.

The then Prime Minister Benazir Bhutto, in an interview with the *New York Times* on 15 May 1994, responded to a question about the 'independence' option stating:

> The Hindus are going to vote for accession to India because they are the minority. If you are talking about the Muslim majority deciding between accession to Pakistan or an independent Kashmir, the Muslim vote could get fractured and we could find ourselves with the status quo, where the Hindu minority accepts Indian rule and the Muslim majority does not accept it.[12]

The answer was limited to the Indian state of Jammu and Kashmir, since that is the only area where there are Hindus. She had carefully avoided answering the question so far as POK and the Northern Areas are concerned. Even within this limited parameter, her answer is interesting. An outcome in Pakistan's favour would lead to a change in the territorial status quo as the entire state would become part of Pakistan. Instead, she said, if 'independence' was an option, the vote would result in a 'status quo'. This was a tacit admission that in such a case, Pakistan would lose the vote in a referendum. Pakistan used the Jammu and Kashmir Liberation Front (JKLF), a pro-independence party, to sponsor terrorism in J&K in the name of Islam. It has not been allowed to take part in elections in POK.

Kargil War

A lost war always leads to a blame game. The Kargil War has evoked considerable debate in Pakistan. The infiltration across the LOC began immediately after the Lahore Summit; preparations had begun earlier. The war wrecked the peace process. Nasim Zehra has given a detailed account of the drama in her book *From Kargil to Coup: The Events That Shook Pakistan*. She says that the decision to launch Operation Koh Paima – as the Kargil adventure was code-named, was made by Musharraf along with a small clique of three generals. Prime Minister Nawaz Sharif received the first briefing on 29 January, but Musharraf did not mention that Pakistani troops had crossed the LOC. This was before Prime Minister Vajpayee's Lahore visit, which took place three weeks later.

By May, India's retaliation had begun, and the matter could not be kept under wraps. Nawaz Sharif received a fuller briefing on 17 May. Nasim Zehra writes that 'the masterminds of Kargil were not seeking permission for the operation they had already launched. The prime minister was being presented with a fait accompli.'[13] The Foreign Minister Sartaj Aziz asked Prime Minister Sharif whether the army's operation 'was not contrary to the undertaking in the Lahore Declaration? Nawaz Sharif's response was "Sartaj Aziz Sahib, can we ever take Kashmir through paperwork? We have an opportunity to take Kashmir".'[14]

It appears from Zehra's account that Nawaz Sharif had still not grasped that the army had crossed the LOC. When this was pointed out to him by the Defence Secretary Lt General Iftikhar Ali Khan, he called a cabinet meeting the next day where the army chief was also invited. Musharraf confirmed that the army had crossed the LOC and took responsibility for the decision. Sharif said, 'Since the army is part of the government, from today onwards we will support the army.'[15]

Like in the past, jehad was used to mobilize the country in 1999 also. The Minister for Religious Affairs, Raja Zafar-ul-Haq said, 'The time is now ripe for jihad.'[16] There was a major difference this time around, though. The drama was now being played out against the background of a nuclearized South Asia after the nuclear tests of the previous year.

Interestingly, just as the Kargil War was beginning to emerge in the public domain in May 1999, Pakistan's Supreme Court gave a judgement, in which it asked the Pakistan government 'to ensure that the people of Northern Areas enjoy their above fundamental rights, namely, to be governed through their chosen representatives and to have access to justice through an independent judiciary inter alia for enforcement of their Fundamental Rights guaranteed under the Constitution'.[17]

The implication was clear – that there was neither democracy nor human rights in the territory under Pakistan's occupation. This was ironic when Pakistan was trying to 'liberate' Jammu and Kashmir on the Indian side of the LOC. The contradiction went unnoticed by India or the international community at the time. The Pakistan Supreme Court's judgement had the result of extending its jurisdiction over a territory that is *not* part of Pakistan under its Constitution. Gilgit-Baltistan has been integrated into Pakistan though the latter claims that the territory has a distinct status in keeping with UN resolutions.

Despite the Supreme Court's orders, it took the Pakistan government a decade to make some cosmetic changes. Pakistan promulgated the Gilgit-Baltistan Order in 2009. The nomenclature of the territory was changed from Northern Areas to Gilgit-Baltistan. An elected assembly was created, but with rather limited powers.

Elections

The irregularities in the 1987 elections in Jammu and Kashmir are blamed for the upsurge of terrorist violence on the Indian side of the LOC. Pakistan-occupied Kashmir did not have elections for the first twenty-three years of its existence. The first election, based on adult franchise, was held in the territory only in 1970. The elections held under the 'Interim Constitution' in 1975 saw the POK chapter (PPP-AK) of the ruling party in Islamabad (PPP) winning the majority. The massively rigged elections came to be known as the 'Tammani elections', after the name of Bhutto's adviser who 'managed' the elections. The term was coined by Bhutto himself.[18]

During the Zia period, there were no elections in 'Azad Jammu and Kashmir' for eight years. The elections of 1985 were held on a party-less basis. This was no different from the situation in Pakistan. If so, the pattern exposes the myth that was 'Azad'; it only follows Pakistan's lead. The JKLF, the pro-independence party founded by Amanullah Khan, was not allowed to participate in 1985 or any of the subsequent elections held in the territory. Ironically, the organization was used by Pakistan to launch the terror campaign in Jammu and Kashmir under the slogan of 'Azadi'.

The defining characteristic of elections in POK is that they bring to power the ruling party in Islamabad. A block of twenty out of fifty-three seats – almost 40 per cent of the total – are reserved. The reserved seats include twelve refugee seats scattered all over Pakistan. These are essentially in the gift of the federal government and the provincial government concerned. This has resulted in a situation where the Karachi-based MQM secured two seats in the POK assembly. This also gives leverage to Islamabad to bring the party of its choice to power in POK.

The regional parties have been completely eclipsed. The contest is between the mainstream parties of Pakistan: PTI, PPP and PML(N). In the last elections in 2021, the Muslim Conference won only one seat in the house of fifty-three. This is in contrast with the situation on the Indian side of the LOC, where the National Conference Party (NCP) and the Peoples Democratic Party (PDP) play a major role in voicing aspirations of the people of Jammu and Kashmir.

The elections in 2021 were held when Imran Khan was prime minister of Pakistan. PTI's tally in the POK assembly went up from two in the previous election to twenty-five seats. PPP got eleven seats while the PML(N) finished with a mere six seats. Imran Khan's ouster in 2022 saw a quick change of guard. The incumbent 'prime minister' of POK, Abdul Qayyum Khan Niazi, who was personally selected by Imran Khan, was ousted through a no-confidence motion and replaced by Sardar Tanveer Ilyas. A no-confidence motion is a normal procedure in democracy, except in this case, it was moved not by the opposition, but by ruling party members. The opposition members boycotted the proceedings. Niazi lost the vote even though his party had an absolute majority. More recently, Tanveer Ilyas has been replaced by Chaudhary Anwar-ul-Haq of the same party – PTI. The changes do not reflect party strength in the house, but the wishes of the oldest party in Pakistan – the army.

Similarly, Imran loyalist Khalid Khurshid has been replaced by Gulbar Khan as chief minister of the Gilgit-Baltistan assembly, even though there is no change in the party position.

Different Trajectories

Though Pakistan has tried to reinvent POK (including Gilgit-Baltistan) in its image in ideological terms, the two have followed different trajectories in terms of political space given to the peoples of POK and Pakistan. Pakistan, under the Zardari government, adopted the Eighteenth Amendment to the Constitution in 2010, which devolved more powers to the provinces. Eight years later, under the Thirteenth Amendment of the POK Constitution in 2018, POK was subjected to greater control by Islamabad. The Gilgit-Baltistan Order of 2018 subjected that region to the same fate. Why do Muslims of POK have less freedom than Muslims of Pakistan?

Earlier, the council headed by Pakistan's prime minister wielded all powers. This was criticized as rule by proxy. In 2018, under the Thirteenth Amendment to the POK Constitution, Pakistan relegated the council to an advisory role. But instead of transferring its powers to the elected assembly, Pakistan has now assumed them directly. It exercises legislative and executive powers over thirty-two subjects in POK.[19] This includes strategic highways, water and electricity, as well as taxation. The POK assembly has been allowed legislative authority on twenty-two subjects. But even this is to be exercised 'with the consent of the government of Pakistan'.[20] This constitutional scheme suggests that POK has been fully integrated into Pakistan, and indeed, has less political space than what has been given to Pakistan's provinces.

Gilgit-Baltistan has been subjected to worse treatment. The Gilgit-Baltistan Order of 2009 conferred limited legislative powers on the elected assembly in respect of sixty-one subjects. The Gilgit-Baltistan Order of 2018 has abolished the entire list. All the legislative and executive powers in the territory are vested in the prime minister of Pakistan. There were widespread protests in the territory against the Gilgit-Baltistan order of 2018. The Supreme Judicial Council of the territory set it aside. The Pakistan government appealed to the Pakistan Supreme Court. The Supreme Court sided with the government in Islamabad and restored the Gilgit-Baltistan Order of 2018.

As mentioned earlier, Pakistan's Supreme Court, in its judgement of 1999, had asked Islamabad to ensure that the people of Gilgit-Baltistan enjoy fundamental rights and representational government. Two decades later, the Supreme Court noted in its judgement of 2019 that the previous judgement had remained unimplemented. But instead of remedying the situation, Justice Saqib Nisar's ruling made the problem worse by strengthening Pakistan's control of the territory. He limited his order to restoring the Gilgit-Baltistan Order of 2018. The operative part of Justice Nisar's judgement was silent on the issue of fundamental rights of the people of the territory, which was cynically invoked to establish the court's jurisdiction and then forgotten. The two judgements two decades apart have managed to integrate Gilgit-Baltistan, even though it does not form part of Pakistan's territory under its Constitution.

POK and Gilgit-Baltistan are effectively integrated into Pakistan after the Thirteenth Amendment to the POK Constitution and the Gilgit-Baltistan Order of 2018. Both changes were made a year before the deletion of Article 370 by India in 2019. India was criticised; Pakistan's actions went unnoticed.

Water, Hydropower Royalty, Connectivity and CPEC

Water and connectivity are the two natural resources of the region. Pakistan draws most of its water from three rivers flowing through POK and Gilgit-Baltistan. This was the result of the Indus Waters Treaty of 1960, which allotted waters of the three western rivers (Jhelum, Chenab and Indus) to Pakistan, while India received waters of the three eastern rivers (Ravi, Beas and Satlaj). India was generous. The treaty gave Pakistan – a lower riparian – 80 per cent of the water despite being one-seventh its size in terms of population. POK, however, has not received the benefit of this bounty. The water usage charge at 15 paise per unit given to POK is one-seventh the rate of Rs 1.10 per unit paid as royalty for hydroelectricity to Punjab and Khyber Pakhtunkhwa. This discriminatory arrangement is justified on the grounds that under Article 161 of Pakistan's Constitution, hydropower royalty or Net Hydel Profit is payable to Pakistan's provinces, while POK does not fall in this category. This is curious logic. Its distinct status did not come in the way of exploiting its resources. This became an issue only when it came to Pakistan making the payment. Even this paltry payment was denied to the territory for the first thirty-six years after the completion of the Mangla dam.

The issues of hydropower royalty and connectivity are important in the context of Chinese investment in the region under the China–Pakistan Economic Corridor (CPEC). POK alone will receive $5.946

billion investment under CPEC. In Gilgit-Baltistan, there are to be infrastructure projects worth $2.129 billion. In addition, there will be a $12 billion investment in the 4,500-MW Diamer-Bhasha dam in the territory.[21] There are a series of five dams to be constructed in Gilgit-Baltistan under the Indus Cascade scheme. An agreement has already been signed for the Diamer-Bhasha dam. This will lead to the inundation of large tracts of land, displacement of the population and damage to the fragile ecology. This may, however, not bring any benefit to Gilgit-Baltistan as Pakistan does not pay it hydropower royalty.

Gilgit-Baltistan is the artery of the CPEC. However, under the Gilgit-Baltistan Order of 2018, control of strategic highways, water and power is vested in Pakistan. Pakistan also controls all the taxation powers. There is a parallel arrangement under the Thirteenth Amendment for POK. This has kept the regions deprived of any benefit from their natural resources, and dependent upon Islamabad for budgetary support.

With the worsening economic situation, in 2023, the people of POK started a protest movement against Pakistan. They are complaining about the shortage of essentials, such as *atta* (flour), and the high electricity tariff. In May 2024, POK witnessed violent clashes in which a police officer was killed and ninety people were injured. The Pakistan government has announced some temporary measures. This includes a subsidy of Rs23 billion.[22] This amounts to a mere $82.43 million (one US dollar equals 279.49 Pakistani rupees). Is this a subsidy? Out of the tax raised in POK and Gilgit-Baltistan, Pakistan retains 20 per cent, while the remaining 80 per cent is given to the territories as a grant by Islamabad. Thus, so-called 'federal' grants do not flow from Pakistan's resources. Islamabad appropriates one-fifth of tax revenue generated from the territories.

Pakistan also announced a partial rollback of the electricity tariff. The revised rate ranges from Rs 3 to Rs 6 per unit.[23] It may be recalled that Pakistan pays POK merely Rs 0.15 paise per unit as 'water use' charges while no hydropower royalty is given to the people of the territory. Thus, even after the downward revision of rates, the electricity generated from the Mangla dam in POK is sold to the POK consumer at twenty to forty times higher prices. Curiously, this is described as the 'export' of electricity from Pakistan to POK, while the dam is in POK where the Indus flows into from Jammu and Kashmir.

Pakistan's Kashmir policy is driven by a combination of interests, ideology and strategy. Staking its claim to Kashmir in terms of religion has made it difficult for Pakistan's leaders to change course even when the country's national interests dictate political accommodation with India. The country is facing an unprecedented economic crisis that requires trimming its defence budget. The blowback of a policy of supporting various extremist groups to carry on jehad in Kashmir has undermined the civil society in that country. The rise of a praetorian state has also undermined democracy in Pakistan. The wishes of the people of POK do not matter. Jinnah's Pakistan has faithfully followed his precept cited at the beginning of the chapter, 'Let the people go to hell.'

20

Terrorism

'ISI embodies the scourge of radicalism that has become a cornerstone of Pakistan's foreign policy.'

–Mansoor Ijaz, a Pakistani-American commentator[1]

In the wake of 9/11, President Musharraf, in a nationally televised address, explained the reasons for Pakistan joining the US-led coalition against terrorism. This was an abrupt turn in the country's policy of creating and supporting the Taliban. Musharraf touched upon Pakistan's interests, but the speech was couched in a religious idiom. He had a difficult task at hand. This was not simply a change in foreign policy alignment. To people who had grown up on the rhetoric of jehad, the change would have appeared a fundamental shift in the ideology the country's civil and military rulers had promoted.

Musharraf was advocating that Pakistan join America to fight against the Islamic emirate that Mullah Omar had proclaimed in Afghanistan. Omar was a product of the Binori mosque in Karachi. The general himself had shaped the military's strategy of using Islamic groups to advance Pakistan's interests in Jammu and Kashmir and Afghanistan. He had to explain the momentous change in terms that would be understood by different constituencies – religious groups as well as the army, which had appointed itself as custodian of Pakistan's ideological frontiers. Musharraf listed Pakistan's material interests in the safety of the country, its prestige, the safety of its nuclear and missile assets. He added, 'In deciding, we must make sure that we are supporting the right cause and it should be according to Islamic tenets. And whatever we do – whatever we are doing is according to the tenets of Islam.'[2]

Musharraf cited the instance where Prophet Muhammad 'entered a friendship treaty with his enemies, the Jews, in Medina'. He added, 'because of the peace treaty with Jews, he was able to fight the infidels of Mecca.' Later, the Muslims fought and defeated the Jews. 'This was possible because there had been a pact with the infidels of Mecca – of a no-war (ph) pact – that Muslims won.' 'If you are facing two problems and you have to choose one, then it is better to take the lesser evil,' he said.[3] As Musharraf described it, in joining the war against terrorism, he had made a tactical choice. The war on terror was the 'lesser evil'.

Two decades later, when the Taliban returned to power in Kabul in 2021, this was celebrated across the political spectrum in Pakistan. Pakistan's alliance with the US proved temporary despite the six decades of military and economic assistance it received from that country. What proved enduring was its relationship with the Taliban. The war against terror was never popular in Pakistan. The common refrain was that it was not 'our' war.

Musharraf went out of power in 2008. The return of a civilian government headed by the PPP did not bring an end to terrorist activities. The 26 November 2008 attacks on Mumbai, commonly known as 26/11, showed that the terrorists' aims were not limited to Jammu and Kashmir. There was no ongoing 'freedom struggle' in Mumbai – the argument often used by Pakistan to justify terrorism in Jammu and Kashmir. Nor was this part of 'disputed territory', even going by Pakistani accounts.

Terrorism has emerged as a global phenomenon. While in other regions this is associated with non-state actors, in the case of Pakistan, it has been part of the state's policy. It is integrated into the Pakistan Army's war-fighting doctrine as asymmetrical warfare. Though Pakistan tries to confuse the issue by calling terrorists freedom fighters, there is a fundamental difference between the two. The success of a national liberation struggle depends upon the support of the people. Terror campaigns by Pakistan-supported groups in Jammu and Kashmir, and Afghanistan, were aimed as much against the civilian population as state forces.

Promoting a Salafist Islam – puritan version of Sunni Islam, brought a reaction and led to the rise of Shia militant groups. The military itself could not remain immune to broader trends in Pakistani society.

There has been radicalization within the army's ranks. The attacks on Musharraf's life involved military personnel.

Jehad in Afghanistan and Kashmir needed a cadre of men who could fight for Pakistan's expansionist aims in neighbouring countries. The army promoted transnational Islam with its stress on Salafist teachings. This helped obtain Arab money and fighters. The patronage given to the Deobandi school, which favours a puritanical conception of Islam, gave a new definition to the ideology of Pakistan. This increasingly influenced the Pakistani state and society.

Madrassas

In this process of mobilizing cadres for jehad in Afghanistan and Kashmir, madrassas have played a key role. Riaz Mohammad Khan, Pakistan's former foreign secretary, cited an article by Ikram Sehgal which mentions that Pakistan has 10,000 madrassas, according to the Ministry of Religious Affairs. The ministry, in fact, places its estimate at about 16,000, considering madrassas not registered with it. The number of madrassa students is roughly 2 million, 3 per cent of all students in schools in Pakistan. Ikram Sehgal also suggested that '18 per cent of madrassas, almost all unregistered, have a "jehadist trend"'.[4]

Riaz Mohammad Khan adds: 'The curricula of almost all madrassas are strictly limited to religious teaching and in some way are more orthodox and rudimentary than the standard introduced at Deoband more than a century ago or than the Dars e Nizami conceived in the late eighteenth century and followed by many non-Deobandi Sunni madrassas.'[5]

President Musharraf, under international pressure, announced madrassa reform in 2002. This included registration, not the banning of madrassas; this legitimized the madrassas.

Jammu and Kashmir

While the world's attention has remained focused on Pakistan's actions in Afghanistan, India was the first to suffer terrorism emanating from that country. Pakistani leaders gave a call for jehad to mobilize support for the 'tribal invasion' in 1947. Pakistan launched Operation Gibraltar in 1965. Regular units of the Pakistan Army were infiltrated in Jammu and Kashmir disguised as mujahideen. The army formations were named after Islamic heroes from battles in distant lands. These have no historical connection with the Indian subcontinent and betray an ideological orientation.

In January 1971, 'Ganga', an Indian Airlines plane was hijacked on its way to Lahore. Bhutto met the hijackers and gave them 'shabashi' (praise).[6] Under the Simla Agreement, Pakistan agreed to respect the LOC and desist from hostile propaganda. Bhutto, however, did not close the option of interfering in Jammu and Kashmir in the future. Speaking in the debate on the Simla Agreement in the Pakistan National Assembly, he said, 'I tell you, Sir, on the floor of this House, with the solemn commitment of the people of Pakistan, that if tomorrow the people of Kashmir start a freedom movement, if tomorrow Sheikh Abdullah or Maulvi Farooq or others start, a people's movement, we will be with them.'[7]

Bhutto's daughter, Benazir, openly gave a call for 'intifada' (uprising) in Kashmir in the late 1980s. This was a call for violence by the JKLF in the name of azadi. While the JKLF was used as the vanguard to initiate a campaign of terror, it was soon marginalized and replaced by hardcore elements. An important terror group active in the Kashmir Valley was Hizbul Mujahideen. Its leader, Syed Salahuddin, headed an umbrella organization of various jehadi groups active in Jammu and Kashmir called the Kashmir Jehad – United Jehad Council, based in the POK capital of Muzaffarabad. In their book *Deception: Pakistan, the United States and the Global Nuclear Weapons Conspiracy*, Adrian Levy and Catherine Scott-Clark wrote, 'Through Musharraf's patronage, LeT (Lashkar-e-Tayyaba) would become the largest Jihadi organization in Pakistan.'[8]

The terror campaign in Jammu and Kashmir targeted Kashmiri Pandits. There was a concerted attempt to change the plural character of the state, which had a 30 per cent minority consisting of Hindus, Sikhs and Buddhists. The terrorists also targeted Muslims who did not subscribe to their extremist philosophy. In 1993, the Hazratbal crisis was staged just when the Third Committee of the United Nations General Assembly dealing with human rights issues was to commence its deliberations. Terrorists took over the Hazratbal shrine. The move was calculated to provoke the Indian security forces. The siege was lifted when the Pakistani move to get a UN resolution adopted against India failed.

While damage to the Hazratbal shrine was avoided, two years later, Charar-e-Sharif could not be saved. In 1995, a group of terrorists led by Mast Gul set fire to the shrine that symbolized the Sufi tradition of the Valley. Mast Gul was a Pathan from Peshawar, not a Kashmiri. He surfaced later in Rawalpindi, where the Jamaat-e-Islami organized a public function to fete him. Mast Gul said, 'I want 5,000 martyrs from the city of Rawalpindi…in fact, every city of Pakistan should contribute martyrs for the Kashmir cause.'[9] Maulana Muhammad Farooq of Harkat-ul-Ansar issued a statement in Muzaffarabad (POK), stating, 'We shall carry the fire of Charar-e-Sharif to all cities of India. Now this fire will raze Delhi and Bombay to [the] ground.'[10] This was a religious war, not a fight for the self-determination of the Kashmiri people.

Pakistan banned JeM and LeT after the attack on the Indian Parliament in December 2001. President Musharraf said, 'No organization will be allowed to indulge in terrorism in the name of Kashmir.'[11] The statement was made after India had moved its troops to the border. Daniel Pearl, the *Wall Street Journal* correspondent, reported in two despatches that no action was taken on the ground to enforce the ban. A July issue of Jaish's magazine urged readers to 'come forward and be a supporter of the warriors of Islam', from 'Kashmir to Palestine', and suggested writing a cheque or draft in the name of Mufti Rafeeq Ahmed, the group's office administrator. In Pearl's report, the bank manager said the Central Bank of Pakistan had issued a directive to freeze the JeM's account, but no action could be taken 'as the account listed in the ad was a personal account'.

Pearl wrote on 2 January 2002, 'The Pakistan government, rather than shutting down militant groups, appears to be trying to narrow their activities to Kashmir.' He added, 'There have been no reports of a crack-down within the Pakistan-controlled section of Kashmir.'[12] Pakistan was trying to hoodwink the world by moving the terrorist bases to POK, rather than closing them down. Daniel Pearl was kidnapped and killed soon thereafter.

The terrorist groups operating in Jammu and Kashmir continued to enjoy immunity even when the military tried to put a temporary hold on groups active in Afghanistan. JeM and the LeT mounted an attack on the Indian Parliament in December 2001, three months after Musharraf's speech in the aftermath of 9/11.

Suicide Attacks and Radicalization

The trend of suicide attacks has picked up with the increasing radicalization of youth in the Kashmir Valley. Burhan Wani, a member of the Hizbul Mujahideen, emerged as the face of the new form of militancy adept at using social media to spread radicalization. The militants have not hesitated to use girls and children as human shields, and to pelt stones on the security forces. They use modern technology and messaging, but the mindset is medieval.

A group called Ansar Ghazwat-ul-Hind, in a statement released in July 2017, stated, 'After the martyrdom of heroic Mujahid Burhan Wani, the Jihad in Kashmir has entered a stage of awakening…'[13] It proclaimed on its Facebook page that its objective was to 'safeguard the Jihad in Kashmir and with Allah's help we will make this Jihad to the last corner of India'. Its aims thus went beyond Jammu and Kashmir. It rejected any notion of democracy, nationalism, UN resolutions or the plebiscite: 'Our Jihad is not for nationhood or nationalism, nor is it for the implementation of Kufria resolutions of Greater Taghoot United Nations, nor is it for Jufria Plebiscite.' It added, 'We perform Jihad only for the supremacy of Allah's and to make Allah's Deen sovereign.'

The organization is named after a prophecy that before the apocalypse, there will be an invasion of India (Ghazwat-ul-Hind), in which India will be defeated.

Ideology

For those who supported the burning of Charar-e-Sharif, the issue went beyond Kashmir. Terrorists want to destroy India's pluralism. The terrorist violence was no longer confined to attacks on Hindu minorities or government institutions. They now covered Muslim places of worship which did not conform to their interpretation of Islam. Charar-e-Sharif was a Muslim shrine.

The link between the terror groups in Jammu and Kashmir and Afghanistan is brought out in the writings of Riaz Mohammad Khan, Pakistan's former foreign secretary. He writes about the three key militant leaders in Kashmir – Fazlur Rehman Khalil, Masood Azhar and Hafiz Muhammad Saeed. 'All three leaders shared strong pan-Islamist views and were committed to the cause of jihad in Afghanistan and Kashmir; two were alumni of the Binori Masjid Darul Uloom.'[14]

The ideology of Pakistan is increasingly influenced by pan-Islamic sentiment. Pakistan uses human rights as a pretext to raise the Jammu and Kashmir issue in international fora. The modern concept of human rights is rooted in liberal values. These groups supported by Pakistan are waging jehad to advance Pakistan's territorial interests.

Riaz Mohammad Khan does not mention the role of Pakistani agencies. Without Pakistan providing sanctuary, training and funding, these groups could not have functioned for such a long time. This link has been extensively recorded in Pakistani and international literature. Adrian Levy and Catherine Scott-Clark quoted Benazir Bhutto in their book *Deception.* She stated that Musharraf told her during her second term as prime minister that 'he wanted to "unleash the forces of fundamentalism" to ramp up the war'.[15] At the time, he was Director-General of Military Operations (DGMO), a key post at the army headquarters. Musharraf approached the JI, the JUI and the Markaz Daawa Al Irshad (MDI), 'who agreed to provide their cadres'.[16]

The army had perfected terrorist violence as part of its toolkit to advance what it perceived as Pakistan's strategic interests abroad. However, the proliferation of armed religious groups soon spread violence inside Pakistan. This was reinforced by the army's attempt to use religious groups against civilian governments. The ISI organized a Long March in July 2012 by the Defence of Pakistan Council to check the PPP government's attempt to normalize relations with India. The Long March had the tacit support of the army chief. Khaled Ahmed wrote that the marchers included 'Maulana Sami ul-Haq, known as the spiritual father of the Taliban'. They also included Fazlur Rehman Khalil, who was once the leader of Harkat-ul-Mujahideen, and was 'often called the post office of Osama bin Laden because he handled his correspondence from Islamabad'.[17]

The then army chief General Kayani's refusal to take action against the Taliban forced the political parties to enter into peace talks with the Taliban. While he remained passive against the growing danger of the TTP, he reacted angrily to the US killing Osama bin Laden. Before retiring, General Kayani did a somersault. In a speech to the cadets of the Pakistan Military Academy in Kakul, he said, 'Any person who believes his opinion to be the final verdict is an extremist…If this is the correct definition of extremism and terrorism, then the war against it is our own war. And a just war too.'[18]

While Kayani belatedly acknowledged that terrorism was a problem inside Pakistan, he delayed action against the TTP. In 2013, when the Pakistan Army was to move against the Taliban in north Waziristan, he insisted on national consensus, delaying the whole operation. When his successor General Raheel Sharif initiated Operation Zarb-e-Azb against the TTP and a host of terrorists in north Waziristan in June 2014, it produced a terrible reaction. This time, the victims were children of army officers studying at Army Public School, Peshawar.

Osama's Killing and the Global Jehad

The discovery that Osama bin Laden was living near the Pakistan Military Academy should have embarrassed Pakistan. But the Pakistan Army remained unrepentant. Khaled Ahmed describes the reaction of Army Chief General Kayani: 'In 2011, he interpreted the killings of Osama bin Laden by the Americans in Abbottabad as being against the interests of Pakistan, reacting against the ruling PPP when it welcomed the assassination.'[19]

John Brennan, US President Barack Obama's homeland security and terrorism adviser at the time, stated, 'I think it's inconceivable that bin Laden did not have a support system in the country that allowed him to remain there for an extended period of time.'[20] Bin Laden was living in a large house with his entire family for more than five years. His presence should have been noticed in the small town.

Bin Laden's killing was greeted with relief by the international community. The Pakistani reaction was different. An article in the *Financial Times* stated, 'Hafiz Saeed, the founder of the Lashkar-e-Tayyaba militant group, was reported to have led funeral prayers for bin Laden in the Pakistani city of Lahore. He called bin Laden a "great man" who had made a sacrifice of martyrdom.'[21] Pakistan's Parliament passed a non-binding resolution, calling to reconsider its relationship with the US 'with a view to ensuring Pakistan's national interests were respected'.[22] Four months later, a bomb attack on the US Embassy in Kabul wounded seventy-seven American and NATO troops. Admiral Mike Mullen, Chairman of the Joint Chiefs of Staff, in a testimony to the Senate Armed Services Committee, stated there was 'credible intelligence' that the attack was carried out with 'ISI support'.[23]

The beginning of this chapter cites a perceptive observation by Mansoor Ijaz about ISI's role in spreading radicalism, which has become the cornerstone of Pakistan's foreign policy. Ijaz has detailed back-channel exchanges between the Zardari government and US officials in the immediate aftermath of Osama bin Laden's killing by US Marines. An embarrassed civilian government feared a military coup and wanted a message to be delivered to General Kayani, Pakistani Army Chief by the US. In exchange, the Pakistani President made a 'critical offer' to the Obama Administration: 'The new national security team will eliminate Section S of the ISI charged with maintaining relations to the Taliban, Haqqani network, etc'. The warning by the US Administration apparently went unheeded. The article does not give details of what the US warning was.[24]

Mansoor Ijaz argued that blacklisting the Haqqani network was futile and 'will have no material impact on the group's military support and intelligence logistics; it is S-Wing that allegedly provides all of this in the first place'.[25] The US did not sanction what was a part of an agency of the Pakistani government.

Terrorist organizations in Pakistan have links with Al-Qaeda and the ISIS. A report in Urdu daily *Jang* on 10 June 2006 stated that Jamaat-ud-Dawa (JUD), which is an incarnation of the old LeT, 'carried out a funeral prayer in absentia for Zarqawi in Lahore'. 'The clerical alliance MMA demanded "fateha" prayer for Zarqawi' in Pakistan's Parliament, but this request was 'denied by the speaker'.[26] It may be recalled that the foundations of the ISIS were laid by al-Zarqawi on his return to Iraq from Afghanistan and Pakistan.

Organizations like LeT and JeM often pride themselves as different from other terror groups involved in sectarian killings. Nevertheless, they reflect the same philosophy which inspires these groups.

Masood Azhar, along with Fazlur Rehman Khalil, was close to bin Laden, who helped Masood Azhar create Jaish-e-Mohammad. The hijacking of Indian Airlines plane IC-814 to Kandahar in December 1999 was organized to secure the release of Masood Azhar. Azhar had organized the Mansehra camp near Abbottabad for terrorist training, which was funded by bin Laden.

On 14 February 2019, a terror attack took place in Pulwama in Jammu and Kashmir on a bus carrying Indian security personnel. A day before, in an identical attack, a suicide bomber in a jeep rammed a bus carrying Iranian troops in the Sistan-Balochistan province of Iran. Twenty-seven Iranian soldiers died. Both attacks originated in Pakistan. Pakistan-supported terrorism has affected not only India and the West but also its Muslim neighbours. Afghanistan has been at the receiving end since the 1980s. Iran, too, is affected. The 2019 attack is not the only one it has suffered from groups based on Pakistani soil.

The Pakistan Army has integrated 'low-intensity conflict' into its defence doctrine. This is a euphemism for a campaign of terrorism. Unless it changes its policy of treating such groups as 'assets' to further its expansionist aims, the problem will continue. The aim of the policy was to 'bleed' India. It is now 'bleeding' Pakistan.

Pakistani leaders and diplomats claim that the country is a victim of terrorism. According to this narrative, this is either the result of joining the US-led war on terror, or the action of external agencies. This view ignores the origin of the problem that lies within Pakistan. A policy of using terror groups to advance Pakistan's strategic interests in Afghanistan and Jammu and Kashmir and suppressing national or ethnic identities in Khyber Pakhtunkhwa and Balochistan, was bound to produce a domestic fallout. As US Secretary of State, Hillary Clinton, said during a visit to Pakistan in October 2011, 'You can't keep snakes in your backyard and expect them only to bite your neighbours. Eventually, those snakes are going to turn on whosoever has them in the backyard.'[27]

Pakistan is a victim – of its own ideology. The ideology is now being defined by multiple actors, including Army and religious groups waging jehad within Pakistan and abroad.

On 22 April 2025, terrorists killed 27 tourists in Pahalgam after identifying them as non-Muslims. Was it a coincidence that the attack came a week after General Asim Munir's rant about the Two-Nation Theory and Kashmir? The incident was calculated to damage the economy of the state, dependent upon tourism. It has been condemned by all sections of Kashmiris. The former chief minister Dr Farooq Abdullah said that Pakistan has always bled Kashmir. The incident showed *jehadi* philosophy behind the terrorist violence.

21

Nuclear Deterrence: Strategy, Ideology or Gamble?

'We must not lose sight of the fact that Kashmir has now become a nuclear flashpoint…'

–Prime Minister Nawaz Sharif in his letter to the UN Secretary-General, 27 May 1999[1]

THE CONCEPT OF NUCLEAR deterrence is rooted in the history of the Cold War. Though the Cold War was driven by ideological considerations, the existential threat posed by a nuclear exchange made both sides keep the issue of deterrence separate. The Cuban missile crisis saw both the US and the Soviet Union stepping back from the precipice. The weapons of last resort were to be used only in the supreme national interest. In 1975, countries on both sides of the political divide signed the Helsinki Accord, pledging not to change the territorial status quo in Europe through the use of force. These two key elements – insulating nuclear policy from ideology and territorial disputes – provided stability to nuclear deterrence. Both these elements are absent from Pakistan's nuclear posture.

Pakistan's leaders talk of a thousand-year war with India. Pakistan combines the First Use policy with the rhetoric of the unfinished agenda of Partition. Linking nuclear posture to a territorial dispute accentuates the risk of escalation. Pakistan's claim on Jammu and Kashmir reflects the Two-Nation Theory. These tactics go beyond any understanding of nuclear deterrence in the conventional sense. Pakistan's risky behaviour can only be explained in terms of its obsession with India. The ideology conditions military thinking and trumps national interest.

The nuclear threat to India was held out in 1987 when A.Q. Khan gave an interview to Indian journalist Kuldip Nayar. The threat was made against the background of a campaign of terrorism in Punjab, though ostensibly, Pakistan linked it to Operation Brasstacks, the Indian military exercise. This was conducted in Rajasthan on the Indian side of the international border. The threat was made even before Pakistan had admitted to having a nuclear weapons capacity. This was followed, two years later, by Operation Zarb-e-Momin, a military exercise launched by the Pakistan Army in late 1989. The military operation was accompanied by ratcheting up of terrorist activities across the LOC in Jammu and Kashmir. Pakistan's Prime Minister Benazir Bhutto gave a speech, calling for a thousand-year war against India. The heightened tensions brought US Deputy National Security Advisor Robert Gates to the subcontinent. Since then, the threat has been held out against India during the Kargil War in 1999, after the attack on the Indian Parliament in 2001, and most recently, after the Pulwama incident in 2019. On each occasion, Pakistan used the threat of nuclear riposte to deter India's response to terrorism sponsored by Pakistan.

The use of the nuclear threat to invite international mediation on Jammu and Kashmir lowers the threshold for triggering a nuclear exchange. Weapons of last resort are brandished at the beginning, rather than the culmination of the cycle of escalation. Even worse is that Pakistan has used the nuclear umbrella to create space for a campaign of terrorism and pre-empt India's conventional response. The four Red Lines enunciated by Lt General Kidwai as head of Pakistan's Strategic Forces Command in 2002 present its policy in defensive terms. This is to disguise an inherently aggressive policy.

The Red Lines were enunciated during the Musharraf period, when a terror attack on the Indian Parliament had brought Indian troops to the international border. Their purpose was to deter an Indian response to a major act of terrorism by a Pakistan-based group. Earlier, Pakistan threatened the use of nuclear weapons in Kargil, when its regular troops, along with mujahideen, had infiltrated across the LOC.

Pakistan's Red Lines relate to the Indian attack inside Pakistani territory, triggering nuclear retaliation. However, during the Kargil War, it held out nuclear threat when the Indian Army was clearing out Pakistani intruders from *within* Indian territory.

Pakistan does not need nuclear deterrence for security. There is no existential threat to Pakistan from India. All four wars in 1947–48,

1965, 1971 and 1999 were initiated by Pakistan. This is borne out both by international sources as well as Pakistani writings. India does not covet Pakistan's territory. It returned Pakistan's territory and 90,000 prisoners of war in 1971 when Pakistan was a defeated nation.

India demonstrated its nuclear capacity in 1974, though it did not follow it up with a weapons programme. Pakistan is believed to have developed nuclear capacity by 1990. During these sixteen years, India did not press its unilateral advantage over Pakistan. Stanford political science professor Scott D. Sagan has argued that 'it is very fortunate that it was India, not Pakistan, that was the first to develop nuclear weapons in South Asia'.[2] He further stated: 'Pakistan military did not possess nuclear weapons before India tested in 1974, and thus was not in a position to argue that preventive war now was better than war later after India developed a rudimentary arsenal.'[3] If Pakistan had conventional as well as nuclear superiority over Indian forces, it would have certainly tried to 'solve' the Kashmir issue on its terms.

Pakistan pursued its covert nuclear programme in the 1980s when it was receiving a large amount of US aid for the Afghan War. It risked losing American aid for the sake of building its nuclear weapon capacity. Was this a military necessity, or a quest for 'parity' with its larger neighbour? Pakistan has blocked negotiations on the Fissile Material Cut-off Treaty in the Conference on Disarmament in Geneva. Its objective is to build up a stockpile of fissile material to expand its nuclear arsenal.

In 2019, Prime Minister Imran Khan, while replying to the debate in Pakistan's Parliament on India's dilution of Article 370 and the Citizenship (Amendment) Act, held out a nuclear threat against India. These were internal changes in India's legal system which do not remotely pose any military threat to Pakistan. Imran Khan's comments showed that nuclear weapons status has not brought restraint but engendered risky behaviour.

Pakistan claims that its nuclear weapons programme is India-specific. This has been constantly repeated by Pakistani leaders, diplomats and generals since it went overtly nuclear in 1998. The attempt is to present Pakistan's actions as posing no threat to other countries and the international non-proliferation regime. This is untrue, as Pakistan contributed to the proliferation of nuclear technology in Libya, Iran and North Korea. Given the extensive presence of terrorist groups within Pakistan, fear of the leakage of nuclear technology to them cannot be easily dismissed.

India's nuclear deterrence is driven by the Chinese threat. India suffered Chinese aggression in 1962. China conducted its nuclear test in 1964. India waited for more than three decades after the Chinese test before following suit, despite having demonstrated nuclear capacity at least since 1974. The 1974 test was not part of a weapons programme. The 1998 tests were not aimed at Pakistan. India does not need nuclear weapons to prevail over that country. India had soundly defeated Pakistan in 1971.

Pakistan seeks to limit the nuclear debate to the subcontinent. This analytical framework does not address India's threat perception. India developed nuclear deterrence against the Chinese threat. There has been Sino-Pak collusion against India since the early 1960s. Limiting the debate to the India–Pakistan bilateral context also diverts attention from China's nuclear proliferation activities that are in violation of its commitments under the Treaty on Non-Proliferation of Nuclear Weapons. China signed the treaty in 1991, nearly a quarter century after it was adopted in 1967. It was responsible for the proliferation of nuclear technology to Pakistan in the interim period and has continued to do so still.

India is committed to a 'no first use' policy, while Pakistan has adopted a 'first use' policy. The former means nuclear weapons will be used only in retaliation against a nuclear strike by the adversary. The latter involves initiating a nuclear strike. Pakistan threatens to do so even against a conventional attack. This is inherently destabilizing. It also widens the use of nuclear weapons to include conventional wars. Pakistan has chosen 'first use' to gain the advantage of offensive while raising the risk of a conventional conflict escalating to the nuclear level.

Deterrence through Ambiguity

Nuclear deterrence is based on a clear understanding of the circumstances in which the nuclear weapons would be used. This is necessary to reduce the risk of a war with horrendous consequences for both sides. Pakistan followed a calculated policy of ambiguity.

It is generally assumed that Pakistan acquired a rudimentary nuclear capacity by 1990. That was the year when US President George H.W. Bush refused to renew the annual certification, under the Pressler Amendment, that Pakistan did not possess a nuclear device. The certification was needed to release US military aid to Pakistan. To avoid losing US military aid, Pakistan needed to maintain deniability about its nuclear capacity. It also wanted to hold out the threat of nuclear exchange to deter India's conventional response to terrorist attacks by Pakistan-based groups. The answer to these two contradictory policy objectives was a policy of ambiguity.

A.Q. Khan gave an interview to Kuldip Nayar in January 1987 claiming that Pakistan had nuclear weapons capacity. Though Khan headed Pakistan's nuclear programme, he could not have spoken to an Indian journalist without General Zia's approval. The interview was given against the background of the Indian Army conducting an exercise, Operation Brasstacks, on the Indian side of the international border in Rajasthan, where there is no territorial dispute. Though Pakistan's leadership may have believed that this would act as a deterrent, it did not happen. The interview was published on 1 March 1987, a month later, when the tensions had already subsided.[4] Nevertheless, this was a blatant attempt at nuclear blackmail by lowering the threshold for nuclear retaliation even before Indian troops had crossed the international border. It also increased miscalculation risks.

Zarb-e-Momin

The Pakistan Army launched its military exercise 'Zarb-e-Momin' close to the LOC in Jammu and Kashmir and the international border in late 1989. The name chosen for the exercise was highly symbolic. It means *strike or blow of the believer*. This showed the ideological orientation of the Pakistan Army, which presents the territorial defence of Pakistan in religious terms.

At the end of the exercise, instead of going back to their normal positions, Pakistani troops remained close to the LOC and the international border. The aim was to provide support to terrorist activities across the border in the Indian state of Jammu and Kashmir. When India started a training exercise in Rajasthan, 'Pakistani planners grew alarmed'. The US Embassy officials in Delhi confirmed that the Indian deployment in Jammu and Kashmir and Punjab did not include tank and artillery, and appeared to corroborate Indian claims that the 'buildup of forces on the border was to prevent cross-border infiltration'.[5] In the midst of border tensions, Prime Minister Benazir Bhutto travelled to POK, and in a passionate speech, threatened a thousand-year war against India. India moved its Strike Corps into Rajasthan, while Pakistan moved its 1st and 2nd Armoured Corps towards the border. However, India did not deploy armour, and Pakistan did not move two strike corps to the front.[6]

After creating a crisis on the ground by exercising close to the border, Pakistan began signalling there was a risk of escalation to the nuclear level. American journalist Seymour Hersh, in an article in the *New Yorker*, mentioned that in the early spring of 1990, intelligence reached Washington that 'General Beg had authorized the technicians at Kahuta to put together nuclear weapons'. American satellites relayed pictures of increased activities at Kahuta, including high explosive tests and 'a truck convoy moving from a suspected nuclear-storage site in Balochistan to a nearby Air Force base'. The article mentioned that the Pakistani government had told Washington that 'India was prepared to send its army across the border'. This was when President Bush decided to send Robert Gates to Pakistan and India with his special messages to President Ghulam Ishaq Khan in Islamabad and to Prime Minister V.P. Singh in New Delhi.

Gates met President Ishaq Khan and General Beg. Pakistan relayed its fear that a 'full-scale ground assault by India could dismember the nation within two weeks'. Hence, Pakistan had 'no option but to go nuclear'. Gates pressed the Pakistani side 'to stop supporting terrorism in Kashmir'. President Ishaq Khan gave his assurance that this would be done. This was conveyed to India but the promise was never kept.

According to the Indian version given in the Kargil Review Committee report, 'the aim of the Gates mission appeared to have been to extract pledges of restraint from both sides. However, Gates did not make any reference to the nuclear issue during his visit to India.'[7]

Pakistani commentator Pervez Hoodbhoy has cited General Beg saying, three years after his 1991 retirement, that, 'Pakistan did not possess a usable nuclear device at that time.' Therefore, his country 'could not have been poised to use such a weapon against India'.[8] The whole episode was a Pakistani charade to continue fuelling the terror campaign in Jammu and Kashmir and pre-empt an Indian response by holding out the threat of escalation to the nuclear level.

Pakistan Army's Doctrine of Offensive Defence

According to Pakistan Army chief General Beg, 'Should there be a war, the Pakistan Army plans to take the war into India, launching a sizable offensive on Indian territory.'[9]

Beg's doctrine of 'offensive defence' was underpinned by a nuclear threat. In October 1989, Beg stated, '...both the nuclear option and the missiles (that Pakistan is developing) act as a deterrence; and those, in turn, contribute to the total fighting ability of the Army, which acts as a deterrent to the enemy.'[10] The statement indicated that nuclear weapons were not only part of a deterrent, but also integrated into the Pakistan Army's war-fighting ability.

1998 Nuclear Tests

Pakistan justified its nuclear tests on 28 May 1998 as a reaction to the Pokhran-II nuclear tests conducted by India on 11 and 13 May 1998. This claim belied logic. Nuclear capacity, including the stock of enriched uranium, cannot be produced in the space of two weeks. Pakistan already had a covert weapons programme. It had held out the nuclear threat to India more than eleven years ago in 1987. Now, it had simply become a declared nuclear weapons state. Pakistan also claimed that its tests were to restore the 'strategic balance' in South Asia. Prime Minister Nawaz Sharif stated, a day after the tests, on 29 May: 'After due deliberations and a careful review of all options we took the decision to restore the strategic balance.'

To see the 'strategic balance' in terms of South Asia deliberately leaves out China.[11] The assumption underlying the claim of 'restoring the strategic balance' was 'parity' with India. This is an article of faith, and its roots go back to the pre-Partition demand of the Muslim League that the minority should have parity with the much larger majority which is the very negation of the principle of democracy.

Nuclear balance does not require 'parity'. As long as a side can inflict unacceptable damage on the other, the purpose is served. What is 'unacceptable' depends upon the psychology of the adversary and its perception by the attacking side. These are intangibles. China, for example, does not have an equal number of warheads and missiles as the US. The quest for 'balance' and 'parity' with India actually disguises Pakistan's quest for escalation dominance, as Lt General Kidwai, now retired, mentioned in his talk at the International Institute of Strategic Studies (IISS) in London in February 2020. Has this added to Pakistan's security? The country lacks strategic depth for dispersing nuclear assets and is densely populated. An unremitting nuclear race, therefore, makes Pakistan's security more perilous. A policy which risks jeopardizing the country's survival cannot be justified in terms of national interest. Its nuclear policy is a reflection of ideology, not deterrence.

Prime Minister Nawaz Sharif's 29 May 1998 statement also made it clear that Pakistan's nuclear weapons are to be used not only to deter nuclear attacks but also to counter conventional threats: 'Our decision to exercise the nuclear option has been taken in the interest of national self-defence. These weapons are to deter aggression, *whether nuclear or conventional*,' [Emphasis added] he said.[12] He was merely repeating what Gen. Zia had conveyed through A.Q. Khan's interview during Operation Brasstacks.

Though unknown in May 1998, barely a year later, the nuclear umbrella would be used by Pakistan to cross the LOC in Kargil. Both nuclear and conventional threats have come from Pakistan. Pakistan's policy is not based on self-defence; this is only used to legitimize a policy chosen for other reasons.

Kargil War and Stability-Instability Paradox

India and Pakistan learned opposite lessons from the 1998 nuclear tests. Indian leaders assumed that the nuclear environment increases the risks and sought to minimize them by adopting a 'no first use' policy. The Pakistan Army assumed that fear of nuclear war will deter Indian retaliation against Pakistan's conventional and sub-conventional threat, and open up space for aggressive action below the nuclear threshold.

Nuclear experts call this the 'Stability-Instability' paradox, where stable nuclear deterrence encourages adventurous action at the lower end of the spectrum, thus creating an unstable balance at the conventional level.

Pakistan infiltrated regular troops disguised as mujahideen across the LOC in Kargil in 1999. The operation began even as the two countries were preparing to hold the Lahore Summit in February 1999.

Pakistan's Prime Minister Sharif wrote a letter to the UN Secretary-General on 27 May, in which he sought the UN's mediation, describing Kashmir as a nuclear flashpoint. The letter mentioned: 'We must not lose sight of the fact that Kashmir has now become a nuclear flashpoint, and its resolution is absolutely necessary for peace and stability in the region.'[13]

The letter was part of Pakistan's old playbook – first, alter the ground situation, and then ask for international mediation in a crisis of its own creation. This had paid handsome dividends in the first war in Jammu and Kashmir in 1947–48, where UN mediation froze the Indian Army's advance, leaving Pakistan in possession of the land it had illegally occupied. The same tactics were being repeated in a nuclearized environment. Prime Minister Nawaz Sharif's letter did not mention the origin of the problem, which began with the Pakistani intrusion across the LOC. Nor did it admit to the presence of Pakistani troops, which the country was forced to acknowledge when it signed an agreement with the Indian government to take the dead bodies of its soldiers and officers from the Indian side of the LOC. 'Kashmir as a nuclear flashpoint' would become the new mantra.

Prime Minister Nawaz Sharif's letter was followed by Shamshad Ahmad's statement on 31 May 1999. Pakistan threatened, 'We will not hesitate to use any weapon in our arsenal to defend our territorial integrity.' The statement did not emanate from any military threat but was meant to pre-empt the Indian response. Pakistan was using the threat of nuclear exchange when it officially claimed that there were no Pakistani troops involved in the intrusion, and the operation was being mounted by mujahideen. Pakistan had lowered the threshold by threatening the use of nuclear weapons in an operation that neither involved the defence of its territory nor danger to its troops, if its official stand was to be believed.

Pakistani actions were premised on two assumptions about Indian and international behaviour. The country assumed that the fear of nuclear exchange would (i) inhibit India from launching a retaliation, and (ii) induce the international community to intervene to prevent escalation. This would, in effect, freeze the situation, leaving Pakistan in possession of fresh territory occupied illegally. Both assumptions were proved wrong. Pakistan succeeded in attracting American mediation, but the mediator demanded that it pull back its forces from Jammu and Kashmir. The outcome was quite different from what Musharraf and his generals had calculated when they embarked on the misadventure.

Pakistan also found, to its horror, that China did not intervene, militarily or politically. Nawaz Sharif made a trip to Washington only after receiving a negative response from Beijing between 27 and 30 June. Earlier, General Musharraf had also failed to draw Chinese support during his visit on 12 June. US President Bill Clinton called upon Pakistan to withdraw its troops from across the LOC. Pakistan had risked nuclear exchange for limited gains and lost on both military and diplomatic fronts.

Pakistan's Red Lines

Pakistan's Red Lines were spelt out in 2002 by Lt General Kidwai as head of Pakistan's Strategic Force Division. The background was military mobilization by both sides following the terror attack on the Indian Parliament. It stated that Pakistan would use nuclear weapons, if:

(i) India attacks Pakistan and conquers a large part of its territory;
(ii) India destroys a large part of its land or air forces;
(iii) India proceeds to the economic strangling of Pakistan; and
(iv) India pushes Pakistan into political destabilization or creates a large-scale internal subversion in Pakistan (domestic destabilization).[14]

No country has used economic 'strangling' as grounds for using nuclear weapons. If this were the case, the Soviet Union and its successor Russia should have launched nuclear weapons at the US, since it has been under various US economic sanctions. India unilaterally extended 'most favoured nation' (MFN) status to Pakistan for more than seven decades, rather than 'strangling' its economy. The MFN status was revoked in response to the Pulwama terror attack in February 2019. Pakistan never extended MFN status to India. Domestic destabilization is too vaguely defined. If this is accepted as legitimate grounds for the use of nuclear weapons, India would have been justified in using nuclear weapons against Pakistan in response to terror attacks on the Indian Parliament in 2001 and on Mumbai in 2008.

Lt General Kidwai, in his speech at the IISS on 6 February 2020, said, 'Pakistan has ensured seamless integration between nuclear strategy and conventional military strategy in order to achieve the desired outcomes in the realms of peacetime deterrence, pre-war deterrence as also in intra-war deterrence if the adversary, having drawn the wrong conclusions, challenges the very foundations of the deterrence theory.'[15]

This gives away the fact that Pakistan's policy goes beyond 'nuclear deterrence' to war fighting. As Kidwai's statement shows, there is no distinction between its 'nuclear and conventional military strategy', both of which are seamlessly integrated. All responsible nuclear powers treat the threshold for triggering nuclear and conventional responses as distinct. Escalating the response to the nuclear level in case of conventional military conflict or economic competition is a reflection of ideology, not deterrence based on rational choices.

Prime Minister Imran Khan

In Pakistan, the civilian leadership does not control nuclear weapons. General Kidwai made a reference to the Pulwama–Balakot incident in his February 2020 speech:

> ...nuclear India should have concluded that in an active military conflict situation, especially a limited one with nuclear-armed Pakistan, while it may be easy to climb the first rung on the escalatory ladder, the second rung would always belong to Pakistan, and that India's choice to move to the third rung would invariably be dangerously problematic in anticipation of the fourth rung response by Pakistan.

The immediate background for the Indian retaliation in Balakot was a terror strike in Pulwama by a suicide bomber. Pakistan's highest political leadership, and the general who once headed Pakistan's nuclear force, were determined to retain space for sub-conventional warfare under the nuclear umbrella.

After the abrogation of Article 370 by India, the then Prime Minister Imran Khan, in a speech in Pakistan's National Assembly on 6 August 2019, stated '...both India and Pakistan are equipped with weapons that you know...' This was a clear hint to nuclear weapons. He said Pakistan might lose out against India in a conventional war. It will thereafter retaliate with nuclear weapons. He had linked Pakistan's nuclear policy to deter not an Indian attack across the international border, but internal changes in Jammu and Kashmir. This was dangerously lowering the nuclear threshold.

Pakistan is developing tactical nuclear weapons and has now embarked upon the pursuit of 'full spectrum deterrence', according to Lt Gen. Kidwai. This is combined with a conscious lowering of the threshold to threaten nuclear exchange against Indian retaliation over terror attacks. Pakistan's Red Lines are deceptively framed; the actual policy followed is inherently aggressive. This cannot be explained in terms of a rational policy of deterrence. It is tinged with ideological blinkers.

22

Economy

> 'Pakistan has become a laggard in South Asia, facing episodes of boom and busts. The country had to approach the IMF for meeting its balance of payments crisis 22 times in the last thirty years.'
>
> –Ishrat Husain, ex-governor of State Bank of Pakistan, writing on 'Seventy-Five Years of Pakistan's Economy'[1]

ISLAM LAYS STRESS ON equality, but the laissez-faire policies followed by the Pakistan government have produced a high degree of inequality in the country. Pakistan has an agrarian economy. The Muslim League was deeply conservative and avoided land reform. Though the political landscape has changed since then, none of the major political parties – PPP, PML(N) and PTI – have sought to bring agriculture into the tax net.

Pakistan has long been ruled by the army. In the army's conception of the state, military prowess is more important than economic development. However, if the army wants Pakistan to be the new Sparta, it does not like the idea of Spartan austerity. The economy is based on high consumption and low savings rates. Together with heavy defence spending, this has made the country perennially dependent upon external assistance. Pakistan is facing an unprecedented economic crisis. The IMF's Stand-by Arrangement allowed it to narrowly avoid a sovereign default in 2023.

Pakistan has been very successful in exploiting geopolitics for financial assistance. During the Cold War in the 1950s, the Afghan War of the 1980s and post 9/11, it received large amounts of foreign aid. Since Ishrat Husain, the former chief of the country's central bank, wrote an article, Pakistan has received three more IMF packages. Beginning with the first

IMF loan in 1958, it has received twenty-five IMF assistance packages with a total of SDR 32.96 billion ($42.848 billion approximately, 1 SDR = 1.32 USD) billion in commitment and SDR 20.85 ($27.105 billion approximately) drawn till now.[2]

This includes a fresh Stand-by Arrangement of $3 billion for nine months, covering July 2023–April 2024. It started negotiations to secure fresh IMF credit soon after the inauguration of Shehbaz Sharif's second government in March 2024. An IMF package of around 7 billion over 37 months was announced in September 2024. The IMF does not follow Islamic banking. It lends money against interest, which is forbidden in Islam. Availing of IMF assistance requires accepting its terms based on modern banking practices. Whenever there is a divergence between ideology and economic interests, Pakistan's elite has chosen the latter.

The Pakistani economy's structural problems and the absence of distributive justice cannot be blamed on the IMF: they result from choices made by Pakistan's civil and military governments. However, the international lenders, by generously bailing out Pakistan at critical moments, may have made it easier for its rulers to avoid economic reforms that will touch elite interests.

Though Jinnah stressed egalitarian order, his instincts and actions were conservative. He opposed the application of Sharia law to agricultural land in a debate in the Central Legislative Assembly in pre-Partition India. Prof. Ishtiaq Ahmad has written that H.M. Abdullah, a private member from Punjab, had introduced a bill 'to allow Muslim women to inherit their share in a family property in accordance with Islamic law'.[3] The Muslim members, including Jinnah, opposed it on the grounds that since agriculture and agricultural property were provincial subjects, the issue of succession could not be included in the bill. Finally, the bill was enacted after excluding agricultural property from its scope. The compromise was accepted, even though this was a departure from Islamic principles. Jurisdiction was a technical issue cited to disguise social preferences for keeping landed property with the male heir. Jinnah was unwilling to hurt the sensibility of the politically powerful constituency, as the Muslim League was dependent on their support.

Jinnah mentioned economic and social justice as objectives to be pursued but gave no blueprint to achieve them. Leftist politicians like Maulana Bhashani from Bengal and Mian Iftikharuddin from Punjab pressed for economic reform but had little influence over state policy. Farzana Shaikh wrote, 'The fear of being seen to compromise the spiritual foundations of Islam, and the hostility of the Muslim League's conservative leadership to any far-reaching economic reforms, undermined the practical influence of a socialist reading of Islam.'[4] This was paradoxical as the demand for an independent Pakistan was often justified in terms of economic justice for Muslims. It was claimed that this was not possible under 'Hindu Raj'. However, post-Partition, the interests of the 'Pakistan ke awam (the people of Pakistan)' remain only a part of political rhetoric.

Pakistan joined the US-led military bloc in the 1950s and enjoyed easy access to bilateral and multilateral lending programmes. Lending from the World Bank came with its own set of underlying economic philosophies. This was reflected in the popularity of the 'trickle-down theory', where the rich could be allowed to grow richer. Their prosperity was supposed to trickle down to their less fortunate brethren, rather than state intervention leading to distributive justice.

Pakistan's anti-communist and pro-Western foreign policy converged with the interests of the landed elite to reinforce the laissez-faire economic policies. Communism was equated with atheism. In a deeply conservative society, religion was used as a bar against the spread of socialist thought. Equality should not have been seen as a foreign precept or a Marxist dogma. It is innate to the spirit of Islam.

Long periods of military rule meant that there were no channels to demand social justice. Civilian politicians avoided the painful political choice of widening the tax base to include agriculture.

Industrialization and Role of the Private Sector

The absence of distributive justice was accompanied by stress on the role of the private sector. Prof. Shahid Javed Burki, who served as Pakistan's de facto finance minister and vice president, World Bank, mentions: 'The main contours of the Jinnah regime's approach towards economic development become visible in the 1948 Industrial Policy.'[5] Except for three areas that were reserved for public ownership, all other sectors were opened to private-sector investment. The reserved sectors were arms and ammunitions of war, the generation of hydroelectric power, and the manufacture and operation of railway, telephone, telegraph and wireless equipment. Burki says that the 'reservation' of these three sectors was an 'academic exercise', as the private sector was not able to invest in these sectors, given the underdeveloped state of the country's industrial sector.[6]

The Muslim League's focus on industrialization in the post-Partition period was a complete turn from the policy followed by Liaquat Ali Khan as finance minister in the Interim Government before independence. He imposed a heavy tax on the industrial sector. The Muslim League's base was the landed aristocracy in the agricultural sector; industrialists were mainly Congress supporters. High taxes were intended to kill the nascent industry which was perceived by the League as the Congress's constituency.

Liaquat followed a policy of prioritizing the industrialization of West Pakistan against the interests of East Pakistan, which was a large grower of jute. The action of Liaquat Ali Khan's government caused agricultural distress in East Pakistan. The chief beneficiary was the small group of business families in West Pakistan that had backed the Muslim League.

Pakistan achieved a high growth rate during Ayub Khan's decade of development. However, this came at a price – it accentuated economic inequalities. Mahbub ul Haq, in a speech in Karachi in April 1968, estimated: 'Only twenty-two family groups controlled at that time about two-thirds of the industrial assets, 80 per cent of the banking and 70 per cent of insurance in Pakistan.' This was a damning indictment of Ayub's policies by the man who served as the country's chief economist in Ayub's government.

Ayub Khan followed a policy of reliance on foreign aid, rather than domestic savings, for economic growth. This increased the debt burden. Akmal Hussain, in his book *A Perspective on Pakistan's Economic History: Growth, Economic Structure, and Governance*, writes,

> The debt servicing as a percentage of total foreign exchange earnings increased from 4.2 per cent in 1960–61 to 34.5 per cent by 1971–72. The magnitude of this figure did not fall for the next three decades. According to official figures, gross foreign aid inflows increased from \$373 million in 1950–55 to \$2,701 million in 1965–70.[7]

Pakistan was very successful in using geopolitics to obtain foreign aid. However, foreign policy cannot be a substitute for sound macroeconomic management. While stressing industrialization, Ayub's government also treated land reforms very lightly.

Distributive justice was no part of the Ayub regime's agenda, but this was the central plank of Bhutto's election programme. Zulfikar Ali Bhutto came to power on the promise of 'roti, kapada aur makaan (food, cloth and shelter)'. His government attempted the nationalization of industries, but did not take up land reforms in the agricultural sector, where most of Pakistan's population was employed. This was no accident. The PPP's electoral base in Sindh and Punjab depended on the support of the landed gentry. Bhutto had gathered an uneasy combination of landed interests and left-wing intellectuals under the umbrella of his party. This enabled him to win the election, but the coalition did not last long. Bhutto soon reverted to the policy of relying on the landed gentry after a brief interlude of socialist rhetoric. He expanded the public sector, but this was only to 'widen the resource base of the regime for the practice of the traditional form of power through state patronage'.[8]

During the Bhutto years, there was a decline in the GDP growth rate. The Zia period saw an increase in GDP growth from 4.9 per cent under the Bhutto regime to 6.6 per cent. This was based on a large amount of foreign assistance received from the US for supporting the Afghan jehad against the Soviet Union. There was also a growth in workers' remittances from the Middle East, which increased from 'US$0.5 billion in 1978 to US$3.2 billion in 1984'.[9]

The high growth of the Zia period could not be sustained because 'the domestic savings rate continued to remain below 10 per cent', Hussain added. 'Development expenditure as a percentage of GDP fell from 7.4 per cent in the 1970s to 3.5 per cent in the 1990s.'[10] The large bouts of external assistance received during the decade-long Afghan War kept the economy buoyant temporarily. There was a 'protracted economic recession in the 1990s'.[11]

The new millennium witnessed 9/11. Musharraf's military regime became the recipient of generous American aid once Pakistan joined the 'Coalition Against Terror. The next two decades also witnessed modest growth rates of 4.7 per cent and 4.4 per cent respectively.'[12]

Defence Expenditure

Pakistan has been run by the military directly or indirectly for much of its existence. The high defence expenditure has left its economy crippled. According to World Bank data compiled by Macrotrends, its defence expenditure has ranged from 6 per cent to 4 per cent of the GDP between 1960 and 2020, tapering down gradually.[13] It has come down slightly to 3.8 per cent of the GDP during the financial year 2021–22.[14]

Looking at the figures for the last six decades, there seems to be little correlation between the high defence budget and any external threat. Defence expenditure started rising in 1963 when India, Pakistan's presumed enemy, was recovering from the 1962 war with China. Its focus was improving defence on its northern frontier and avoiding a two-front war. That year, Pakistan's defence expenditure was $0.228 billion, or 3.65 per cent of its GDP. It rose sharply to $0.448 billion (5.9 per cent of its GDP) by 1965, when the second India–Pakistan war broke out. Did Pakistan's rulers sense India's weakness in the aftermath of the 1962 war, and decide to exploit it? The military build-up was a prelude to Pakistan launching Operation Gibraltar in 1965 with infiltration in Jammu and Kashmir.

After the 1965 war, which proved to be a major setback for Pakistan, there was no rethinking on following an aggressive policy. Defence expenditure went up both in absolute terms and percentage of GDP. It increased to $0.55 billion or 6.73 per cent of the GDP in 1966. It reached $0.748 billion or 6.74 per cent of the GDP in 1971, when the third India–Pakistan war took place.[15] The upward trajectory had started three years before the East Pakistan crisis broke out. It was, once again, driven by the choices made by Pakistan's military rulers rather than any external compulsion. In 1969, General Yahya Khan had taken over as the new army chief. While the high level of military expenditure continued to claim resources, the 'decade of development' was petering out.

After the 1971 war, there was a three-year period when the defence budget came down in absolute terms, though it remained above 6 per cent of the GDP. By 1975, the defence budget had exceeded pre-1971 levels, even though the army's defence responsibilities had halved with the loss of the eastern wing. It stood at $0.77 billion in 1975 (as against

$0.74 billion in 1971).[16] This was under the civilian government of Zulfikar Ali Bhutto.

The year 1979 was another watershed. The Soviet intervention in Afghanistan had taken place the previous year. Pakistan joined the US-supported war in Afghanistan in the 1980s, and the military's fortunes revived. For the next decade, military expenditure remained above 6 per cent of the GDP. There was no threat from India. The Soviet Union was in the process of consolidating its hold in Afghanistan – a task in which it never succeeded.

After the Geneva Accords and the Soviet Union's withdrawal from Afghanistan, Pakistan's western flank was secure. India was battling Pakistan-supported terrorism in Jammu and Kashmir. There was a civilian government in power in Islamabad. The military expenditure was increased by Benazir Bhutto's government, just as her father had done after the 1971 war. The civilian government most likely did not control Pakistan's India policy, or there was a civil-military consensus on a policy of confrontation with India.

In absolute terms, there has been a steady, unbroken trend of rise in defence expenditure till 2018, even though there was an occasional dip in the ratio between defence spending and the GDP. Naturally, in the competition for resources, the military had the upper hand, even though there was no ostensible threat to justify the high levels of expenditure.

Low Savings and Investment Rates

Pakistan's high defence expenditure was combined with low savings and low investment rates that resulted in slow economic growth. The differential between savings and investment rates brought increasing debt.

In the 1970s, the savings rate was 7.4 per cent, while the investment rate was 17.7 per cent. During the 1980s, the savings rate was 7.7 per cent, while the investment rate was 18.7 per cent. In the 1990s, the savings rate went up to 14 per cent, while the investment rate came down marginally to 18.3 per cent. During the 2000s, the domestic savings rate was 14.6 per cent, while the investment rate rose slightly to 18.4 per cent. During the second decade of the new millennium, the savings rate fell to 9.3 per cent, while the investment rate came down to 15.4 per cent. Hussain H. Zaidi wrote for *Hilal*, the Pakistan

Armed Forces magazine, 'It is obvious that the level of investment has always exceeded that of domestic savings. The difference has been met through external borrowing, which has resulted in the accumulation of debt.'[17]

The former governor of the State Bank of Pakistan, Ishrat Husain, enumerated some of the factors behind the country's economic decline. He said, 'The largest setback to the country has been the neglect of human development.' Comparing Pakistan's case with India, he said, 'Science and technology, which are the drivers of productivity and efficiency, have been neglected and innovation is missing from the production structure. Modi is personally leading the move to transform India into an advanced technological power; 16 unicorns were added only in one year.'

He ended his article on a depressing note:

> Pakistanis consume more than they save – both the government as well as households. They import more than export, have low investment rates in private and public sectors but aspire to grow beyond their means. Unless these recurrent imbalances of fiscal, trade, financial, savings investment gap are bridged the situation would remain unchanged.[18]

China–Pakistan Economic Corridor

Today, China has emerged as Pakistan's largest bilateral lender. According to an IMF report, China's loan to Pakistan stood at $23.651 billion in the period ending December 2023, surpassing that of Paris Club lenders (Japan, France) at $7.541 billion and Saudi Arabia at $6.661 billion. Multilateral creditors including the IMF, World Bank and Asian Development Bank have lent much more – $46.509 billion.[19]

Pakistan's increasing reliance on China for borrowing may lead it into the same debt trap Sri Lanka found itself in earlier. The CPEC funding has two streams – concessional financing to infrastructure projects and loans with 17 per cent returns on investment in US dollar terms. Interestingly, these loans by the Chinese government are only to the Chinese companies executing the projects. Curiously, the Pakistani government has been prevailed upon to extend sovereign guarantees for loan repayment by private companies. Normally, governments provide such guarantees only where the government itself is the borrower.

Thus, the commercial as well as foreign-exchange risks of the Chinese investors have been fully secured. Most of these projects financed by China under the CPEC are in the power sector. Stringent financing terms translate into high electricity tariffs.

Pakistan is overwhelmed by Chinese exports. The Chinese exports to Pakistan accounted for $23.1 billion in 2022, while Pakistan's exports to China the same year were worth $3.03 billion.[20] According to the Chinese ambassador to Pakistan, Jiang Zaidong, China has directly invested $25.4 billion in Pakistan.[21] Thus, China's annual trade surplus is more than 80 per cent of cumulative Chinese investment in Pakistan. The bulk of Chinese financing is in the form of credit rather than investment.

Trade with India

Pakistan's economic policies reflect a high degree of pragmatism. Despite the stress on Sharia, the country's successive civil and military governments did not hesitate to receive assistance from Western donors, including the IMF. Their lending policies are based on the market economy rather than Islamic practices. However, Islamabad reverts to a deeply ideological position when it comes to trading with India.

It has denied India the MFN treatment, which is obligatory under General Agreement on Tariffs and Trade (GATT) and World Trade Organization (WTO). Contrary to the nomenclature, the term means treating India on par with its other trading partners. In rejecting this, Pakistan has not only breached its obligations under GATT and WTO but also foregone the commercial benefit that access to the largest economy in the subcontinent would have brought it.

The fear of being swamped by Indian exports is highly overblown. Pakistan has a competitive advantage in light industries. India's subcontinental size makes it more cost-effective for industries in its western region to import from Pakistan than from industrial centres on its eastern side.

Social Safety Net and Financial Inclusion

According to the IMF report 'Pakistan Economy: Selected Issues', 2017, there are three components of Pakistan's social safety net. 'At the federal level, the Benazir Income Support Program is the main social safety net.' This is complemented by smaller programmes such as Zakat and Bait-ul-Mal, which are in keeping with Islamic practice. Overall, expenditures on social safety nets, excluding subsidies and provincial programmes, represent 0.54 per cent of GDP, well below the South Asia average as well as the emerging markets' average.[22] The IMF report mentions, 'Public spending on social safety nets in Pakistan remains relatively low amid still high poverty. About 30 per cent of the population still lives below the poverty line.'

Pakistan has not invested in its people. According to the United Nations Development Programme (UNDP) report released in September 2022 cited in an article in the Pakistani journal the *Friday Times*, 'Pakistan has dropped seven slots in the Human Development Index (HDI) 2021-2022.' 'The country now ranks 161 out of 192 countries.' Bangladesh stands at 129 while India stands at 132. West Pakistan looked down upon East Pakistan when they were part of the same country. Ayub Khan has described the eastern wing in derogatory terms in his memoir *Friends Not Masters*. Today, Pakistan is behind Bangladesh in parameters like life expectancy, years of schooling and gross per capita income. The article mentioned, 'The report stated that life expectancy at birth in Pakistan is 66.1 years, expected years of schooling are eight while the gross per capita national income is $4,624.' It further quoted, 'Life expectancy at birth in Bangladesh is 72.4 years, expected years of schooling are 12.4 while the gross per capita national income is $5,472.'[23]

Eschewed Tax Base

Pakistan has an eschewed tax base, where the major share of revenue comes from indirect taxes and large swathes of the economy are exempt from income tax. The indirect taxes account for up to 80 per cent of the total taxes budgeted for collection during financial year 2023–24. Their impact on the poor is much higher.

Imran Khan was fond of talking about social justice. As prime minister, he made no attempt to change Pakistan's tax base which penalizes the poor. The charge applies equally to politicians on the other side of the political divide who are now ruling Pakistan.

Debt Trap

Miftah Ismael, former finance minister, said in a TV interview that there is a real risk that Pakistan is now facing a debt trap.[24] He was being polite. It has already slipped into one.

The definition of a debt trap is where the loan repayment exceeds the revenue receipt. According to the official budget figures, Pakistan's debt service payment of Rs 7.303 trillion exceeded the federal government's share of revenue of Rs 6.9 trillion by Rs 416 billion in the financial year 2023–24, ending June 2024.[25] This means that the government had to borrow more even to pay existing debts.

The problem seems to be getting worse as the debt burden is increasing faster than the federal government's income. According to Pakistan's budget for FY 2024–25, the debt payment of Rs 9.775 trillion will exceed the net income of the federal government of Rs 6.979 trillion by Rs 2.796 trillion. The debt payment went up from Rs 7.309 trillion in FY 2023–24 to Rs 9.775 trillion in FY 2024–25. The federal government's net income has only marginally increased.

The Future?

The 2022 floods in Pakistan caused enormous damage to the economy, and suffering for millions of people. Climate change is a global phenomenon. Pakistan's authorities are right to point out that the country has very small emissions. There is a need for international support, particularly from the developed countries, which account for a major part of global emissions. However, not all the problems can be traced to the recent floods.

The economy was already facing severe problems when Pakistan signed the Extended Finance Facility agreement with the IMF in 2019. This was followed by a Stand-By Arrangement, which was a nine-month facility to cover the interim period before the new government was elected. As soon as Shehbaz Sharif returned to power, his government started negotiating a longer-term agreement.

Low savings and low investment rates have been a constant feature of Pakistan's economy since the 1960s. This was before the COVID pandemic, the Ukraine crisis or the 2022 floods. These chronic problems of the economy are due to choices made by Pakistan's elite.

Pakistan's tax-to-GDP ratio for FY 2023–24 is projected at 9.9 per cent, though the figure agreed with the IMF was 10.8 per cent.[26] According to an estimate by Dr Ikramul Haq, Pakistan's tax-to-GDP ratio has dwindled to 6.5 per cent.[27] Major sectors of the economy are outside the tax net – agriculture (22.7 per cent) and retail (18 per cent). Together, they account for over 40 per cent of Pakistan's GDP. Yet, their contribution to tax collection is negligible.

According to World Bank figures, Gross Domestic Savings for Pakistan in 2023 were 6.4 per cent of the GDP. This figure for Bhutan was 21.41 per cent (2022); 23.8 per cent for Sri Lanka (2023); 25.8 per cent for Bangladesh (2023); 29.2 per cent for India (2023) and 46.6 per cent for China (2022).[28]

Pakistan's economic conditions require fundamental changes. The budget for FY 2024–25 presented in June 2024 showed that Shehbaz Sharif's government was either unable or unwilling to attempt them.

The army claimed its pound of flesh. Defence is part of the federal government's responsibility. Therefore, the defence burden has to be seen in terms of the federal government's share of revenue. The budget has allocated Pakistani rupees 2.122 trillion to the defence sector. There is an additional provision of Rs 662 billion for military pensions. Thus, the total amount allocated to the defence sector is Rs 2.784 trillion. The federal government's net revenue is projected as Rs 10.377 trillion. The military has appropriated more than a quarter (26.83 per cent) of the revenue available despite the country's dire economic crisis.

The revenue projections are based on a GDP growth rate of 3.6 per cent for FY 2024–25. Last year, the economy grew by 2.38 per cent, according to the Pakistan Bureau of Statistics.[29] A sharp increase in GDP growth at a time when IMF conditions are expected to bring contractionary pressures in the economy may not be too realistic. A shortfall in revenue and growth projection will mean the share of military expenditure or debt payments will be still higher than the above figures suggest. Pakistan's deepening crisis is a result of decades of living beyond its means, as the former governor of the State Bank of Pakistan candidly admitted.

Reforms need political consensus, which is impossible in an increasingly polarized environment. The PTI wrote a letter to the IMF in February 2024, stating that Shehbaz Sharif's government is 'a government without legitimate representation, carries no moral authority to govern, and, in particular, to carry out taxation measures'. It asked the IMF to 'ensure' '…an audit of at least thirty percent of the national and provincial assemblies' seats' 'prior to the grant of finance facility that is to burden the people of Pakistan with further debt'.[30]

The letter conveyed that in a divided polity, the Shehbaz Sharif government's authority is challenged, and giving Pakistan a loan would be risky business. Pakistan is unwilling to control defence expenditure. All four wars with India were initiated by Pakistan. There is hardly any justification for spending 26 per cent of the total revenue of the federal government on defence when the country boasts of full-spectrum nuclear deterrence. Successive governments have failed to widen the tax base to include agriculture. This will affect the interests of the landed gentry, who control Pakistan's politics and the army. Neither the federal budget nor the provincial budgets for FY 2024–25 have included agricultural income in the tax net.

Though ideology plays a large role in determining Pakistan's policies in other spheres, its economic choices are driven by the elite's interests. The only exception is its trade with India, which reflects a deeply ideological approach bereft of any economic logic. High defence expenditure is disproportional to any real or perceived external threat. It reflects only an ideological choice to achieve 'parity' with its bigger neighbour.

23

Imran Khan and Riyasat-e-Madina

'We sided with the US in the war on terror but they came here and killed him, martyred him.'

–Imran Khan on the killing of Osama bin Laden by US commandos[1]

IMRAN KHAN GREW IN stature after losing power. He not only drew large crowds but was also one of the few politicians who could criticize the army. Usually, the fate of the Pakistani ex-prime minister is political exile or oblivion. Bhutto was hanged. Benazir and Nawaz Sharif spent long years in the Middle East after they were eased out. What explains his hold on the Pakistani imagination? Is he only a passing figure in the country's history? A cricketer and a playboy who turned to politics only to discover faith? His vision of 'Naya Pakistan (New Pakistan)' is anchored in the concept of 'Riyasat-e-Madina' which goes back to Islam's early history.

The events of 9 May 2023 changed the situation dramatically. Imran's arrest by the Pakistan Rangers was followed by the attack on the Army GHQ and the ransacking of the Lahore Corps commander's residence. This was described by the ISPR as a 'black day' in Pakistan's history. It marks the point of no return in Imran's relationship with the military. He has become the most controversial politician in the country.

Imran was sentenced to prison in three different cases and disqualified from participation in elections. The cases include the Toshakhana case (selling a state gift from a foreign dignitary), leaking a secret cyber cable and the Iddat case, for marrying his third wife before she had completed the mandatory waiting period after divorce. The charges may appear frivolous. But it is worth recalling that Nawaz Sharif, his predecessor, was removed from the prime minister's office for not declaring the payment he never received from his son's company! At the time, Imran had colluded with the army against Nawaz Sharif. It is not any act of omission or commission, but the power equation with the army that seals the fate of politicians in Pakistan.

Imran Khan's confrontation with the army started building up in 2021. It began with differences over the appointment of the ISI chief. Imran regarded the appointment of the spy chief as the prime minister's prerogative; the army chief thought otherwise. Imran later blamed the army chief, General Qamar Javed Bajwa, for his ouster in 2022. He also claimed foreign (US) interference and accused the Shehbaz Sharif regime of being an 'imported government'. He has since criticized General Asim Munir, Bajwa's successor. He also attacked the ISPR and a few generals by name. If he was trying to drive a wedge between the top leadership of the army by selectively criticizing some officers, the attempt seems to have backfired spectacularly. The army as an institution does not tolerate interference in its internal working.

Imran Khan found himself accidentally thrust into the role of an anti-establishment hero. He owes his political career to the military's patronage. In this, he may be no different than Bhutto or Nawaz Sharif. He benefited from the political void created by Musharraf, who exiled leaders of both the mainstream parties – PPP and PML(N). This was filled by religious parties. Imran Khan supported Musharraf's military coup. He also supported the referendum held by Musharraf in 2002, which was boycotted by all the democratic parties.

The army paved the way for Imran Khan's victory in the 2018 elections by easing out Nawaz Sharif's democratically elected government before the completion of its term. Imran's democratic credentials are of recent origin.

Imran Khan's rise in politics reflects Pakistan's trajectory since Partition. There was a deepening of Pakistan's Islamic identity, especially post 9/11. A policy of fighting the Taliban in Afghanistan paradoxically led to a rise in the influence of religious parties in Pakistan. Jehadi groups chased by the US forces in Afghanistan found sanctuaries in Pakistan. Musharraf accommodated the MMA, a group of pro-Taliban religious parties, in government in the two frontier provinces as well as at the federal level. Musharraf and the MMA went out of power in 2008. However, the army continued to rely on religious groups. Imran Khan was the choice of the military after it had undermined the PPP and PML(N) governments in turn. His public speeches harking back to the glories of early Islam capture the public sentiment.

Imran also capitalized on the growing anti-Americanism in Pakistan. His public stance on the Afghan war was based on opposition to American policies. A *Financial Times* article stated, 'In 2013, as chair of his Pakistan Tehreek-e-Insaf party, Khan threatened to block NATO supply routes after US drone strikes in Pakistan.'[2] In September 2019, as prime minister, Imran Khan stated in an address to the Council on Foreign Relations that 'Pakistan, by joining the U.S. after 9/11, committed one of the biggest blunders'. He added, 'The groups that were close to the Pakistan army, the army was now trying to kill them.'[3] He seemed to regret a change in that polity, and not the army's past association with the terror groups.

In June 2020 Prime Minister Imran Khan in a speech in Pakistan's Parliament criticized the US government's action and described Osama bin Laden as a 'martyr'.[4] It took a year before the PTI information minister issued a clarification, 'It was a slip of the tongue. He had clarified it.'[5] An article in the *New York Times* mentioned, 'The prime minister at first said bin Laden was merely "killed" by the Americans, but quickly corrected himself to say the leader of Al-Qaeda was "martyred".'[6] Given the context, the original expression 'killed' was the slip of the tongue, which the prime minister corrected to 'martyred.' The correction was important given his domestic constituency.

Musharraf's choice to join the coalition against terror was a tactical move. But people on Pakistan's streets saw his actions as a compromise with the Americans. There was a widespread perception that the war against terrorism was not 'our war'. This dented the army's image as a custodian of Pakistan's ideological frontiers. This was the beginning of attacks on military establishments, including two attacks on Musharraf's life. Ironically, Imran, who was the military's creation, is now a beneficiary of the anti-army sentiment.

'Taliban Khan'

Imran Khan is sometimes known by the moniker 'Taliban Khan' in the Pakistani press. He advocated negotiations with the Taliban and opposed launching a military operation in north Waziristan.[7] Imran Khan's pro-Taliban stance earned him rich political dividends in Khyber Pakhtunkhwa. Historically, the province was the stronghold of the ANP, which had a secular agenda. It espoused the cause of Pashtun nationalism and stressed distributive justice. ANP formed the government in Khyber Pakhtunkhwa in 2008. In the 2013 elections, it was replaced by Imran Khan's PTI which formed the government. The PTI's success followed a spate of targeted violence against senior ANP leaders. In the 2024 elections, 'Independents' supported by Imran won a comfortable majority (ninety-one out of 145 seats) at the provincial level. In the elections to the Pakistan National Assembly, the ANP, the main opposition party, got two seats.

Imran professes concern for minority rights but shows scant interest in protecting them. The TTP carried out a twin suicide bombing at the All Saints' Church in Peshawar on 22 September 2013, leaving 127 worshippers dead and over 250 injured. It was the deadliest attack on the Christian minority in the history of Pakistan. Pervez Hoodbhoy has written, 'Imran Khan briefly visited the Church, but his remarks were less than sensitive and seemed to obliquely justify the attack.' He has cited columnist Saroop Ijaz:

> He is crystal clear in his absolute defence of the terrorists. Mr. Khan is no 'apologist', he is an 'advocate', an 'ally'. Whether he does it out of fear or single-digit IQ no longer matters, he is for murder in the name of faith. His vision of 'Naya Pakistan' has the PTI as a political wing of the non-corrupt Tehreek-e-Taliban Pakistan (TTP).[8]

Imran Khan had earned the trust of the Taliban. In early 2014, the Taliban leader Mullah Fazlullah named him as a member of the Taliban team to negotiate with the government.[9] Khaled Ahmed writes, '... Fazlullah had named Imran Khan in his panel, thus creating a situation where PTI would be talking to itself while pretending to talk to the TTP. Mercifully, Khan begged off from this absurd scenario.'[10]

After the terrorist attack on the Army Public School in Peshawar in January 2015, in which 150 persons, including 132 children, were killed, Imran Khan visited the school accompanied by his then-wife Reham Khan and Khyber Pakhtunkhwa Chief Minister Pervez Khattak. They were met with slogans of 'Go Imran Go' and 'Go Khattak Go' by the protesting parents.[11] Imran countered by suggesting that some of the parents appeared to be 'political workers'. This triggered a response by an angry parent: 'We have formed an association, the Shaheed Peshawar Association, which has no political affiliation, and we gathered outside the APS to ask the PTI chairman who is responsible for our children's deaths.'[12]

Prime Minister Imran Khan in an opinion piece in the *Washington Post* on 22 June 2021 blamed the US government for having 'pressured Pakistan for the very first time to send our troops into the semiautonomous tribal areas bordering Afghanistan'.[13] He said this did not stop the insurgency but led to mass displacement of the people internally. It is curious logic that restoring law and order in its territory is not the normal duty of the state. Imran Khan was averse to giving bases to the US but did not comment on the Taliban using sanctuaries in Pakistan to launch attacks on the coalition forces in Afghanistan.

Imran Khan stated, 'In the past, Pakistan made a mistake by choosing between warring Afghan parties, but we have learned from that experience.'[14] Pakistan has never been neutral. It supported the Taliban even when it was receiving US military and economic assistance in the name of fighting them during the first two decades of the new millennium.

The Taliban's capture of power in Kabul in 2021 marked the fulfilment of Pakistan's long-standing goal of achieving 'strategic depth'. However, it brought an unexpected outcome for the Pakistani establishment. By mid-2022, the TTP cadres began returning to Pakistan. There was an increase in incidents of exhortation and killings in Khyber Pakhtunkhwa. Imran stated that his party workers were also being attacked. He said that the Taliban kills US supporters. It should spare his party which has similar thinking as the Taliban.[15]

Imran Khan on Jinnah's Speech of 11 August 1947

Imran Khan tries to appropriate Jinnah for his electoral purposes by quoting him in his speeches. In his address as prime minister to the

Pakistan National Assembly on 6 August, and in the POK assembly on 14 August 2019, he categorically refuted that Jinnah's speech of 11 August 1947 was a 'secular' speech. He said it reflected 'Islamic Sunnah'. Imran also quoted from Islamic history to show that the Jewish minority enjoyed protection in Riyasat-e-Madina. The minorities in his country would be more comfortable if they had the protection of the Constitution, rather than a faith to which they do not belong.

Imran Khan claimed that his family elders – Zaman Khan and Jehangir Khan – took part in the Pakistan movement. He posted on his X (formerly Twitter) handle and Facebook account that they attended the Round Table Conference. He also claimed Zaman Park in Lahore is named after his family. Prof. Ishtiaq Ahmad, a noted historian, pointed out that Zaman Khan and Jehangir Khan were never invited to the Round Table Conference. It was a different Jehangir who participated in the conference. This was Sir Jamshed Jehangir, a Parsi gentleman based in Karachi. Zaman Park is a looted property. It belonged to Hindus originally.[16]

Imran Khan's inconsistencies have not hurt his public image. His supporters have accepted his raunchy past, political grandstanding, and expressions of piety without question. No other leader would enjoy this extraordinary prerogative.

Prime Minister

Imran Khan came to power at the federal level in 2018 with the army's patronage and the support of religious parties like the TLP. His government had a six-member majority in the Pakistan National Assembly. It could not survive without the intervention of the 'neutrals'. Imran had coined this phrase to describe the army when it was his partisan. When it really became 'neutral', he turned against his erstwhile benefactors.

The most striking aspect of the 2018 elections was the emergence of the TLP. Imran Khan benefited from an unstated partnership with the new entrant to national politics. Though it got no seats in the national Parliament, the TLP served its purpose by undercutting the PML(N)'s votes in many constituencies. Overall, the vote share of religious parties went up from 5.6 per cent in the 2013 elections to 9 per cent in 2018.

Under pressure from the TLP, Prime Minister Imran Khan dropped his choice of economic adviser, Princeton University economist Atif R. Mian, who is an Ahmadiya.[17]

Imran, in his inaugural speech after being elected as Pakistan's prime minister in August 2018, promised to make Pakistan an ideal state on the lines of 'Riyasat-e-Madina'. This was a reference to the first community of Muslims founded by the Holy Prophet in the seventh century. Pervez Hoodbhoy writes that, arguably, 'Zia-ul-Haq and Imran Khan have been the only Pakistani leaders who introduced significant changes bringing Pakistan closer to an Islamic state.'[18]

Imran Khan's rhetoric of social justice and the welfare state touches a deep chord among the masses who are facing unprecedented economic hardships. He combines 'fairness' with a call for an 'Islamic welfare' or 'fellahi' (welfare) state rooted in the history of early Islam. This is most comforting, though it does not touch the basic problems of low savings, low investment and high defence expenditure. The Pakistani people do not need charity. The welfare programme in a modern economy has to be matched with better resource mobilization. Imran Khan, like his predecessors, has shied away from this difficult task.

Though Imran makes reference to the welfare state, the rule of law and the Constitution in his speeches, the dominant theme is religion. In his November 2019 speech, he only made two passing references to the fellahi regime. Most of the speech was devoted to early Islamic history. He gave the example of compassion and mercy shown by Prophet Muhammad after his victory over Mecca. He also cited the example of Nelson Mandela. But his treatment of his political opponents was far from the ideals of the Holy Quran and the Prophet's life. It was also different from the reconciliation offered by Mandela to his political adversaries. Imran chose the slogan of 'ehtisab' (accountability) to drive Nawaz Sharif and Asif Zardari into political oblivion. His opponents saw the process as a cover for vindictiveness. Anticipating criticism, the then prime minister Imran said he was sometimes described as 'be-reham' (merciless). But he explained that mercy can only be shown to the poor and the dispossessed. Those who have robbed the state do not deserve it. None can be above the law. While the opposition leaders were harassed, the treatment of the government figures was quite different. Military generals were not subjected to action by the National Accountability Bureau.

Imran Khan, as prime minister, dissolved the Parliament before the vote on the 'no-confidence motion' against him in April 2022. The National Assembly could be restored only with judicial intervention on 7 April 2022. When eventually the vote took place just after midnight on 10 April, the no-trust motion was carried by 174 votes.[19] His party members resigned from the National Assembly as well as provincial assemblies in Punjab and Khyber Pakhtunkhwa to press the demand for early elections at the national level.

Under Imran Khan, Pakistan's economy was plunging in early 2022. In violation of the agreement signed by his government with the IMF, Imran Khan cut petroleum prices and increased subsidies. Paradoxically, he was saved from his follies by the PDM, the alliance of opposition parties. They were in a hurry to unseat him before the term of Army Chief Gen. Bajwa ran out in October 2022. This was necessary to deny Imran the chance to pick Bajwa's successor, who would have helped him cement his hold on the government for the next five years. In the bargain, the PDM took over the biggest liability – the Pakistan government – at a time when the country was facing its worst economic crisis. Shehbaz Sharif faced the dilemma of carrying out painful economic reforms to qualify for IMF assistance when polls were due. This proved to be a boon for Imran. The public anger at the worsening economic situation was transferred to the PDM government headed by Shehbaz Sharif, and the army, which was seen as backing the latter.

Opposition Leader

Imran Khan enjoyed the support of the army in his earlier phase as an opposition leader. But after being eased out of power in 2022, he fell afoul of the army. This was a new situation. Failure to grasp the difference proved his undoing. He continued to berate not only the civilian leadership but also the army.

The violence that followed Imran Khan's first arrest on 9 May 2023 was described by the ISPR, the military's media arm, as 'Black Day'.[20] The statement issued by the ISPR said the group had done what the 'eternal enemy' could not do in seventy-five years.[21] The point about the eternal enemy was a reference to India. Blaming India for Pakistan's internal troubles is part of the standard script used by the Pakistan Army and politicians when in trouble.

The hard-hitting statement by the ISPR mentioned that after Imran's arrest, 'attacks were made on Army property and installations in an organized manner'. It warned that in case of any further attack against the security forces, there would be severe 'retaliation', 'the responsibility for which will be on this very group that wants to push Pakistan into a civil war and has expressed it multiple times'.[22]

After his release by the Supreme Court's orders, Imran Khan, in a speech, renewed his attacks on the army. He recalled the events of 1971 when East Pakistan broke away. He said that instead of inviting the party which had won the majority, a military operation was launched against them. He further added that pitting the army against the largest political party (PTI) would lead to the break-up of Pakistan in so many parts that it would be difficult to pick up the pieces. Repeated references to the events of 1971 were calculated to draw attention to the role of the army as well as Bhutto in the break-up of the country.

Is Imran leading a protest movement? Or simply using the people's grievances? What explains his popularity? As Pakistani commentator Raza Rumi wrote:

> The social classes that inhabit unelected institutions share Mr Khan's weltanschauung which comprises exhibitions of public religiosity, hatred for traditional political elites, citing 'corruption' as the biggest issue, and a convenient, varying dose of anti-Americanism. This is why Mr Khan is a formidable foe for the ancien regime. He is their creature and nemesis at the same time.[23]

The 'unelected institutions' is a reference to the judiciary and the military. Raza Rumi's comment provides useful insight into the mindset of the educated middle class, which is the backbone of these two institutions. However, the class origin of the Pakistani establishment does not explain the crowd that attacked the Army GHQ and ransacked the Lahore Corps commander's residence. Some of them were shown on social media looting food from the kitchen. This included frozen strawberries and 'falsas'. While the former is a luxury item, the latter is a common fruit found in northern India and Pakistan.

It is difficult to explain the crowd behaviour in terms of the charisma of an individual. Attacking army installations is a high-risk venture in Pakistan. The people are facing economic distress. The inflation rate is running above 30 per cent, while the food inflation is still higher at 48 per cent. The country witnessed riots over the distribution of *atta* in 2022. If it is a protest movement against the dire economic condition of the people, it will endure much after Imran Khan has become a footnote in history.

Imran Khan, with his lavish lifestyle, is an unlikely icon for the impoverished masses. His economic programme did not include widening the tax base. Nor did he attempt land reforms. The slogan of fairness and equity (*insaf*) was about punishing his political rivals who were supposed to have looted the country. This may be true. But a campaign against corruption is no substitute for an economic programme. His 'messaging' is of a different nature; he tries to rely on faith and Islam's past glory.

Imran Khan not only reflects Pakistan's ideology but is also shaping it. He is giving it a push towards deeper Islamization. His philosophy is rooted in the social contract of the seventh century, while Arab states are trying to liberalize their societies. The anti-American strand in Pakistan's national discourse predates the rise of Imran Khan. He has only reinforced it. The beauty of Islam is the idea of equality. Imran Khan's life and career may be furthest from this high principle. The PML(N) and PPP leadership may accuse him of corruption, but to the masses, he is the leader who is promising to lead the nation back on the righteous path.

What is intriguing is that, in the aftermath of 9 May 2023, several senior army officers were dismissed. This suggests that Imran had sympathizers within the officer corps. The ISPR statement cited earlier accused Imran of attempting to push Pakistan into a civil war. Imran has repeatedly referenced the events of 1971. However, he is no Sheikh Mujibur Rahman, nor are the people of Punjab an oppressed majority – unlike the Bengalis, who were. Punjab holds the lion's share of political influence as well as control over the country's ultimate power structure – the army.

'Independents' backed by Imran Khan secured the largest number of seats in Pakistan's Parliament in 2024, though they fell short of a majority. The government has been formed by Shehbaz Sharif, with the support of the PPP, while PTI supporters sit in opposition in the National Assembly. However, they have secured a comfortable majority in Khyber Pakhtunkhwa and have formed the government there. Meanwhile, Imran Khan remains behind bars. The army can engage in political engineering, but managing an economy in free fall will not be easy. The situation remains highly unpredictable.

There was some improvement in PTI's position with the Supreme Court's ruling that the party was entitled to its share of reserved seats. But the arrest and court martial of Faiz Hameed, the former ISI chief who was close to Imran, suggest that the noose may be tightening again.

Imran Khan has often boasted that he will play to the last ball. But the cricketer now finds himself on an unfamiliar wicket, facing the army. The attack on army installations on 9 May has brought the full weight of the military down on PTI supporters. Opposing the army in Pakistan is very different from opposing a civilian regime. Nawaz Sharif and Benazir Bhutto both returned to power after clashing with the army, though their truces with the establishment were short-lived. Will Imran have a second innings?

At present, this looks difficult. He is seventy-two, with no clear line of succession or second-tier leadership. Imran has often claimed that his party is the largest in Pakistan. He overlooked the fact that the largest party in Pakistan is the army. While he may not return to power, his political trajectory has shown that the centre of gravity in Pakistan's politics has shifted further towards religious fundamentalism.

24

Conclusion

'The two-nation theory which we had used for the fight for Pakistan had created not only bad blood against the Muslims of the minority provinces but also an ideological wedge between them and the Hindus of India.'

–Chaudhry Khaliquzzaman, who became president of Pakistan Muslim League after Jinnah, in his memoir *Pathway to Pakistan*[1]

THE FLOODS IN PAKISTAN in 2022 caused massive damage to the country's economy and left millions homeless. The floods were the result of global warming caused by industrialized countries. Pakistan has very low per capita emissions. Extreme weather events have impacted other parts of the world as well. The fragile economies of developing countries have fewer resources to cope with their after-effects. Pakistan has also been in the throes of a deepening economic crisis, much before the floods or the COVID-19 pandemic. It signed an agreement for a nearly $7 billion loan under the Extended Finance Facility of the IMF in September 2024. This is the twenty-fifth package of IMF assistance the country has received.

Unlike climate change, Pakistan's economic problems are of its own making. They have persisted despite the generous assistance received from the international community. Does the 'Ideology of Pakistan' equip it to cope with the twin threats of climate change and under-development?

The ideology of Pakistan is anchored in the past. The combination of high defence expenditure, low savings rate and low tax-to-GDP ratio has pushed the country into a debt trap, leaving no resources to meet new challenges. The economic crisis comes at a time of deep political polarization in the country. Imran Khan, the principal opposition leader, has been sentenced to a three-year prison term and disqualified from participation in elections for five years. Without political consensus, it would be difficult for the government to undertake the unpopular measures required to restore economic stability.

Soon after the election of the Shehbaz Sharif government, Imran wrote a letter to the IMF, suggesting that future assistance be linked to fair elections. The divide in Pakistan's society extends beyond civilian politics to a growing disillusion with the role of the military. The challenge to the army's legitimacy comes not from outlying areas, but from the largest province – Punjab, which also accounts for the bulk of recruitment in the army.

The IMF report on Article IV consultations with Pakistan of October 2024 mentions, 'In 1980 Pakistan had higher per capita GDP (PPP terms) than many regional peers, but its living standards since have fallen behind.'[2] This reflects a long-term trend of relative decline, except for interludes where foreign aid boosted the economy, such as during the Cold War and post 9/11 period. But geopolitics cannot be a substitute for sound economic management. Pakistan has repeatedly been on the verge of default. Despite the dire economic situation and prodding by the IMF, the tax base remains narrow. The poor bear a disproportionately high burden, with indirect taxes accounting for 80 per cent of the total tax collection. The increased inequalities have created social unrest. Islam lays stress on equality, yet in Pakistan, elite interest has trumped faith.

The ideology of Pakistan provides no solution to the existential problems the country faces. Pakistan is an agricultural country; it depends upon rivers which draw water from the melting of glaciers. With global warming, the melting of Himalayan glaciers is expected to increase and cause more frequent floods. According to a Yale University study, glaciers in the Karakoram range, 'could vanish by the end of the century. Correspondingly, meltwater is expected to increase until around the 2050s and then begin to decline.'[3] The Indus basin is particularly vulnerable 'because snow and ice melt comprise as much as 72 percent of river runoffs in the upper Indus, compared with between 20 and 25 percent in the Ganges and Brahmaputra rivers (the last two depend on monsoon rain)'.[4]

Meltwater increase in the next few decades will cause more frequent floods. Once the glaciers have melted beyond a point, the process will reverse and there will be drought. Pakistan is seeking to build five dams in the upper reaches of the Indus river in Gilgit-Baltistan, which is part of POK. It has signed an MOU with China for the construction of the Diamer-Bhasha dam. Pakistan might benefit from the hydropower, but this will also affect the fragile ecology of the region. There will be less and less meltwater available after 2050.

Imran Khan, as prime minister, was fond of calling for insaf and an Islamic fellahi state. He provided no programme to address the rising inequalities in Pakistan. He alone is not to be blamed for a system built by Pakistan's civil-political elite over seven decades. Agriculture and retail are both exempt from income tax. The former benefits the rural landed gentry, which controls the legislatures, and the latter, the urban business class. Pakistan has an eschewed taxation system with 80 per cent of revenue coming from indirect taxes. Their incidence falls on the poor. In September 2023, the IMF Managing Director Kristalina Georgieva gave curt advice to Pakistan's caretaker prime minister Anwar-ul-Haq Kakar: 'Please collect more taxes from the wealthy and please protect the poor people of Pakistan.'

The idea of Pakistan was fundamentally different from the Westphalian system where the nation state was defined in terms of geography, not the king's religion. This was expressly rejected by both Iqbal and Maududi. The influence of ideology over state policy is not something that is immutable, as shown by the collapse of communism in Russia and Eastern Europe. China, under Xi Jinping, is reverting to increased party control, but the party is practising a blend of market economy and nationalism. The communist ideology is based on economic interests, not faith. Sovereignty belongs to the party in China; it belongs to the divine in Pakistan according to the Objectives Resolution, which has become the cornerstone of the Constitution.

In Pakistan, the role of ideology has strengthened because of the choices made by the Pakistani rulers. They have shown enormous pragmatism where it suits their interests. Pakistan effortlessly changed from being a camp follower of the West to an all-weather friendship with communist China. In both phases, it insulated the domestic polity from the Western or the Chinese model. The ideology did not constrain it from exploiting Muslim East Pakistan. Nor has it stopped it from exploiting POK, which is paid remuneration for its water resources at one-seventh the rate paid to projects in Punjab or Khyber Pakhtunkhwa. The economic policies followed by successive Pakistani rulers have accentuated inequalities, which goes against the principle of equality preached by Islam. Pakistan has, however, allowed ideology to shape its policy towards India, which is an extension of the Two-Nation Theory espoused by the Muslim League.

The February 2024 elections have exposed Pakistan's political fault lines. The PML(N) formed the government despite finishing second to PTI-supported 'Independents'. In Pakistan today, no party has a countrywide presence. Effectively, both PML(N) and PPP have become regional parties. The former is largely confined to Punjab while the latter has a presence mostly in Sindh. The success of PTI-backed candidates partly reflects the economic distress for which the PDM coalition was blamed. But it also shows the impact of ideology. Imran's appeal to religion and anti-Western discourse finds an echo among the masses. This reflects the median of Pakistan's society.

The census highlights a curious twist of history. The country's eastern wing was more populous than its western wing in 1947. Their history of uneasy coexistence was marred by a consistent attempt to deny the numerical majority of East Pakistan. Today, Pakistan has a larger population (241.427 million) than Bangladesh (173.297 million).[5] Pakistan is behind Bangladesh in terms of all socio-economic indicators, but it has a higher population growth rate. Pakistan's population growth rate (1.98 per cent) exceeds that of other Islamic countries – Malaysia (1.09 per cent), Bangladesh (1.03 per cent), Iran (0.7 per cent) and Turkey (0.56 per cent). India's population growth rate is 0.81 per cent, while China's growth rate dropped to negative 0.02 per cent in 2023.[6] Unchecked population explosion is the third biggest problem the country faces, next to climate change and economic reforms. 40.1 per cent of Pakistan's population was below the poverty line in 2023–24.[7] The GDP growth rate (2 per cent) is not sufficient to make a dent in the poverty level, given the high rate of population growth (1.98 per cent).

The conception of a state based on religion was inherently flawed. It led to the partition of the subcontinent and the uprooting of millions of people. As Wali Khan said, this was not simply the partition of India, but the partition of the Muslim community. With Bangladesh breaking away from Pakistan in 1971, what the League called 'Muslim India' is now divided into three parts, attenuating its political strength. The supreme folly of what Jinnah achieved is that the Muslims in the Muslim-majority states did not need Pakistan. Their numerical majority gave them a permanent safeguard of their interests. The Muslims of the Muslim-minority provinces, who were in the vanguard of the Pakistan movement, suffered the consequences of Partition. As Khaliquzzaman has written, 'The two-nation theory which we had used for the fight for Pakistan had created not only bad blood against the Muslims of the minority provinces but also an ideological wedge between them and the Hindus of India.'[8]

General Asim Munir, addressing a conference of ulema on 8 August 2024, said, 'Those who do not accept Shariat and Constitution, we do not recognize them as Pakistanis.'[9] The meaning was clear. Faith defines citizenship. And the final arbiter to judge an individual's acceptance of Shariat and Constitution is the army. In the triangular contest between the army, Imran Khan and the Tehreek-e-Taliban Pakistan, each is trying to use religion against the other. Shariat is invoked to delegitimize opponents. The contest to shape ideology is deepening its role in the country at a time when it is facing its worst economic crisis.

General Munir gave the call for accepting Sharia and the Constitution to an audience of the clergy. He said no one would be allowed to spread anarchy. Was this a caution to them against straying into the lay domain? There was perhaps another audience he was targeting – Imran's suspected followers within the army. This may be an index of radicalization within the army. But the use of religious idiom deepens the problem, coming as it does from the highest echelon of the army.

General Asim Munir, in his speech to Overseas Pakistanis on 16 April 2025, reminded his audience that they 'belong' to a superior 'ideology'. He stressed the Two-Nation Theory while reaffirming his determination to hold on to Balochistan. The Baloch never wanted to join the Pakistani state; they do not find religion a sufficient basis of nationality. Hatred for Hindu India remains the only basis for Pakistan's identity seven decades after Partition. As Pakistan's internal problems mount, its army falls back on religion-based ideology.

Will Pakistan break free from the trap of ideology that has placed it in a needless conflict with its bigger neighbour, and has created chaos inside? This will release much-needed resources for the development of the people of Pakistan. It does not face a threat from India. All four wars – 1947, 1965, 1971 and 1999 – were started by Pakistan. Its army's calculation that the threat of escalation to the nuclear level will deter India's conventional response to its sub-conventional warfare went disastrously wrong during the Kargil War.

Pakistan must also accept that the war on terror is its 'own' war. General Kayani acknowledged this in his speech in 2012 at the Pakistan Military Academy at Abbottabad. But the fleeting recognition by the then army chief has faded from public memory. The Pakistani Army's bets on the Taliban providing strategic depth in Afghanistan, and Imran Khan proving to be a pliant stakeholder, have gone spectacularly wrong. What lessons has it drawn from the twin fiascos? After achieving nuclear deterrence, does Pakistan still need strategic depth in Afghanistan? Normalization of relations with India will give Pakistan a peace dividend in terms of lower defence expenditure, and let that country emerge as a transit hub between India's growing market, Central Asia and West Asia.

There is also the other Pakistan, of Faiz Ahmad Faiz, Nayyara Noor (the singer) and Anwar Maqsood, a very courageous satirist. During my stint in the Indian Consulate, I had the privilege of knowing many distinguished Pakistanis. I was touched by the warmth of the people. I came to know Habib Jalib, the revolutionary poet. I called on Mir Saheb, the founder of *Jang*. I had the privilege of being invited by Maulana Edhi to his home. I was introduced to Pakistan's Constitution by Justice Dorab Patel. The port town had a thriving business community. Many from that generation have passed away. But Pakistan continues to have highly talented people. Do they have political space to make the changes their country needs?

Was Jinnah the sole spokesman of the 'Muslim India'? Maulana Azad, Maulana Hussain Madani, Rafi Ahmed Kidwai and other Muslims chose India. Post-Partition, India continued to be enriched by the contributions of Muslims in various fields. At least three served as presidents of the republic – Dr Zakir Husain, Fakhruddin Ali Ahmed, and Dr A.P.J. Abdul Kalam. There were distinguished members of the Sikh, Christian and Parsi communities who have rendered enormous service to the nation. No country is perfect. But the fact that India, with an overwhelming Hindu population, chose a Constitution that provides equal opportunity to all people shows the spirit of tolerance the country has. This choice was made despite the trauma of Partition based on religion.

There were courageous leaders like Badshah Khan and his brother Dr Khan Saheb in undivided India, who wanted NWFP to be part of India. This was a refutation of the Muslim League's Two-Nation Theory by an overwhelmingly Muslim-majority province. The Muslim League won by a narrow margin in a referendum in NWFP boycotted by the Khudai Khidmatgar under the Khan Brothers. In a departure from the practice followed in Bengal, Punjab and Sindh where provincial assemblies were given the choice to join either dominion, the British ordered a referendum in NWFP, where the Congress government led by Dr Khan Saheb had the majority in the assembly. Wali Khan in *Facts Are Facts* states, 'The referendum was held only in six districts of the province, and six Agency Areas adjacent to the Frontier were excluded along with the tribal areas.' 'The population of the entire Frontier province was seventy to eighty lakhs.' However, there were only 5,72,799 voters and the votes polled were merely 2,92,118. Votes in favour of Pakistan were 2,89,244 (50.5 per cent).[10]

While Dr Khan Saheb was assassinated on 9 May 1958 in Pakistan, Badshah Khan spent long years in exile. He had a great sense of disappointment with the Congress leaders who accepted the Partition plan without consulting him. He died on 20 January 1988 in Peshawar. He was buried in Jalalabad in Afghanistan, as per his wishes. Despite the ongoing civil war in that country, both sides agreed to a ceasefire during his funeral in a tribute to the cause of Pashtun nationalism he espoused. He was a devout Muslim who adopted non-violent methods. His legacy has enormous significance for a region that has come to be associated with the Taliban and Al-Qaeda after 9/11. His son Wali Khan carried on the secular tradition.

Acknowledgements

MY THANKS TO MY countless friends in Karachi, who gave me an insight into Pakistan. My posting there coincided with Operation Clean-up, the first military crackdown against Muhajirs, who gave birth to the idea of Pakistan. I had the privilege of knowing some eminent figures like Meiraj Mohammad Khan, Justice Dorab Patel, Sardar Sherbaz Mazari and Habib Jalib.

I would like to thank the US Library of Congress and the United Nations Dag Hammarskjold Library for some of the research material used for this book.

I would also like to thank Shahram Sarmadee for helping me gain access to Urdu publications.

My grateful thanks to Bloomsbury, and in particular Nitin and Srishti for their effort in giving shape to this book.

Notes

Chapter 2 The Ideologies of Pakistan

1 Sir Muhammad Iqbal, Presidential Address to the 25th Session of the All-India Muslim League, Allahabad, 29 December 1930.
2 Justice Dorab Patel, *Testament of a Liberal* (Oxford University Press, 2004), 139.
3 Ibid., 136–137.
4 Dorab Patel, *Testament of a Liberal*, 170.
5 Ayub Khan, *Friends Not Masters: A Political Autobiography* (Oxford University Press, 1967), 196.
6 Justice Muhammad Munir, *From Jinnah to Zia* (Vanguard Books, 1979), 25.
7 Jayanta Kumar Ray, *Democracy and Nationalism on Trial: A Study of East Pakistan* (Indian Institute of Advanced Study, 1968), 57.
8 Qudratullah Shahab, *Shahabnama* (Sang-e-Meel Publications, 1987), 293.
9 Sir Syed Ahmad Khan, Speech at Lucknow, 1887.
10 Farzana Shaikh, *Making Sense of Pakistan* (C. Hurst & Co., 2009), 24.
11 Roy Jackson, *Mawlana Mawdudi and Political Islam: Authority and the Islamic State* (Routledge, 2010), 59.
12 Sir Muhammad Iqbal, Muslim League Presidential Address, 1930.
13 Ibid.
14 Pervez Hoodbhoy, *Pakistan: Origins, Identity and Future* (Routledge, 2023), 289.
15 Pervez Hoodbhoy, *Pakistan: Origins, Identity and Future*, 112.
16 Maulana Maududi, *Masla Qaumiyat* (Deen-e-Mohammadi Press, 1935), 50.
17 Ibid., 100.
18 Ibid., 103.
19 Farzana Shaikh, *Making Sense of Pakistan*, 36–37.
20 Ishtiaq Ahmed, *Jinnah: His Successes, Failures and Role in History* (Penguin Random House, 2020), 312.
21 Ayub Khan, *Friends Not Masters*, 196.
22 Munir, *From Jinnah to Zia*, 74.
23 Ibid.
24 Ibid.
25 Ibid.

26 Ibid.
27 Ibid., 109.
28 Shahab, *Shahabnama*, 1157–1158.
29 Shahab, *Shahabnama*, 1153.
30 Najam Sethi, 'Fallout', *Friday Times*, 3 April 2020.
31 Altaf Gauhar, *Ayub Khan: Pakistan's First Military Ruler* (Oxford University Press, 1998), 346.
32 Khaled Ahmed, *Sleepwalking to Surrender: Dealing with Terrorism in Pakistan* (Penguin Random House, 2016), 7.
33 Ibid.
34 Faizal Devji, *Muslim Zion: Pakistan as a Political Idea* (C. Hurst and Co. Publishers, 2013), 16.
35 Aitzaz Ahsan, *The Indus Saga and The Making of Pakistan* (Jumhoori Publications, 2013), 350.

Chapter 3 Two-Nation Theory

1 Muhammad Ali Jinnah, Presidential Address to the Muslim League, Lahore, March 1940.
2 Akbar S. Ahmed, *Jinnah, Pakistan, and Islamic Identity: The Search for Saladin* (Routledge, 1997), 110.
3 Ibid.
4 Sir Syed Ahmad Khan, *Asbab-e-Baghawat-e-Hind* (Sang-e-Meel Publications), 3.
5 Ibid., 5.
6 Ibid.
7 Ibid., 8.
8 Ibid., 8.
9 Ibid., 9.
10 Ibid., 11.
11 Thomas R. Metcalf, *Ideologies of the Raj* (Cambridge University Press, 1997; online edition 2008), 50.
12 Wali Khan, *Facts Are Facts: The Untold Story of India's Partition* (Vikas Publishing House, 1987), 3.
13 Sir Syed Ahmad Khan, Speech in Lucknow, 1887.
14 Sir Syed Ahmad Khan, Speech in Meerut, 1888.
15 Ibid.
16 Chaudhry Khaliquzzaman, *Pathway to Pakistan* (Longman, 1961), 12.
17 Khaliquzzaman, *Pathway to Pakistan*, 12.
18 Ibid., 43.
19 Ibid.
20 Niaz Murtaza, 'National Myths', *Dawn*, 11 April 2017.

Chapter 4 Lahore Resolution

1 Chaudhry Khaliquzzaman, *Pathway to Pakistan* (Longman, 1961), 345.
2 V.P. Menon, *Transfer of Power* (Orient Blackswan Private Limited, 1957), 58–59.
3 Ibid., 66.
4 Ibid., 80.
5 Ayesha Jalal, *The Sole Spokesman* (Cambridge University Press, 1985), 55.
6 Ibid., 56.
7 Bipin Chandra, *India's Struggle for Independence 1857-1947* (Viking, 1988), 431.
8 Menon, *Transfer of Power*, 66.
9 Ibid., 81–82.
10 Khaliquzzaman, *Pathway to Pakistan*, 207.
11 H.V. Hodson, *The Great Divide* (Oxford University Press, 1969), 83.
12 Ibid.
13 Edward Penderel Moon, *Divide and Quit* (Chatto & Windus, 1961), as cited by Hodson in *The Great Divide*, 83.
14 Hodson, *The Great Divide*, 83.
15 Ibid.
16 Khaliquzzaman, *Pathway to Pakistan*, 342.
17 Ibid., 343.
18 Ibid., 344.
19 Ibid.
20 Ibid., 236–237.
21 Penderel Moon, *Divide and Quit*, 20.
22 Ishtiaq Ahmed, *Jinnah – His Successes, Failures and Role in History* (Lightstone, 2020), 248, citing Khurshid Ahmad Khan Yusufi, *Speeches, Statements and Messages of the Quaid-e-Azam*, Vol. 2 (Bazm-i-Iqbal, 1996).
23 Jalal, *The Sole Spokesman*, 57.
24 Khaliquzzaman, *Pathway to Pakistan*, 234.
25 Hodson, *The Great Divide*, 79.
26 Ibid.
27 Ishtiaq Ahmed, *Jinnah – His Successes, Failures and Role in History*, 209.
28 Hodson, *The Great Divide*, 88.

Chapter 5 Cripps Mission, Cabinet Mission Plan and Nehru's Statement of July 1946

1 H.V. Hodson, *The Great Divide* (Oxford University Press, 1964), 164.
2 V.P. Menon, *Transfer of Power* (Orient Blackswan Private Limited, 1957), 132.

3 Menon, *Transfer of Power*, 133.
4 Penderel Moon, *Divide and Quit* (Chatto and Windus, 1961), 27.
5 Ibid.
6 Menon, *Transfer of Power*, 153.
7 Ibid.
8 Penderel Moon, *Divide and Quit*, 46.
9 Hodson, *The Great Divide*, 139.
10 Ibid., 140.
11 Ibid., 142.
12 Ibid., 153.
13 Penderel Moon, *Divide and Quit*, 51.
14 Ibid., 48.
15 Ibid.
16 Transfer of Power, Field Marshal Viscount Wavell to Lord Pethick-Lawrence, Telegram, R/3/1/112: ff 15-16, New Delhi 16 July 1946.
17 Maulana Azad, 'The Call for Direct Action', in Sheila McDonough (ed.), *Mohammed Ali Jinnah: Maker of Modern Pakistan* (D.C. Heath & Co., 1971), 57.
18 Hodson, *The Great Divide*, 165.
19 Ibid., 169.
20 Ibid., 164.
21 Muhammad Ali Jinnah, First Presidential Address to the Constituent Assembly of Pakistan, 11 August 1947.
22 Venkat Dhulipala, *Creating a New Medina: State Power, Islam, and the Quest for Pakistan in Late Colonial North India* (Cambridge University Press, 2016), 389.
23 Maulana Azad, 'The Call for Direct Action', in Sheila McDonough (ed.), *Mohammed Ali Jinnah: Maker of Modern Pakistan*, 59.

Chapter 6 Muslims for a United India

1 Maulana Hussain Ahmad Madani, *Muttahida Qaumiyat aur Islam* (Idarat Tulue Al Islam, Qaumi Ekta Trust, 1938), 51–57.
2 S. Irfan Habib, *Maulana Azad: A Life* (Aleph Book Company, 2023), 126.
3 Ibid., 135.
4 Shamsul Islam, *Muslims Against Partition of India: Revisiting the Legacy of Patriotic Muslims* (Pharos Media and Publishing, 2017), 191.
5 Ibid., 192.
6 Ibid., 140.
7 Ibid., 148.
8 Wilfred Cantwell Smith, *Islam in Modern History* (Princeton University Press, 1957), 282.

9 Maulana Hussain Ahmad Madani, *Muttahida Qaumiyat aur Islam* (Qaumi Ekta Trust, 1938), 37–46.
10 Madani, *Muttahida Qaumiyat aur Islam*, 37/43.
11 Ibid.
12 Madani, *Muttahida Qaumiyat aur Islam*, 38/44.
13 Madani, *Muttahida Qaumiyat aur Islam*, 51/57.
14 Madani, *Muttahida Qaumiyat aur Islam*, 54.
15 Maulana Maududi, *Masla Qaumiyat* (Idara Tarjuman-ul-Quran, 1935), 53–54.
16 Madani, *Muttahida Qaumiyat aur Islam*, 51/57.
17 Shamsul Islam, *Muslims Against Partition of India*, 85.
18 Ibid., 190.
19 Shamsul Islam, *Muslims Against Partition of India*, 192.
20 Abdul Ghaffar Khan, *The Frontier Gandhi: My Life and Struggle, Autobiography of Abdul Ghaffar Khan*, trans. Imtiaz Ahmad Sahibzada (Rupa Publications, 2021), 174.
21 Ibid., 175.
22 Ibid., 177.
23 Ibid., 178.
24 Ibid., 201.
25 Ibid.
26 Ibid., 201–202.
27 Ibid.

Chapter 7 Jinnah's Speech of 11 August 1947

1 Chaudhry Khaliquzzaman, *Pathway to Pakistan* (Longman, 1961), 320–321.
2 Muhammad Ali Jinnah, First Presidential Address to the Constituent Assembly of Pakistan, 11 August 1947.
3 Ibid.
4 Muhammad Ali Jinnah, Presidential Address to the Muslim League, Lahore, March 1940.
5 Jinnah, First Presidential Address to the Constituent Assembly of Pakistan.
6 Wali Khan, *Facts Are Facts: The Untold Story of India's Partition* (Vikas Publishing House, 1987), 160.
7 Ibid.
8 Ibid., 143.
9 Ibid.
10 Munir, *From Jinnah to Zia*, 32.
11 Ibid.
12 Liaquat Ali Khan, Constituent Assembly Debates, National Assembly of Pakistan.

13 Munir, *From Jinnah to Zia*, 37.
14 Ibid., 34.
15 Ibid.
16 'The Objectives Resolution', *Islamic Studies* 48, no. 1 (Spring 2009): 114.
17 Ibid.
18 Jinnah Papers, *Pakistan: Struggling for Survival, 1 January-30 September 1948*, First Series, Vol. VII, Editor-in-Chief, Z.H. Zaidi; Quaid-I-Azam Papers Project, Culture Division, Government of Pakistan.
19 Akbar S. Ahmed, *Jinnah, Pakistan, and Islamic Identity* (Routledge, 1997), 197.
20 Ibid., 175.
21 Ibid., 176.
22 Ibid.
23 Ibid.
24 Ibid., 36.
25 Ibid.
26 Ayesha Siddiqa, 'A Friendship Fit for a King', *Friday Times*, 28 April 2007.
27 Khaliquzzaman, *Pathway to Pakistan*, 320–321.
28 Ishtiaq Ahmed, *Jinnah: His Successes, Failures and Role in History*, 502–503.
29 Khurshid Ahmad Khan Yousufi, *Speeches, Statements and Messages of the Quaid-e-Azam, Vol. II* (Bazm-e-Iqbal, 1996), as cited by Ishtiaq Ahmed in *Jinnah: His Successes, Failures and Role in History*, 1306.
30 R.J. Moore, 'Jinnah and the Pakistan Demand', *Modern Asian Studies* 17, no. 4 (1983): 529–561, as cited in Farzana Shaikh, *Making Sense of Pakistan* (Columbia University Press, 2009), 69.
31 Farzana Shaikh, *Making Sense of Pakistan*, 60.

Chapter 8 Divine Sovereignty

1 'The Objectives Resolution', *Islamic Studies* 48, no. 1 (Spring 2009): 91.
2 Ibid.
3 Ibid.
4 Ibid.
5 Ibid.
6 Munir, *From Jinnah to Zia* (New Era Press, 1901), 37.
7 Ibid., 36.
8 'The Objectives Resolution', *Islamic Studies* 48, no. 1 (Spring 2009), 95.
9 Ibid., 100.
10 Ibid., 104.
11 Ibid., 105.
12 Ibid., 114.
13 Ibid.
14 Ibid., 115.

15 Ibid., 117.

16 'I Have Been Removed Repeatedly But You Keep Bringing Me Back, Says Re-Elected PM-N Head Nawaz', *Dawn*, 3 October 2017.

Chapter 9 The 'Other' Nation

1 Sheikh Mujibur Rahman, *The Unfinished Memoirs* (University Press Bangladesh, 2012), 56.

2 Ibid.

3 Sherbaz Khan Mazari, *A Journey to Disillusionment* (Oxford Pakistan Paperbacks, 1999), 56.

4 Syed Badrul Ahsan, 'When Mr. Jinnah Came to Dhaka', *Dhaka Tribune*, 4 March 2020.

5 Ibid.

6 Sheikh Mujibur Rahman, *The Unfinished Memoirs*, 104.

7 Ahsan I. Butt, *Succession and Security: Explaining State Strategy against Separatists* (Cornell University Press, 2017).

8 Jayanta Kumar Ray, *Democracy and Nationalism on Trial*, 50.

9 Ayub Khan, *Friends Not Masters*, 184.

10 Mussarat Jabeen, Amir Ali Chandio and Zarina Qasim, 'Language Controversy: Impacts on National Politics and Secession of East Pakistan', *South Asian Studies: A Research Journal of South Asian Studies* 25, no. 1 (January–June 2010): 109.

11 Ibid., 111.

12 Jayanta Kumar Ray, *Democracy and Nationalism on Trial*, 35–36

13 Ibid., 38.

14 Ibid., 10.

15 Sherbaz Mazari, *A Journey to Disillusionment*, 56.

16 Ibid., 38.

17 Ibid., 64.

18 Jayanta Kumar Ray, *Democracy and Nationalism on Trial*, 76.

19 Altaf Gauhar, *Ayub Khan: Pakistan's First Military Ruler* (Sang-e-Meel Publications, 1993), 346.

20 Chaudhry Muhammad Ali, *The Emergence of Pakistan* (Columbia University Press, 1967), 298.

21 Ibid., 299.

22 Ibid.

23 Ibid.

24 Ibid., 204.

25 Jayanta Kumar Ray, *Democracy and Nationalism on Trial*, 158.

26 Ibid., 334–335.

27 Ibid., 96.

28 Sherbaz Mazari, *A Journey to Disillusionment*, 136.
29 Ibid., 137.
30 Altaf Gauhar, *Ayub Khan: Pakistan's First Military Ruler*, 325.
31 Ibid., 328.
32 Sherbaz Mazari, *A Journey to Disillusionment*, 142.
33 Altaf Gauhar, *Ayub Khan: Pakistan's First Military Ruler*, 332.
34 Sherbaz Mazari, *A Journey to Disillusionment*, 175.
35 Ibid., 173.
36 Ibid., 179.
37 Ibid.
38 Ibid.
39 Ibid., 180.
40 Ibid., 181.
41 Ibid., 182.
42 Ibid.
43 Ibid., 183.
44 Ibid.
45 Ibid., 185.
46 Ibid., 186.
47 Ibid., 190.
48 Ibid., 192.
49 Ibid., 208.
50 Ibid., 212.
51 Ibid., 213.
52 Telegram from the Consulate General in Dacca to the Department of State, https://history.state.gov/historicaldocuments/frus1969-76v11/d19
53 PTV News Official, 8 August 2024.

Chapter 10 Who Is a Muslim?

1 Munir, *From Jinnah to Zia* (New Era Press, 1981), 95.
2 'The Objectives Resolution', *Islamic Studies* 48, no. 1 (Spring 2009), 95.
3 Munir, *From Jinnah to Zia*, 95.
4 Fahad Chaudhry, 'Under Pressure Govt Backtracks on Atif Mian's Appointment; Removes Economist from Advisory Council', *Dawn*, 7 September 2018.
5 Waseem Ashraf Butt, 'Minaret of Ahmadi Place of Worship Removed in Gujranwala', *Dawn*, 12 December 2022.
6 Imran Sadiq, 'Historic Building Demolished, Ahmadiyya Place of Worship Vandalised in Sialkot', *Dawn*, 24 May 2023.
7 Imtiaz Ali, 'Ahmadi Place of Worship Vandalized in Karachi', *Dawn*, 25 July 2023.

8 Part IX: Islamic Provisions, The Constitution of Pakistan.
9 Farzana Shaikh, *Making Sense of Pakistan* (Oxford University Press, 2016), 91.
10 Article 260 (3), The Constitution of Pakistan.
11 Farzana Shaikh, *Making Sense of Pakistan*, 104.

Chapter 11 Minority Rights

1 Munir, *From Jinnah to Zia* (New Era Press, 1981), 33–34.
2 Ibid.
3 Ibid.
4 Census of Pakistan 1951, 'Population According to Religion', Table 6.
5 'CJ Lauds Parliament for Correcting Historic Wrong,' *Dawn*, 9 June 2010.
6 Ibid.
7 Ibid.
8 Marva Khan, 'Constitutional Comparison and Analysis of Discrimination against Religious Minorities in Pakistan and India', *LUMS Law Journal* 1, no. 1 (2014): 28.
9 Ibid.
10 Ibid.
11 Ibid.
12 FIDH-HRCP, 'Minorities under Attack: Faith-based Discrimination and Violence in Pakistan', 10 March 2015, 7.
13 Article 227(1), The Constitution of Pakistan.
14 FIDH-HRCP, 'Minorities under Attack: Faith-based Discrimination and Violence in Pakistan', 10 March 2015, 7.
15 Ibid.
16 Ibid.
17 Dorab Patel, *Testament of a Liberal* (Harvard University Press, 1956), 212.
18 Asif Aqeel, 'Problems with the Electoral Representation of Non-Muslims', *Herald*, 1 July 2018.
19 Ibid.
20 Ibid.
21 Ibid.
22 Ibid.
23 Ibid.
24 FIDH-HRCP, 'Minorities under Attack: Faith-based Discrimination and Violence in Pakistan', 10 March 2015, 10.

Chapter 12 Nationality, Language and Ideology

1 Munir, *From Jinnah to Zia* (New Era Press, 1981), 1.

2 Hamidul Haq Chowdhury, *Memoirs*, as cited by Dorab Patel, *Testament of a Liberal*, 1.
3 Ibid.
4 Munir, *From Jinnah to Zia*, 4.
5 Nilofer Afridi Qazi, 'My Grandmother and the 1973 Constitution', *Friday Times*, 9 May 2023.

Chapter 13 Khyber Pakhtunkhwa

1 Dorab Patel, *Testament of A Liberal* (Harvard University Press, 1956), 136–137.
2 Wali Khan, *Facts Are Facts* (Vikas Publishing House, 1987), 143.
3 Christophe Jaffrelot, *The Pakistan Paradox: Instability and Resilience* (Random House, India, 2015), 153.
4 Dorab Patel, *Testament of a Liberal*, 130.
5 Ibid.
6 Ibid., 131.
7 Ibid.
8 Ibid., 136–137.
9 Ibid., 136.
10 Christophe Jaffrelot, *The Pakistan Paradox*, 157.
11 Ibid., 159.
12 Ibid.
13 Ibid.
14 Khadim Hussain, 'Political Cost the ANP Paid in Its Fight against Extremists' (Pak Institute for Peace Studies, August 2013), 4.
15 Ibid.
16 Ibid.
17 Ibid.
18 Isabel Hilton, 'The Pashtun Code: How a Long-ungovernable Tribe May Determine the Future of Afghanistan', *New Yorker*, 3 December 2001.

Chapter 14 Sindh

1 Sherbaz Mazari, *A Journey to Disillusionment* (Oxford University Press, 1999), 262.
2 Ibid., 41.
3 Asma Faiz, *In Search of Lost Glory: Sindhi Nationalism in Pakistan* (Hurst Publishers, 2021), 36.
4 Ibid., 15.
5 Ibid., 37.

6 Narendra Singh Sarila, *The Shadow of the Great Game: The Untold Story of India's Partition* (HarperCollins, 2009), 206.
7 Asma Faiz, *In Search of Lost Glory*, 55.
8 Ibid., 56.
9 Ibid., 41–43.
10 Mohammad Ali Mahar, 'What Ails Karachi?', *Friday Times*, 26 January 2023.
11 Ibid.
12 Asma Faiz, *In Search of Lost Glory*, 44.
13 Mohammad Ali Mahar, 'What Ails Karachi?'.
14 Ibid.
15 Sherbaz Mazari, *A Journey to Disillusionment*, 66.
16 Jaffrelot, *The Pakistan Paradox*, 121.
17 Sherbaz Mazari, *A Journey to Disillusionment*, 260.
18 Ibid.
19 Benazir Bhutto, *Daughter of the East: An Autobiography* (Hamish Hamilton, 1988), 165–166.
20 Sherbaz Mazari, *A Journey to Disillusionment*, 542.

Chapter 15 Balochistan

1 Pervez Hoodbhoy, *Pakistan: Origins, Identity and Future* (Routledge, 2023), 222.
2 Ibid.
3 Selig S. Harrison, *In Afghanistan's Shadow: Baluch Nationalism and Soviet Temptations* (Carnegie Endowment for International Peace, 1981), 22.
4 Harrison, *In Afghanistan's Shadow*, 23.
5 Hoodbhoy, *Pakistan: Origins, Identity and Future*, 222.
6 Harrison, *In Afghanistan's Shadow*, 24.
7 Ibid., 25.
8 Hoodbhoy, *Pakistan: Origins, Identity and Future*, 222.
9 Ibid.
10 Ibid.
11 Frederic Grare, *Balochistan: The State Versus the Nation* (Carnegie Endowment for International Peace, 1 April 2013), 7.
12 Sherbaz Mazari, *A Journey to Disillusionment*, 292.
13 Ibid.
14 Ibid.
15 Ibid., 305.
16 Harrison, *In Afghanistan's Shadow*, 37.
17 Ibid.

18 Ibid., 151.
19 Grare, *Balochistan: The State Versus the Nation.*
20 Ibid.
21 International Crisis Group, 'Pakistan: The Forgotten Conflict in Balochistan', 2007, 1.
22 Ibid.
23 Ibid., 7.
24 Grare, *Balochistan: The State Versus the Nation.*
25 Human Rights Watch, 'Pakistan: Rampant Killings of Shias by Extremists', 29 June 2014.
26 President General Pervez Musharraf's Address to the Nation, 20 July 2006, as cited by International Crisis Group, 'Pakistan: The Forgotten Conflict in Balochistan', 2007, 2.
27 Ibid.
28 2006: Aftermath of Nawab Akbar Bugti's Death', *Dawn*, 30 May 2011.
29 Meena Z. Khwaja, Abid Q. Suleri and Babar Shahbaz, 'Natural Resource Allocation in Balochistan and NWFP: Reasons for Discontent', Working Paper Series 111, Sustainable Development Policy Institute, November 2009, 4.
30 Fasih Uddin, 'Analysing 7th NFC Award and Its Implications', December 2020.
31 'Balochistan Package and Ownership of Natural Resources', *Dawn*, 21 December 2009.
32 Malik Asad, 'Bizenjo Coerced over Census Results, SC Told', *Dawn*, 14 November 2023.
33 Saleem Shahid, 'Balochistan Budget 2024-25: Nosherwani Announces Rs. 956 Bn Surplus Budget', *Dawn*, 22 June 2024.
34 Syed Irfan Raza, 'PPP Set to Form Govt. in Balochistan, Says Sarfaraz Bugti', *Dawn*, 19 February 2024.

Chapter 16 Muhajirs

1 Shahid Javed Burki, *Pakistan under Bhutto, 1971–1977* (Macmillan Press, 1980), 19.
2 Mohammad Ali Mahar, 'What Ails Karachi?', *Friday Times*, 26 January 2023.
3 Reema Abbasi, 'Urdu: The Language of Defiance', *Dawn*, 23 February 2020.
4 Web Archive, US Library of Congress, 'Muttahida Qaumi Movement'.
5 Vazira Fazila-Yacoobali, 'The Battlefields of Karachi: Ethnicity, Violence and the State', *Journal of the International Institute*, University of Michigan, 4, no. 1, (Fall 1996).
6 Rafia Zakaria, *The Upstairs Wife: An Intimate History of Pakistan* (Beacon Press, 2015), 136.
7 Rafia Zakaria, *The Upstairs Wife*, 136.

8 Rafia Zakaria, *The Upstairs Wife*, 171.
9 Vazira Fazila-Yacoobali, 'The Battlefields of Karachi: Ethnicity, Violence and the State', *Journal of the International Institute*.
10 Jaffrelot, *The Pakistan Paradox*, 171–172.
11 Farhan Hanif Siddiqi, 'Intra-Ethnic Fissures in Ethnic Movements: The Rise of Muhajir Identity Politics in Post-1971 Pakistan', *Asian Ethnicity*, 11, no. (1), (2010), 25–41, as cited by Jaffrelot in *The Pakistan Paradox*, 171–172.
12 Adeel Khan, 'Ethnic Nationalism and the State in Pakistan', Doctor of Philosophy thesis, Faculty of Arts, University of Wollongong, 2001, as cited by Jaffrelot in *The Pakistan Paradox*, 171–172.
13 Jaffrelot, *The Pakistan Paradox*, 174.
14 'What Altaf Said…', *Dawn*, 23 August 2016.
15 Ibid.
16 Muhammad Feroz Iftikhar, 'Legally Muhajir', thesis for the Institute of Business Administration, May 2017, 40.
17 Ibid.

Chapter 17 Army

1 Ishtiaq Ahmed, *The Pakistan Military in Politics: Origins, Evolution, Consequences (1947–2011)* (Amaryllis, 2013), 237.
2 C. Christine Fair, *Fighting to the End: Pakistan Army's Way of War* (Oxford University Press, 2014), 238.
3 Husain Haqqani, *Pakistan: Between Mosque And Military* (Carnegie Endowment for International Peace, 2005), 26.
4 Ibid.
5 Trading Economics.
6 Maj. Gen. (Retd) Muhammad Akbar Khan, *Raiders in Kashmir* (National Book Foundation, 1975), 37.
7 Altaf Gauhar, *Ayub Khan: Pakistan's First Military Ruler*, 212.
8 Farzana Shaikh, *Making Sense of Pakistan*, 154.
9 Ibid., 106.
10 Brigadier (Retd) Mohammad Yousaf, *Silent Soldier: The Man Behind the Afghan Jehad General Akhtar Abdur Rahman Shaheed* (Jang Publishers, Lahore, 1991), 40.
11 Ibid., 48.
12 Ibid., 46.
13 Ibid., 78.
14 Farzana Shaikh, *Making Sense of Pakistan*, 168.
15 Barbara Crosette, 'Pakistan Asks Talks on Atom Spread', *New York Times*, 7 June 1991.
16 Najam Sethi, 'Right or Wrong', *Friday Times*, 31 January–6 February 1991.

17 Ibid.
18 Ibid.
19 Ibid.
20 Ishtiaq Ahmed, *The Pakistan Military in Politics*, 238.
21 Ibid., 237.
22 Stephen P. Cohen, *The Pakistan Army* (University of California Press, 1984), 103.
23 C. Christine Fair, *Fighting to the End*, 238.
24 Stephen P. Cohen, *The Pakistan Army*, 70.
25 Khaled Ahmed, *Sleepwalking to Surrender*, 116.
26 Farzana Shaikh, *Making Sense of Pakistan*, 156.
27 Ibid., 157.
28 Ibid., 156.
29 Stephen P. Cohen, *The Pakistan Army*, 70.
30 Khaled Ahmed, *Sleepwalking to Surrender*, 116.
31 Farhan Bokhari and Matthew Green, 'Pakistan Navy Officers Face Court Marshal', *Financial Times*, 4 August 2011.
32 Ibid.
33 Yaqoob Malik, 'Terrorists Attack Kamra Air Base: Nine Attackers Dead, Plane Damaged', *Dawn*, 16 August 2012.
34 Khaled Ahmed, *Sleepwalking to Surrender*, 22.
35 Ibid.
36 Raza Rumi, 'A Coup That Failed', *Friday Times*, 27 May 2023.
37 Ibid.
38 'Anarchy Is Spread through Social Media: COAS Munir', *Dawn*, 8 August 2024.

Chapter 18 Afghanistan

1 S.K. Lambah, Durand Line, *Indian Foreign Affairs Journal* Vol. 7, no. 1, January–March 2012, 51–52.
2 International Crisis Group, 'The Problem of Pashtun Alienation', 5 August 2003, 1.
3 Vartan Gregorian, *The Emergence of Modern Afghanistan: Politics of Reform and Modernisation 1880–1946* (Stanford University Press, 1969), 187.
4 Vartan Gregorian, *The Emergence of Modern Afghanistan*.
5 Ibid., 159.
6 Farzana Shaikh, *Making Sense of Pakistan*, 54.
7 Farzana Shaikh, as cited in Durand Line by S.K. Lambah, 51.
8 Rashid Ahmad, *Descent into Chaos: How the War against Islamic Extremism Is Being Lost in Pakistan, Afghanistan and Central Asia* (Allen Lane, 2008), as cited in Durand Line by S.K. Lambah, 51–52.

9 Barnett R. Rubin, *The Search for Peace in Afghanistan: From Buffer State to Failed State* (Yale University Press, 1995), 127.
10 Barnett Rubin, *The Search for Peace in Afghanistan*, 127.
11 Riaz Mohammad Khan, *Afghanistan and Pakistan: Conflict, Extremism, and Resistance to Modernity* (Woodrow Wilson Center Press with Johns Hopkins University Press, 2011), 43.
12 Barnett Rubin, *The Search for Peace in Afghanistan*, 139.
13 Steve Coll, *Ghost Wars* (Penguin, 2004), 410.
14 'General Assembly "Appalled" by Edict on Destruction of Afghan Shrines; Strongly Urges Taliban to Halt Implementation', UN General Assembly Press Release GA/9858, 9 March 2001.
15 Kathy Gannon, 'I Is for Infidel: From Holy War to Holy Terror, 18 Years Inside Afghanistan' (Public Affairs, 2005), as cited in Khaled Ahmed, *Sleepwalking to Surrender*, 188.
16 Riaz Mohammad Khan, *Afghanistan and Pakistan*, 226.
17 International Crisis Group, 'Pakistan's Tribal Areas: Appeasing the Militants', 11 December 2006, 19.
18 Riaz Mohammad Khan, *Afghanistan and Pakistan*, 229.
19 'FM refrains from Calling Osama bin Laden Martyr or Terrorist', *Dawn*, 21 June 2021.
20 'The Taliban Get Down to the Tedious Business of Running a Country', *The Economist*, 7 September 2021.
21 Luis Martinez, 'Mullen Stands by His Comments', ABC News, 30 September 2021.
22 Shafiq Ahmad, 'Who Is Who in Taliban Interim Government', *Anadolu Agency*, 9 September 2021.

Chapter 19 Jammu and Kashmir

1 Sheikh Abdullah, *Flames of the Chinar: An Autobiography* (Viking, 1993), 60.
2 'Assembly Debates', National Assembly of Pakistan, 11 July 1972.
3 Akbar Khan, *Raiders in Kashmir*, 23.
4 Muhammad Yusuf Saraf, *Kashmiris Fight For Freedom,* Vol. 2 (Ferozesons, 1979), 860.
5 Akbar Khan, *Raiders in Kashmir*, 23.
6 Muhammad Yusuf Saraf, *Kashmiris Fight For Freedom*, 860.
7 United Nations Security Council (1957), 'India: Documents submitted as annexes to the statements made by Mr. Krishna Menon at the 762nd, 763rd and 734th meeting of the Security Council', pages 44–77, as cited in D.P. Srivastava, *Forgotten Kashmir: The Other Side of the Line of Control* (HarperCollins, 2021), 98–99.

8 United Nations Security Council (1957), 'Pakistan's Foreign Minister Feroz Khan Noon's Statement in 770th Meeting of the UN Security Council', 18 February 1957.

9 J. Hayat, 'Azad Jammu & Kashmir (AJK): Prospects for Democratic Governance amidst Ambiguous Sovereignty, Absence of Self-determination and Enduring Conflict', Ph.D. thesis for Suhr Institute of Political Science, Research Unit Peace and Conflict Studies, Frei Universitat Berlin, 2014), page 79, as cited in Dinkar P. Srivastava, *Forgotten Kashmir: The Other Side of the Line of Control*, 50.

10 Altaf Gauhar, *Ayub Khan: Pakistan's First Military Ruler*, 237.

11 'Assembly Debates', National Assembly of Pakistan, 11 July 1972, as cited in Dinkar P. Srivastava, *Forgotten Kashmir: The Other Side of the Line of Control*, 140.

12 Claudia Dreifus, 'Real-Life Dynasty; Benazir Bhutto', *New York Times*, 15 May 1994.

13 Nasim Zehra, *From Kargil to the Coup: Events That Shook Pakistan* (Vanguard Books, 2018), 163.

14 Nasim Zehra, *From Kargil to the Coup*, 162.

15 Ibid., 165.

16 Ibid., 171.

17 Al-Jehad Trust vs Federation of Pakistan, Supreme Court of Pakistan (1999), 1401.

18 Saraf, *Kashmiris Fight For Freedom*, 1357.

19 'Azad Government of State of Jammu and Kashmir Act III of 2018, Art 31 (3) and (4), Third Schedule', as cited in Dinkar P. Srivastava, *Forgotten Kashmir: The Other Side of the Line of Control*, 225.

20 Ibid.

21 D.P. Srivastava, *Forgotten Kashmir*, 317.

22 'AJK: PM Shehbaz Approves Immediate Provision of Rs 23 Bn to Region', *Business Recorder*, 13 May 2024.

23 Ibid.

Chapter 20 Terrorism

1 Mansoor Ijaz, 'Time to Take on Pakistan's Jihadist Spies', *Financial Times*, 11 October 2011.

2 President Musharraf's speech, *Washington Post*, 19 September 2001.

3 President Musharraf's speech, *Washington Post*, 19 September 2001.

4 Riaz Mohammad Khan, *Afghanistan and Pakistan*, 246.

5 Ibid., 267.

6 Saraf, *Kashmiris Fight for Freedom*, 1378.

7 'Assembly Debates', National Assembly of Pakistan, 11 July 1972, as cited in Dinkar P. Srivastava, *Forgotten Kashmir: The Other Side of the Line of Control*, 267.
8 Adrian Levy & Catherine Scott-Clark, *Deception: Pakistan, the United States and the Global Nuclear Weapons Conspiracy* (Penguin, 2007), 241.
9 Umer Farooq, 'The Mast Gul Factor', *Herald*, 10 August 2016.
10 Hashim Qureshi, 'Charar-e-Sharif, Discretion, Kidnappings', JKDLP Blog, December 1995, https://hashimqureshi-jkdlp.blogspot.com/1995/12/charar-e-sharifdiscretion-kidnappings.html.
11 'In Musharraf's Words: A Day of Reckoning', *New York Times*, 12 January 2022.
12 Daniel Pearl, 'Pakistan Clamps Down on Islamic Militants to Avert War with India, Terror at Home', *Wall Street Journal*, 2 January 2002.
13 Zulfikar Majid, 'Zakir Musa Named Al-Qaida Commander in Kashmir', *Deccan Herald*, 27 July 2017.
14 Riaz Mohammad Khan, *Afghanistan and Pakistan*, 214.
15 Adrian Levy & Catherine Scott-Clark, *Deception*, 240.
16 Ibid., 241.
17 Khaled Ahmed, *Sleepwalking to Surrender*, 49.
18 Ibid., 47.
19 Ibid.
20 James Lamont, Richard McGregor and Farhan Bokhari, 'Pakistan: Caught Off-guard', *Financial Times*, 4 May 2011.
21 Daniel Dombey, James Lamont and Farhan Bokhari, 'US Lays Bare Mistrust of Pakistan', *Financial Times*, 4 May 2011.
22 Amy Kazmin and Farhan Bokhari, 'Critical Time for US and Pakistan, Says Kerry', *Financial Times*, 15 May 2011.
23 Mansoor Ijaz, 'Time to Take on Pakistan's Jihadist Spies', *Financial Times*, 11 October 2011.
24 Ibid.
25 Ibid.
26 Khaled Ahmed, *Sleepwalking to Surrender*, 44.
27 James Lamont, 'Clinton Warns Pakistan on Militant "Snakes"', *Financial Times*, 21 October 2011.

Chapter 21 Nuclear Deterrence: Strategy, Ideology or Gamble?

1 Letter dated 27 May 1999 from Prime Minister Nawaz Sharif to the UN Secretary-General, circulated as document no. A/54/118 S/1999/633, 2 June 1999.
2 Scott D. Sagan and Kenneth N. Waltz, *The Spread of Nuclear Weapons, An Enduring Debate* (W.W. Norton, 2012), 140.
3 Sagan and Waltz, *The Spread of Nuclear Weapons*, 140.

4 Abbas Nasir, 'Down Memory Lane', *Dawn*, 25 August 2018.

5 Mushahid Hussain, 'Pakistan "Responding to Change"', *Jane's Defence Weekly*, 14 October 1989, 779, as cited in Devin T. Hagerty, *Nuclear Deterrence in South Asia: The 1990 Indo-Pakistani Crisis*, 98.

6 Ibid.

7 Record of Discussion with I.K. Gujral (24 September 1999) and Record of Discussion with B.G. Deshmukh (26 October 1999), as cited in the Kargil Review Committee report, 66.

8 General Mirza Aslam Beg, interviewed by Ikramullah, *The News*, Islamabad, 3 December 1992, as cited by Pervez Hoodbhoy, 'Nuclear Issues between India and Pakistan: Myths and Realities', paper for Stimson Center.

9 Mushahid Hussain, 'Pakistan "Responding to Change"', *Jane's Defence Weekly*, 14 October 1989, page 779, as cited in Devin T. Hagerty, *Nuclear Deterrence in South Asia: The 1990 Indo-Pakistani Crisis*, 98.

10 *Jane's Defence Weekly*, 14 October 1989, as cited in the Kargil Review Committee report, page 191.

11 Australian Parliament Report on the 1998 Indian and Pakistani Nuclear Tests, 53.

12 Ibid.

13 Letter dated 27 May 1999 from Prime Minister Nawaz Sharif to the UN Secretary-General, circulated as document no. A/54/118 S/1999/633, 2 June 1999.

14 Peter R. Lavoy, *Pakistan's Nuclear Posture: Security and Survivability*, Semantic Scholar, 2007, 4–5.

15 'Keynote Address and Discussion Session with Lieutenant General (Retd) Khalid Kidwai', IISS, 6 February 2020.

Chapter 22 Economy

1 Ishrat Husain, 'Seventy-Five Years of Pakistan's Economy', *The News*, 19 August 2022.

2 International Monetary Fund, *Pakistan: History of Lending Commitments as of February 28, 2025*, Washington, DC: International Monetary Fund, 2025.

3 Ishtiaq Ahmed, *Jinnah: His Successes, Failures and Role in History*, 164.

4 Farzana Shaikh, *Making Sense of Pakistan*, 119.

5 Shahid Javed Burki, *Pakistan under Bhutto*, (St Martin's Press, 1980), 16.

6 Ibid., 64.

7 Akmal Hussain, *A Perspective on Pakistan's Economic History: Growth, Economic Structure and Governance* (Oxford University Press, 2012).

8 Ibid.

9 Ibid.

10 Ibid.
11 Ibid.
12 Hussain H. Zaidi, 'Saga of Pakistan's Economy since 1947', *Hilal*, August 2018.
13 Macrotrends, Pakistan Military Spending and Defence Budget 1960–2023
14 Yousuf Nazar, 'Demystifying Pakistan's Military Spending: Why Is There No Transparency', *Friday Times*, 6 June 2022.
15 Macrotrends, Pakistan Military Spending and Defence Budget 1960–2023.
16 Ibid.
17 Hussain H. Zaidi, 'Saga of Pakistan's Economy Since 1947', *Hilal*, August 2018.
18 Ishrat Husain, 'Seventy-Five Years of Pakistan's Economy', *The News*, 19 August 2022.
19 International Monetary Fund, 'Pakistan: Second and Final Review under the Stand-by Arrangement', 10 May 2024, 32.
20 Trade Economics.
21 The PM's visit to China, 4 June 2024.
22 International Monetary Fund, 'Pakistan Economy: Selected Issues', 2017, 9–11.
23 'Pakistan Down in Human Development Index by Seven Places', *Friday Times*, 9 September 2022.
24 'You Won't Believe This: Miftah Ismael Exposes Jaw-Dropping Details of Budget 2023–24', posted on YouTube, 10 June 2023.
25 *Business Recorder*, Budget, 10 June 2023.
26 International Monetary Fund, Pakistan Staff Country report, Volume 2023, Issue 260, 18 July 2023.
27 Ikramul Haq, 'Malice towards None & All: Sorry IMF, We Are Incorrigible!', *Friday Times*, 29 July 2023.
28 World Bank, Gross Domestic Saving as percentage of GDP.
29 'GDP Growth for the Current Year', *Business Recorder*, 23 May 2024.
30 Sabih Ul Hussnain, 'Letter to IMF: Imran Khan Asks Fund to Condition Loan to Elections Audit', *Friday Times*, 28 February 2024.

Chapter 23 Imran Khan and Riyasat-e-Madina

1 Salman Masood, 'Pakistan's Prime Minister Suggests that Osama bin Laden Was a Martyr', *New York Times*, 26 June 2020.
2 Stephanie Findlay, 'A Win for Pakistan: Imran Khan Gambles on Taliban Ties', *Financial Times*, 29 September 2021.
3 'A Conversation with Prime Minister Imran Khan', Council on Foreign Relations, 23 September 2019.

4 Salman Masood, 'Pakistan's Prime Minister Suggests that Osama bin Laden Was a Martyr'.
5 'PM Imran Calling Osama bin Laden a Martyr Was a "Slip of the Tongue": Fawad', *Dawn*, 27 June 2021.
6 Salman Masood, 'Pakistan's Prime Minister Suggests that Osama bin Laden Was a Martyr'.
7 'PTI against the Military Operation in NW: Imran Khan', *Dawn*, 16 August 2012.
8 Saroop Ijaz, 'From Apologist to Ally', *Express Tribune*, 23 September 2013, as cited in Pervez Hoodbhoy, *Pakistan: Origins, Identity and Future*, 405.
9 Khaled Ahmed, *Sleepwalking to Surrender*, 13.
10 Ibid.
11 Asad Zia, 'Sour Note: Chants of "Go Imran, Go" Greet PTI Chief at APS', *Express Tribune*, 14 January 2015.
12 Ibid.
13 Imran Khan, 'Pakistan Is Ready to Be a Partner for Peace in Afghanistan, but We Will Not Host U.S. Bases', *Washington Post*, 21 June 2021.
14 Ibid.
15 Qamar Cheema, 'Dr Ishtiaq Ahmed on Return of Taliban: Why Is Pakistan Confused?' YouTube, 13 August 2022.
16 Ibid.
17 Fahad Chaudhry, 'Under Pressure Govt Backtracks on Atif Mian's Appointment; Removes Economist from Advisory Council', *Dawn*, 7 September 2018.
18 Hoodbhoy, *Pakistan: Origins, Identity and Future*, 279.
19 Sana Chaudhry, 'A PM No More: How the Historic Move to Eject Imran Khan through a No-trust Vote Unfolded', *Dawn*, 8 April 2023.
20 Iftikhar Shirazi, '"An Example of Hypocrisy": Army Declares Violence in Wake of Imran's Arrest a "Black Chapter"', *Dawn*, 10 May 2023.
21 ISPR Statement, 9 May 2023.
22 Iftikhar Shirazi, '"An Example of Hypocrisy": Army Declares Violence in Wake of Imran's Arrest a "Black Chapter"'.
23 Amber Rahim Shamsi, 'Imran Khan Crisis: Is Pakistan Facing Its Own January 6 Moment?', Al Jazeera, 17 March 2023.

Chapter 24 Conclusion

1 Khaliquzzaman, *Pathway to Pakistan*, 390.
2 IMF, Pakistan: 2024 Article IV Consultation and Request for an Extended Arrangement under the Extended Fund Facility, 10 October 2024.

3 Vaishnavi Chandrashekhar, 'As Himalayan Glaciers Melt, a Water Crisis Looms in South Asia', *YaleEnvironment360*, 3 October 2022.

4 Ibid.

5 'Worldometer', www.worldometers.info.

6 Ibid.

7 'Pakistan Overview', *World Bank*, https://www.worldbank.org/en/country/pakistan/overview, accessed on 6 April 2025.

8 Khaliquzzaman, *Pathway to Pakistan*, 390.

9 'Anarchy Is Spread through Social Media: COAS Munir', *Dawn*, 8 August 2024.

10 Wali Khan, *Facts Are Facts: The Untold Story of India's Partition*, 131.

Index

About the Author

Dinkar P. Srivastava is a former Indian diplomat. He served in the Ministry of External Affairs and was posted to Pakistan, the United States and the European Union. As Director/Joint Secretary, UN Political Division in the Ministry of External Affairs, he was part of India's successful lobbying efforts to prevent internationalization of the Jammu and Kashmir issue. In his long career he has dealt with human rights, terrorism, Indian candidature for permanent membership of the United Nations Security Council, Pokhran II nuclear tests and the Kargil conflict.

Srivastava was a member of the Indian delegation to the World Conference of Human Rights. He was involved in the drafting of the National Human Rights Commission statute. He was also an adviser to the Indian delegation to the International Court of Justice in the case of the shooting down of Pakistani spy plane Atlantique. As India's ambassador to Iran, he negotiated the MOU for Indian participation in Chabahar Port.

He is the author of *Forgotten Kashmir: The Other Side of the Line of Control.*